American Woodworker

TOOL SMARTS

Routers and Router Tables

>> *How to Choose and Use the Most Versatile Power Tool in the Workshop*

American Woodworker

TOOL *SMARTS*

Routers and Router Tables

》》 *How to Choose and Use the Most Versatile Power Tool in the Workshop*

Introduction by Randy Johnson,
Editor, *American Woodworker* Magazine

FOX CHAPEL
PUBLISHING

Published by Fox Chapel Publishing Company, Inc., 1970 Broad St., East Petersburg, PA 17520, 717-560-4703, www.FoxChapelPublishing.com

American Woodworker, ISSN 1074-9152, USPS 738-710, is published bimonthly by Woodworking Media, LLC, 90 Sherman St., Cambridge, MA 02140, www.AmericanWoodworker.com.

Library of Congress Control Number: 2011000926
ISBN-13: 978-1-56523-508-3
ISBN-10: 1-56523-508-8

Library of Congress Cataloging-in-Publication Data

Routers and router tables. -- 1st ed.

   p. cm. -- (Toolsmarts)

Includes index.

ISBN 978-1-56523-508-3

1. Routers (Tools) 2. Workbenches. 3. Cabinetwork.

TT203.5.R687 2011

684'.083--dc22

                    2011000926

To learn more about the other great books from Fox Chapel Publishing, or to find a retailer near you, call toll-free 800-457-9112 or visit us at *www.FoxChapelPublishing.com*.

Printed in China
First printing: August 2011

What you can build with this book...

CHOOSING A ROUTER, *page 8*

Knowing the unique features of each type of router will help you fine-tune your choice.

ROUTER TABLES TO BUILD, *page 40*

These four designs, with their accessories, will provide great choices to meet whatever your needs are.

ROUTER TECHNIQUES, *page 128*

The variety of ways that a router can be used, whether cutting, panel raising, grooving, joining, or even carving, is what makes it such a useful feature in your shop.

JOINING WOOD WITH THE ROUTER, *page 172*

A tell-tale sign of any well-built piece of furniture is its joints. But to achieve precise joinery, you must learn accurate use of your router.

p. 8

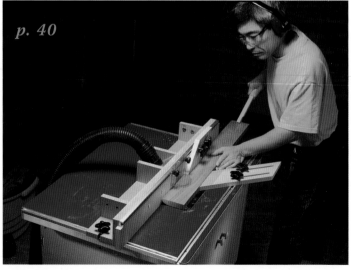

p. 40

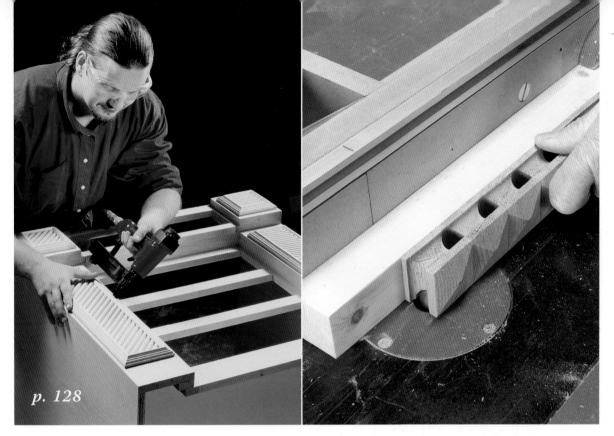

p. 128

p. 172

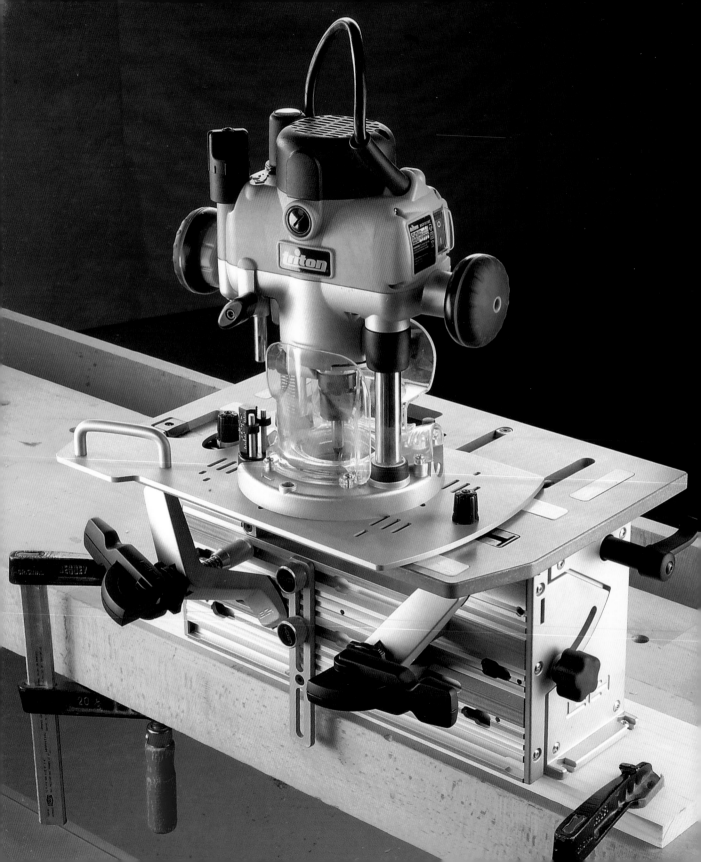

Choosing a Router

Most routers fall into one of three categories: small, medium, and large. Knowing the unique features of each type of router will help you to fine-tune your choice.

The smallest router is commonly referred to as the trim router, so named because it's designed primarily for trimming plastic laminates. Its compact size also makes it handy around the shop for routing small profiles, grooves, and details.

The midsize router packs about twice the horsepower of the trim router and can handle a wide variety of routing tasks, from edge molding to dadoing to a variety of router table applications. Most midsized routers accept both 1/4" and 1/2" diameter bits, allowing you to expand your bit options. If you're in the market for your first router, a midsize router combo kit, which includes both a fixed base and a plunge base, is a good choice.

On the top end of the scale are the large fixed and plunge base routers. If you need a router to make raised panel doors or deep mortises, you'll want the power of a large router to drive the large bits needed for such work.

Most woodworkers eventually end up with two or three routers in order to take advantage of the features and benefits of each style.

« **This plunge router** makes joints easily with the help of a jig.

by GEORGE VONDRISKA

Tool Test

POWERHOUSE ROUTERS FOR THE ROUTER TABLE

What's the one thing you need most when you're shaping dozens of raised panels on a router table? Power! These 3-hp monsters deliver plenty.

There are two completely different kinds of 3-hp routers: fixed-base and plunge. Both types have 15-amp motors with variable speed (a must for big bits), soft start (so your arm isn't wrenched when turning the machine on in a hand-held cut) and feedback circuitry (which helps the motor maintain rpm as it bears into a heavy cut).

There's a huge difference between fixed-base and plunge routers, however, in how easy they are to use in a router table. Adjusting some of these big routers can be a real headache. Few of them have been specifically designed to be used upside down in a router table, but some manufacturers are clearly catching on.

FIXED-BASE ROUTERS

A fixed-base router is our first choice for use in a router table. It has two distinct advantages: it's easy to change a bit quickly and it's easy to adjust the bit's height. Making a coarse height adjustment is a simple matter of loosening a clamping mechanism and twisting or lifting the router's motor (Photo 1). To change bits, all you have to do is remove the router motor from the base (Photo 2). The collet is right out in the open.

PLUNGE ROUTERS

A powerful plunge router is a great tool for cutting large dadoes and mortises, but the features that make it handy for hand-held work get in the way when you hang the machine in a router table (Photo 3). Adjusting the bit height is awkward on most plunge routers because there's no coarse height adjustment. Instead, you end up turning and turning a micro-adjust knob. Changing bits can be even more of a hassle, particularly when the bit has a large diameter, like a panel-raiser (Photo 4).

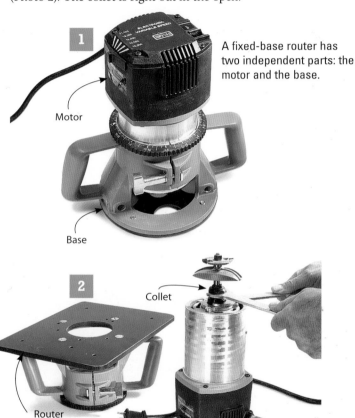

1

A fixed-base router has two independent parts: the motor and the base.

Motor

Base

2

Collet

Router table insert

STAFF

Changing any bit on a fixed-base router is a breeze. All you've got to do is remove the motor.

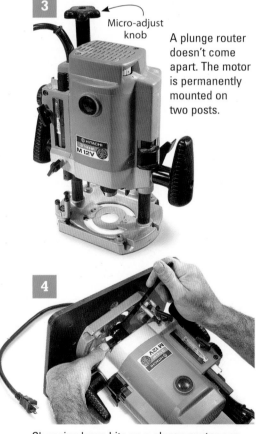

3

Micro-adjust knob

A plunge router doesn't come apart. The motor is permanently mounted on two posts.

4

STAFF

Changing large bits on a plunge router can be difficult, particularly if the base has a small opening. You can't retract the motor to give you more room around the collet.

ROUTER TABLE-FRIENDLY FEATURES

Discombobulating problems crop up when you turn a router upside down and tuck it under a router table. Labels are difficult to read. Switches are backward. Whether you choose a fixed-base or a plunge router for your router table, here are some features that make any machine safer and easier to use.

Micro-adjust knob

A micro-adjust knob is a must-have on a plunge router. It should project beyond the motor so you can easily wrap your hand around it. These knobs are included on some routers, but available as accessories on others.

Speed control

The speed control should be front and center, right where you can see it. Your safety depends on having a big bit spinning at the right speed, especially when it starts up. Some speed controls are mounted on top of the motor, out of sight when the router is upside down.

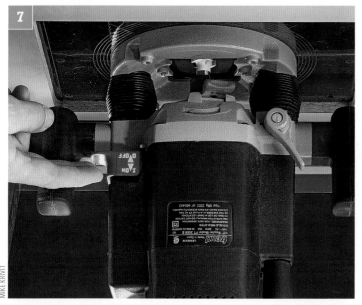

The on/off switch should be easy to reach and easy to read. A router ought to be unplugged when you change bits. It's usually pretty dark under a router table, though. Can you be sure the router is turned off when you plug it back in? A big slider switch like this is the next best thing to having an externally mounted switch on your router table.

The hole through the router's metal base ought to be large enough for big bits to pass through. Many metal bases have holes that are too small because they're designed to accommodate template guides. Changing big bits is difficult with a plunge router that has a small opening (see Photo 4, page 11).

Plunge Routers Off the Table

Our favorite 3-hp router for a router table is a fixed-base machine, but when you want to stretch your tool dollars as far as they'll go, a big plunge router makes a lot of sense. You can't make stopped dadoes and mortises with a fixed-base router, after all.

Out of the table, a 3-hp plunge router is large and heavy (most weigh 12 to 13 lbs.), but it's a great machine to drive big bits. Take a wide roundover bit, for example (see photo, right). It's risky and impractical to make this huge cut in one pass, but with a plunge router you can lower the bit in stages, taking one small last bite for an ultra-smooth surface. Of course, you can do this with a fixed-base machine, too, but a plunge router has a multi-step depth stop that allows you to repeat the same series of measured cuts over and over again.

Setting the exact depth of cut is certainly critical when you're using a plunge router to make dadoes and mortises. A good depth guide makes a huge difference, and they vary widely in quality from one machine

to another. The best ones have a clearly marked scale that can be adjusted to the zero mark when your bit is even with the bottom of the router (see photo below). Then you lift a rod connected to the scale to directly indicate how deep the cut should go. The scales on other routers cannot be "zeroed out," so you must count off 1/16-in.

marks from an arbitrary starting point on the scale to set the depth of cut.

A dust shroud is a fairly new and very welcome addition to many plunge routers (see photo below). The shroud directs chips and dust to a small exhaust port. Hook up a vacuum and you can rout virtually dust-free.

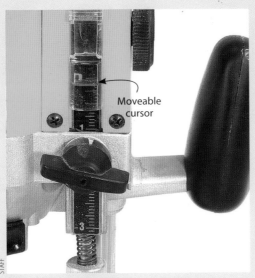

The depth-of-cut guide on a plunge router should be legible and easy to "zero out," so you don't have to make a lot of test cuts to hit an exact depth.

Moveable cursor

A dust shroud keeps that obnoxious stuff from flying all over your shop. Cutting dadoes and mortises is pretty much dust-free.

Dust port

by SETH KELLER

8 Great Reasons to Own a Plunge Router

PLUNGE ROUTERS GO WHERE NO OTHER ROUTER CAN

The plunge router deserves a place in every shop. Routing chores, such as mortising, stopped dados and inlay pattern work, are safer and easier to perform using a plunge router. Its unique base allows the motor housing to ride up and down on a pair of posts fixed to the base. The plunge mechanism is spring-loaded so the motor housing always wants to spring up to the top of the posts. A lock/release lever allows free up-and-down movement of the router housing or locks it in place at a given depth. The depth of cut can be preset, allowing you to position the router over the work and plunge the bit to an exact depth. The depth stop works much like the stop does on a drill press.

Plunge routers have been around for years. Some die-hard users of fixed-base models may argue that a fixed-base router can do everything that a plunge router can do, but they don't realize what a great, unique tool the plunge router is. Here are eight things a plunge router can do with ease that present a challenge for a fixed-base model.

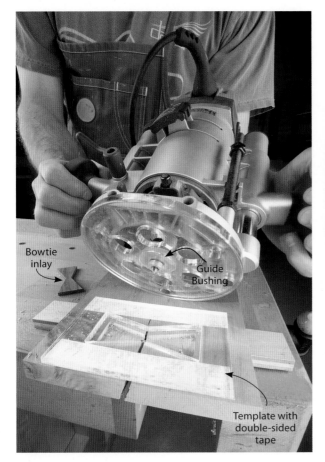

Bowtie inlay

Guide Bushing

Template with double-sided tape

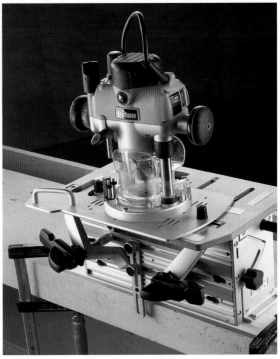

1 GREAT TEMPLATE ROUTERS

Template routing with guide bushings is trouble-free when you use a plunge router. Just set the router over the template, turn it on, plunge the bit to the preset depth and rout. The plastic bowtie inlay template, shown above, would probably have a few battle scars if a fixed base router had been used. You may get away with tipping it into the cut for a while, but sooner or later that template would be nicked.

2 REQUIRED BY SOME JIGS

A plunge router is a must when it comes to sophisticated jigs for making joints. These jigs cut mortises, tenons, dovetails, and a whole lot more, but they simply can't perform all their operations without the use of a plunge router.

Inlay

3 IDEAL FOR INLAY GROOVES

The plunge router is ideally suited for stringing and delicate inlay work, often called captured inlay, because the plunge mechanism allows a smooth entrance and exit from the cut. Try tipping your fixed-base model into a cut like this and your cut will likely be misaligned right where the groove starts. This is one operation you definitely want to get right the first time, and a plunge router is the surest way to get the job done well.

Start block

Edge guide

Stop block

Micro-adjust knob

Gauge

4 BURN-FREE STOPPED FLUTES

There's no better way to mill stopped grooves and flutes than by using a plunge router. This type of milling is safer and simpler than using a fixed-base router. All you need to cut perfect flutes is a start block, a stop block, and an edge guide. With the router set on the start block, plunge the bit to the preset depth and press the lock lever as you make the cut along the length of the board. At the end of the cut, release the plunge lock lever and the bit retracts off the workpiece, leaving you with the cleanest flutes possible. You won't leave burn marks, as you might if you tipped the router in or waited for it to spin down before extracting it at the end of the cut.

5 ON-BOARD SCALE FOR FINE ADJUSTMENTS

Micro-adjustable depth knobs make fine-tuning a plunge router simple. Small changes in bit height can be frustrating to make on some fixed-based routers. Plunge routers allow you to read and fine-tune the depth right on the router's face.

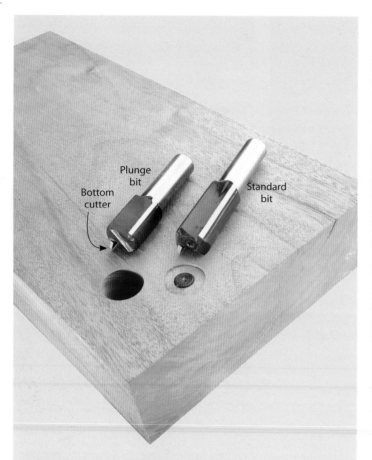

Plunge bit

Bottom cutter

Standard bit

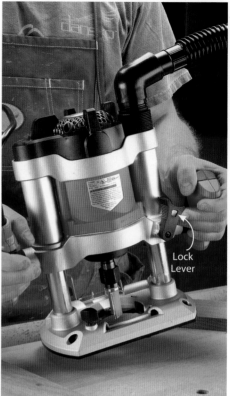

Lock Lever

Use the Right Bit for Plunging

Take advantage of bits designed for a plunge router. Plunge-cutting straight bits have bottom cutters that allow the bit to bore a hole as it is plunged into the work. Bits without a bottom cutter aren't capable of making plunge cuts, because they bottom out in the center.

6 BUILT-IN BIT PROTECTION

One advantage a plunge router has over a fixed-base model is bit protection. A plunge router automatically surrounds and protects your expensive bits when it's not in use. Just push your finger to disengage the lock lever and the spring-loaded mechanism retracts the housing, lifting the bit into the safety of the router base. This protects your bits, your fingers, and your benchtop from accidental nicks.

Stepped turret

7 A STAR AT CUTTING MORTISES

Cutting mortises is much easier with a plunge router than with a fixed-base model. A deep mortise can be cut without overtaxing the router or the bit. An adjustable stepped turret is the key. It allows a plunge router to make a series of relatively shallow but ever deeper cuts. You don't have to tip a spinning bit into the work as you would with a fixed-base router. A simple twist of the plunge router's stepped turret allows to you increase the depth-of-cut setting for the next pass, guaranteeing a cut that's not too deep.

8 BEST FOR SOME SPECIALIZED BITS

Some popular bits are best used with a plunge router. A keyhole/picture-hanging groove, for example, would be virtually impossible with a fixed-base router. To create this keyhole groove requires the bit to plunge down into the stock, slide laterally to cut the groove and then reverse-plunge to create the keyhole on the opposite end. These specialized bits have cutters on the top, bottom, and side. Imagine lifting the bit up out of the cut while using a fixed-based router. On second thought, don't even try to imagine it.

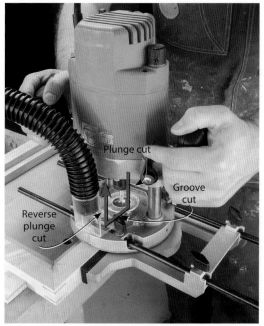

Plunge cut

Groove cut

Reverse plunge cut

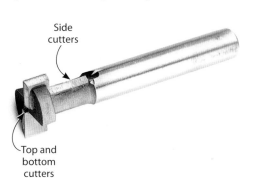

Side cutters

Top and bottom cutters

by RICHARD TENDICK

Trim Routers

THEY'RE VERSATILE AND EASY TO MANAGE

Take a good look around your shop. How many routers do you own? Most woodworkers have a couple midsize routers and a plunger. If this describes your set, you're missing one: the trim router. It can make your workshop life a whole lot easier.

A trim router is a surprisingly versatile tool. Although it only accepts 1/4-in. shank bits, you can put it to work cutting grooves, inlays, and molding profiles as well as flush-trimming edging, banding, and laminate. Its small size is a huge asset, not a liability. For many jobs, it's much more comfortable to use than a larger router.

Trim routers cost from under $100 to several hundred. With such a big range in prices, we found clear differences in the overall usefulness and quality of the 12 models gathered for this test. Read on to learn about their role in the shop, features to look for, individual profiles of each machine, and our recommendations.

THE VERSATILE TRIM ROUTER

Easy To Handle

A trim router's small size is a big plus when you must rout lots of edges. It's particularly easy to balance a trim router's small baseplate on a narrow edge. A large, heavy router with its big baseplate is prone to tipping.

EDITOR: TOM CASPAR • ART DIRECTION: DAVID SIMPSON • PHOTOGRAPHY: VERN JOHNSON

Despite their small size, most trim routers have plenty of power for cutting small profiles, grooves, and hinge mortises. Many of these jobs don't require the extra power of a larger, bulkier router.

It's easy to guide a trim router with one hand. This frees your other hand to trail the cord around or reposition the workpiece. Large routers generally require two hands.

Ideal for Delicate Work

A trim router is better-suited for fine and delicate work than a larger router is. Cutting this recess for a butterfly inlay, for example, requires a fragile 1/8-in. bit. With a large, heavy router, you can easily overpower and break this bit. You'll have a much better feel for how the cut is progressing when using a lightweight trim router.

An Inexpensive Dedicated Router

A trim router is the least expensive type of router to add to your tool kit. Reserve your workhorse midsize and plunge routers for big jobs. You can dedicate a trim router to a single job you must repeat throughout the course of a project, such as cutting molding, as shown here. Pick it up whenever you need it; the router will always be ready to go.

Screw adjust

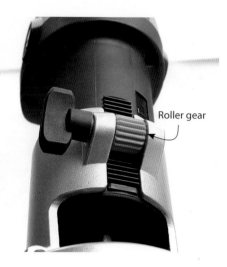

Roller gear

FEATURES

Depth-of-Cut Adjustment

This is by far the most important feature of a trim router. We prefer routers that have a screw mechanism to adjust the depth of cut, but most don't have it.

A screw makes it much easier to achieve a precise setting, because you can easily raise or lower the bit by a few thousandths of an inch. This degree of precision is often essential with the bits you're likely to use. When you set the depth of an inlay groove or adjust a small roundover bit to cut a full radius, a few thousandths can make a big difference.

Trim routers without a screw adjust rely on a much simpler, less reliable system. Basically, you slide the base by hand up or down on the motor housing. Some of these routers have a roller gear to assist you. This is a good feature, but the gear has a much coarser pitch than a screw adjust does, so it isn't as sensitive. It can be quite difficult to achieve a precise setting

with routers that don't have a screw adjust because the base usually doesn't slide smoothly. It often sticks, slips, and sticks again. Lubricating the motor housing can alleviate this problem, but the lubricant wears off and must be renewed.

Trim routers with a screw adjust or roller gear have another important benefit: a mechanical interlock between the base and motor housing. When the base is tightened, it can't accidentally move up or down. If you make a heavy cut with machines that don't interlock, vibration may cause the motor to slip down inside the base, leading the bit to cut deeper. This isn't a common problem, though, since trim routers aren't generally intended for heavy cuts.

Baseplate for Template Guides

We prefer trim routers with baseplates that accept template guides of any size. A template guide allows you to trace around a pattern. It's particularly useful for routing round, oval, or butterfly-shaped inlay, a job well-suited for a trim router.

Many trim routers accept Porter-Cable-style template guides, which come in a variety of sizes. Some trim routers accept only one special 3/8-in.-dia. guide that's supplied with the router. No other sizes are available. A few trim routers don't accept any kind of template guide.

Template guide

Base Style

Trim routers have two different base styles. Some bases wrap completely around the motor housing; others attach in cantilever fashion to one side of the motor. We prefer the wraparound style.

You must loosen both kinds of bases from the motor housing to adjust the bit's depth of cut. Cantilevered bases tend to tilt a little when you tighten them back onto the motor, which changes the depth of cut—not much, but enough to be annoying. Wraparound bases don't shift when you tighten and lock them, so the depth of cut doesn't change.

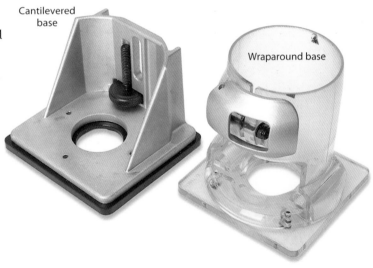

Cantilevered base

Wraparound base

Comfortable Grip

Trim routers are designed to be held with one hand. Some are much more comfortable than others, but you can't be sure if one fits your hand until you try it. We like models with a cushioned motor housing that swells just above your fingers. The larger top makes it easier to grip the router between cuts, when it's not supported by a workpiece.

Stop mark

A Clear View

Sometimes you want to clearly see the bit as it's cutting. If you've drawn start and stop marks for a molding, for example, you'll want to see them through the router's base and inside the opening around the bit. Visibility is much better on routers with clear plastic bases; others have black phenolic bases you can't see through.

Some routers have LED lights to illuminate the bit and workpieces, which can prevent costly mistakes.

Variable Speed and Soft Start

We really like variable speed and soft start on large, powerful routers, but they're really not necessary features on trim routers.

Variable speed is most useful with large-diameter bits, which you must slow down for safety. Trim routers, of course, aren't designed to handle large bits. Variable speed is useful in cutting plastic with a trim router, however. Slowing the bit's speed reduces the chance of melting the plastic as you cut it.

With soft start, the bit ramps up to speed when you turn on the machine. That's fine with a big router with a large startup torque, but this feature's benefit is barely noticeable with the much smaller startup torque of a trim router.

ACCESSORIES

Offset and Tilting Bases

If you'll be using your trim router with plastic laminate, you may need two additional bases. Offset and tilting bases are only available for a few routers. Generally, they come in a laminate-trimming kit that also includes a standard base.

An offset base is handy for scribing and other jobs with little clearance (see photo, right). The bit goes into a collet mounted inside this base. The bit is driven by a belt that's connected to a drive pulley mounted on the end of the motor's shaft.

A tilting base is used with a flush-trim bit to get into corners or trim angles greater than 90 degrees (see photo, right).

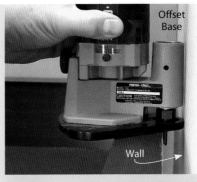

Offset Base

Wall

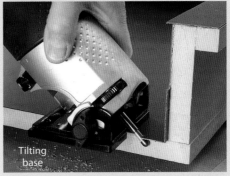

Tilting base

Edge Guide

An edge guide is useful when cutting any type of groove, especially for inlay. We prefer models that either come with an edge guide or have one available as an accessory.

Unfortunately, none of the guides are as precise as the best guides on larger routers. When cutting a groove for inlay, for example, we'd prefer to use a guide with a micro-adjust knob for widening the groove or for fine-tuning the distance between the wood's edge and the groove. Trim router edge guides aren't that sophisticated.

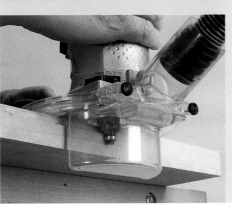

Dust Collection

Routing can create a cloud of fine dust that's unhealthy to breathe. You can capture that dust right at the source with a vacuum hose that attaches to a dust port. The Bosch trim routers are the only models with this accessory.

by DAVE MUNKITTRICK

Router Tables

THE VERSATILITY OF A SHAPER AT A FRACTION OF THE COST

The router revolutionized home shop woodworking. It's an incredible tool, capable of doing anything from edge-shaping to making sliding dovetail joints. It didn't take long for innovative woodworkers to discover that mounting their router in a table adds a whole new dimension to an already useful tool.

A router table offers many benefits:

■ **Safety**

Router table routing is safer than hand-held routing (Photo 1).

■ **Versatility**

With a router table you can do things that are impossible to do with a hand-held router. You can put an edge profile on narrow stock or small parts, make raised-panel doors, lock miters, and drawer joints.

■ **Stability**

Freehand routing is inherently unstable. The slightest tip or bump and you'll be starting the job over. A router table and fence support and guide your stock for a stable ride over the cutter.

Today there are literally hundreds of manufactured tables that when combined with a 1-1/2- to 3-hp router approach, if not equal, the capabilities of a full-sized shaper. No single table system is perfect, but you can find one that will meet your needs.

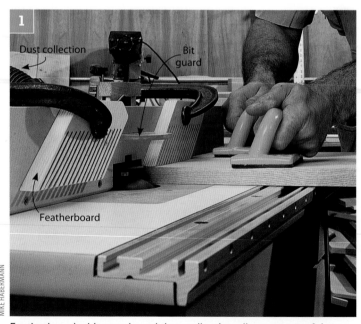

Dust collection

Bit guard

Featherboard

Featherboards, bit guards and dust collection allow you to safely do things with a router table that would be impossible with the router alone.

BENCHTOP OR FLOOR MODEL

Router tables come in two basic types: benchtop (Photo 2) and floor model (Photo 3).

Floor models are our first choice. They offer the size and stability you need to handle large stock and big routers.

The benchtop models are small and light enough to be both portable and storable. If you really need a portable, storable router table, or you know you'll always be working with small stock, then a benchtop router table is a good choice.

A word of warning: A benchtop router table set on a typical workbench is uncomfortably high. You want your router-table top height to fall in the 34- to 40-in. range. Unless you have a bench that's under 25-in. tall, you'll need to build a separate bench for your benchtop router or set it up on a pair of low sawhorses.

THE FENCE

The fence is the heart of any router table system. Here's what we think makes a great fence:

One-Piece vs. Two-Piece Fences

A one-piece fence is the clear favorite. By one piece we simply mean a fence with the main body made from a single piece of metal. A one-piece fence guarantees a continuous surface in a single plane for guiding your stock.

Two-piece fences are modeled after shaper fences where the infeed and outfeed halves move independently. This is handy on a shaper where the cutters remove

Benchtop router tables are portable and storable. Capable of handling most routing operations, they're the way to go when shop space is extremely limited.

Floor model router tables have larger tops and longer fences to better support and guide large stock.

1/32 in. from the stock width with each pass. However, on a router table this is a big hassle because 99 percent of your routing tasks require no offset and getting a two-piece fence perfectly aligned can be a chore.

Dual-Position vs. Single-Position Fences

We preferred the flexibility of a dual-position fence. A dual-position fence clamps to the edges of the tabletop (Photo 4), allowing it to be positioned on either side of the router. This is a big advantage on tables with offset router mounts. It allows you to work with a shallow or deep setback depending on the amount of support your stock requires.

A single-position fence is secured to the top through slots or by metal T-slots. It can only be placed on one side of the router.

Subfence

Don't buy a router table that won't accommodate a subfence (Photo 5). The best subfence systems are simple-to-make pieces of MDF that slide along slots in your main fence. A subfence can be made long or tall to guide long or vertically positioned stock. They are easy to offset for edge jointing (Photo 6).

T-Slots

A T-slot in the main fence works best for attaching subfences and accessories. Some manufacturers cut the T-slots in the subfence instead (Photo 7). But, this kind of subfence is trickier to make yourself.

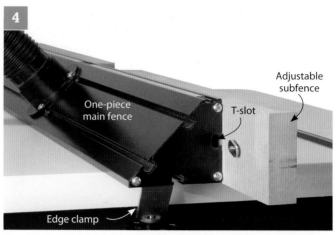

Here's what to look for in a router-table fence: Edge clamps allow you to position the fence anywhere on the table. A one-piece main fence doesn't have the alignment hassles of a two-piece fence. T-slots make convenient attachment points for subfences and accessories.

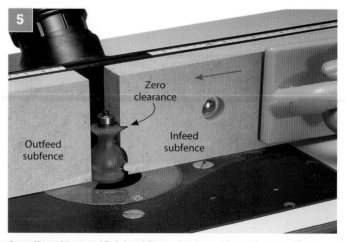

An adjustable sacrificial subfence is a must-have feature. The subfence allows you to adjust the fence opening to accommodate any sized bit. With the main fence secure, you can even push the infeed fence into a spinning bit and create a zero-clearance opening to eliminate chip-out.

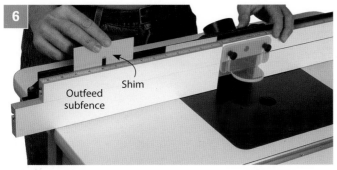

A subfence allows you to offset the outfeed fence with shims for edge jointing. Some manufacturers include shims, but you can easily make your own from paper, cardboard, or plastic laminate.

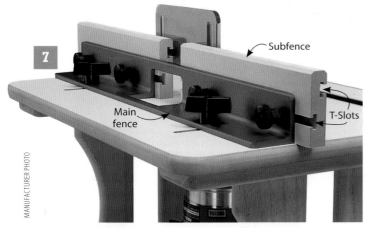

MANUFACTURER PHOTO

T-slots in the subfence work great, but in order to make your own subfence, you'll need to purchase a specialized router bit. We prefer the easy-to-make subfence shown in Photos 4 and 5.

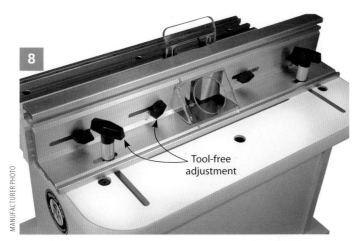

MANUFACTURER PHOTO

Tool-free adjustment knobs are the only way to go. The last thing you need to keep track of is another screwdriver or Allen wrench.

Tool-Free Adjustments

The best fence systems use top-mounted knobs to secure the fence to the table (Photo 8). Knobs under the table make adjustments unnecessarily cumbersome. Subfence adjustments should also be tool-free.

Dust Collection

Routers create gobs of dust and shavings so there's no excuse for a table to come without dust collection. Most models had good dust collection built right into the fence. As long as the fence is near the bit, these designs performed well. Cabinet-style bases offer the possibility of retrofitting a hose in the enclosed cabinet where the chips missed by the fence dust port can be extracted.

THE TABLE TOP

The router-table top has two simple but crucial functions. It must support the weight of a router without sagging and provide a flat, obstruction-free surface to run your stock over. A router-table top's worst enemy is sag. This creates all kinds of problems because the board you are machining must conform to the dip in your table.

To help prevent a sagging top, remove that heavy router when it's not going to be used for long periods of time.

Missing Safety Features

We're sticklers when it comes to safety. That's why we were disappointed when bit guards and external power switches were sold as accessories. We feel they should be included with every table!

Most manufacturers include a small bit guard attached to the fence. For operations where the fence can't be used, such as putting an edge profile on a curved piece, this guard is useless. Fortunately there are a number of good aftermarket guards available for larger bits and freehand work (Photo A). We think these guards should be included as standard equipment so users aren't tempted to try to work without them.

We felt the same way about external power switches (Photo B). Should the need arise, you don't want to be feeling for the power switch that's tucked in under the table. That off button should be right up front.

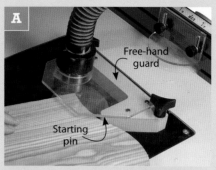

Bit guards are essential for safe hand-held routing. Unfortunately, specialized guards are sold as accessories.

An external power switch adds safety and convenience. It beats the heck out of fumbling around under the table looking for the on-off switch. In an emergency, it becomes an important safety feature.

Top Material

Router-table tops are made from one of three basic materials:

1. Metal
2. MDF
3. Phenolic resin

Phenolic resin is the best choice for a router-table top. It offers the strength and durability of metal but will never rust or corrode. Phenolic resin is so strong it's used in the landing gear of fighter jets and as skids for nuclear missiles on submarines. Unlike MDF, you can set a phenolic top in a steam bath overnight and it won't lose its shape or strength.

Metal tops also offer strength and stability. But, steel can rust and requires preventative maintenance just like cast iron, and aluminum is prone to leaving gray metallic streaks on your stock.

Most router-table tops have an MDF core. High-pressure plastic laminate (p-lam) applied to the top and bottom of a thick core make the best MDF tops. The p-lam provides a slick surface and greatly increases the strength of the MDF core.

9

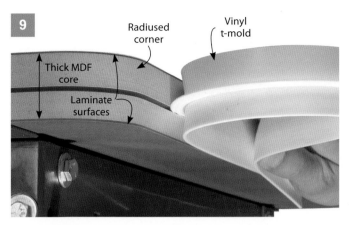

Radiused corner

Vinyl t-mold

Thick MDF core

Laminate surfaces

The best MDF tops are at least 1-1/16-in. thick and faced on both sides with high-pressure plastic laminate for a slick, durable, sag-resistant surface. Vinyl T-molding protects the raw MDF edges and radiused corners protect you when you back into them.

10

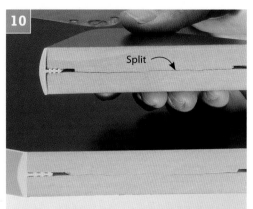

Split

Vinyl T-molding has a downside. It caused splits in a number of the tops we tested. These splits flared the edges of the top, ruining the flatness of the surface.

11

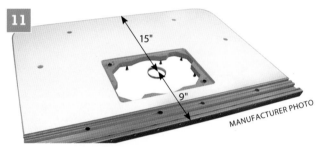

15"

9"

MANUFACTURER PHOTO

An offset router mount, when combined with a dual-position fence, allows you to choose the amount of table support between you and the router depending on which side of the bit you mount the fence.

Tip:

No matter what kind of top you buy, put a straightedge on it right away. If it sags in the middle, send it back and get a new one.

Moisture is a real problem for MDF. Get it wet and it's ruined, and long-term exposure to humid conditions can cause MDF to swell and weaken. This leads to sagging over time.

Most manufacturers use vinyl T-molding to protect the edges of MDF tops (Photo 9). This is a good thing, but it can cause a serious problem (Photo 10). As shown in the photo, the T-molding can cause the MDF to split and flare the edges, which leads to a less-than-flat top. We're at a loss to explain why this problem appeared on some tables but not on others.

Offset Router Mounts

Routers are either mounted dead center on the table, or they're offset to the front or back of the table. Offset router mounts (Photo 11) are a real advantage when combined with a dual-position fence. For most routing operations it's good to have the router positioned close to the operator. It makes feeding the stock and adjusting the router easier. Occasionally, you need extra support for raising panels or edging wide stock. With an offset router you can flip the fence to the other side of the table, giving you extra table support.

Direct-Mount vs. Mounting Plates

Some router tables use a direct-mount where the router is fastened directly to the tabletop (Photo 12). Others have router mounting plates that allow you to lift the router out of the table for bit changes and hand-held operations (Photo 13).

If you don't mind dedicating a router or a router base to your table, we think a direct-mount top has several advantages over mounting plates. It's a stronger, smoother top because there's no large cutout for a mounting plate which weakens the top, and there's no mounting plate to level flush with the top. On the downside, removing the router for hand-held work requires unscrewing the base from the top. That's why it's best to devote a router or an extra base to a direct-mount table.

Mounting plates replace the base plate on your router. The router is attached to the mounting plate, which in turn hangs in a rabbeted hole cut into the table's top. This system makes it easy to lift the router and mounting plate out of the table for bit changes and hand-held work. If yours is a one-router shop, like mine, a mounting plate is what you want.

The best plates are made from metal or phenolic resin to resist sagging. Plates should fit flush or have levelers.

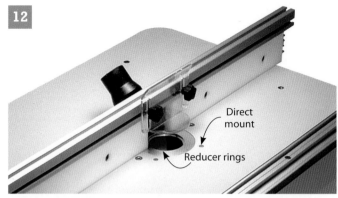

12

Direct mount

Reducer rings

Direct mounting the router to the top creates an uninterrupted surface free of catch points caused by a mounting plate. Direct mounting also requires a much smaller hole, which results in a stronger top. On the downside, it's a hassle to remove the router for hand-held work.

13

Reducer rings

Leveling screws

Mounting plates allow you to easily lift the router and mounting plate out of the table for bit changes and hand-held work. On the downside, you need to level the plate with the top, and the large cutout can weaken the top.

Predrilled or DIY Router Mounting

Predrilled plates eliminate the chance of screwing up your mounting plate or top with misplaced holes. Some manufacturers include a DIY mounting kit, while others leave you to go it alone. If it's available, we strongly recommend having the manufacturer drill the holes.

THE BEST BASE

There are three types of bases; the cabinet, the open stand and the folding stand. Cabinet bases are our first choice for floor (Photo 14) and benchtop models. Made from melamine, a plastic-coated MDF product that weighs a ton, cabinet bases provide a rock-solid foundation for your router-table top.

Cabinet-style bases allow you to enclose the area under the table with doors. This makes it easy to add a second dust collection point under the table by simply drilling a new dust port into the back of the cabinet. Doors also help to muffle that screaming router.

We didn't care for the open stands on the floor models. They are lighter than the cabinet bases, making them less stable and prone to scooting around the floor when machining large, heavy stock.

Folding stands all have one major defect— they wobble. Believe me, you don't want a router table that moves! If you need a portable router table, we suggest you stick to the benchtop models.

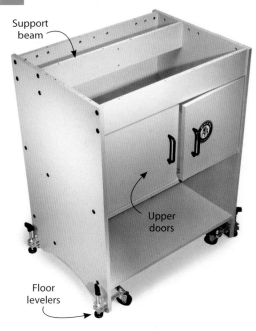

Support beam

Upper doors

Floor levelers

Three things to look for in a floor-model cabinet base:

Doors create an enclosed space under the table for additional dust collection. They also help quiet a screaming router.

A support beam for the top.

Levelers for uneven floors.

by DAVE MUNKITTRICK

Router Lifts

ADDING CONVENIENCE AND PRECISION TO MAXIMIZE ROUTER TABLE PERFORMANCE

For the serious router table user, the benefits of owning a router lift are huge. Strap a 3-1/4-hp variable-speed router into one of these lifts and you have a routing system that can't be beat for convenience, power, and accuracy. With a router lift, all your height adjustments can be made from the top of the table instead of underneath and bit changes no longer require removing the router from the table.

A router lift is essentially a router-table mounting plate with an attached carriage that holds the router. A removable crank handle inserts into the mounting plate and turns to raise and lower the carriage with incredible precision. A dial built into the plate or fastened onto the crank measures height adjustments in 1/64-in. or finer increments. Most lifts do not give you a cumulative readout. In other words, you have to keep track of the number of crank revolutions for height changes greater than 1/16 in. Some lifts allow you to zero out the height indicator.

Router lifts allow bit-height adjustments from the top of the table. No more groping under the table to release and adjust the router motor.

MIKE KRIVIT

Above-the-table bit changes can be made with most router lifts. That means you no longer have to drop the router out from under the table to change bits.

This is a great feature because it makes it possible to set your bits to exactly the same height every time you use them. For example, it practically eliminates the need for test cuts whenever you make stiles and rails for panel doors.

Router lifts eliminate the three biggest complaints router table users have. Above-the-table height adjustments (Photo 1) eliminate the most common complaint: the need to awkwardly grope under the table to adjust the bit height. Above-the-table bit changes (Photo 2) do away with having to remove the router to change bits. Finally, accurate micro-adjustments are a reality with a lift (Photo 3). Still, as

someone who just graduated from a hole cut in a piece of plywood, I was skeptical. After all, a router lift costs as much as a good router. But once I tried a lift, it didn't take long for me to become a believer.

All the lifts we tested performed well. The height adjustments were smooth and accurate. Backlash (that slop you feel in the handle when changing directions) was minimal and most lifts have backlash eliminators. We found that carriage travel varied quite a bit among brands. A router lift should have at least 3 in. of carriage travel. This allows you to start a tall bit low in the table and gradually raise it as you cut deeper with each pass.

MIKE KRIVIT

Router lifts make super-accurate micro-adjustments. You can confidently make adjustments as small as 1/1,000 in.

In the end, your choice of lift will depend on your particular circumstances. The main consideration is the size and type of router you own and whether you want to permanently mount it in your table.

CAN I USE MY OLD ROUTER AND TABLE?

For most fixed-base routers, the answer is yes. Your old router table should work fine, but there are two important considerations: Don't assume a router lift plate will fit the opening in your table. Check the router lift plate sizes and compare them to your current mounting plate's size. We also recommend you add cross bracing under your router tabletop. Router lifts are heavy, weighing 7 to 20 lbs. Add a 3-hp or larger router and you can almost guarantee that your top will sag over time without some added support.

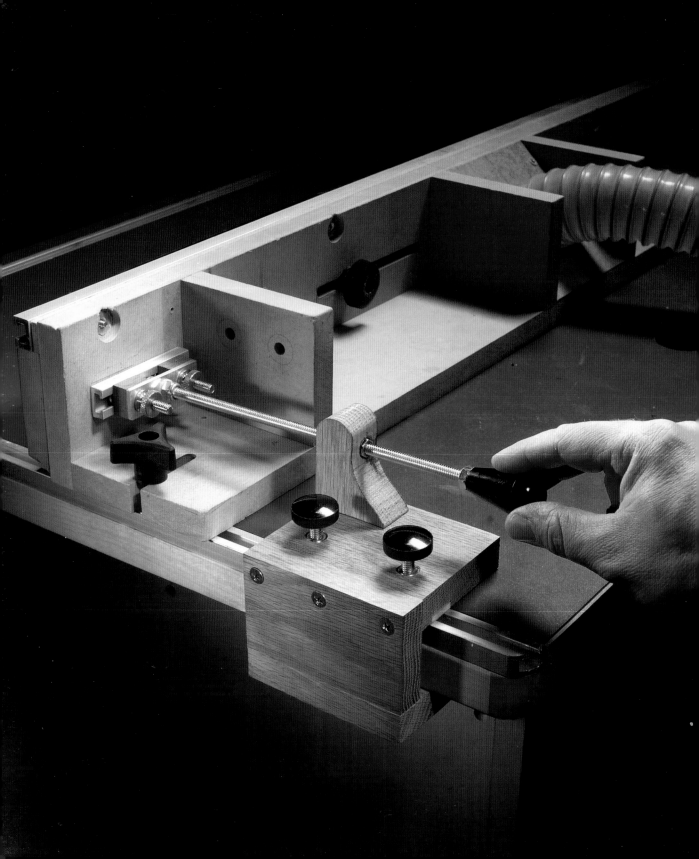

Router Tables to Build

Woodworking has a long tradition of woodworkers building their own router tables. In the following chapter you'll find four table designs and several useful accessory options.

If you have a tight budget, consider building the $100 Router Table. Simple no-frills materials keep the price down, yet the design still includes many useful features and accessories, including an easy-to-adjust zero-clearance fence and tilt-top design for easy router adjustment. The design even allows for the addition of optional dust collection, an external switch, and router bit storage. If your shop has limited space, the Mobile Router Center should meet your needs. Its fold-up design includes casters, so the table takes up less space than a full size table and easily wheels out of the way when not in use. It even includes onboard storage for your router, fence, and accessories. If you want a router table with all the bells and whistles, such as a large extra rigid top, then make sure to check out the American Woodworker Router Table or the Next Generation Router Table.

You will also see additional tips on ways you can improve your existing router table. You could even create your own hybrid router table using just the features you like best.

《 Building your own router table allows you to add the features you need or want, including this "two cent" micro adjuster.

by BILL HYLTON

$100 Router Table

AS EASY TO USE AS IT IS TO BUILD

Sometimes, less really is more. Take router tables, for instance. It's not at all difficult to ring up a big tab for a manufactured router table, complete with a new router, loaded with convenience, durability, adjustability, and precision. But to me, the compelling thing about a router table is that it converts a portable power tool into a stationary power tool and thus expands its utility and versatility.

A router table can be simple and quite inexpensive to make without sacrificing functionality. A basic table can be just as versatile, accurate, and easy to use as one of those grandees but cost far less.

I just finished making a $100 router table (excluding the router). I bought most of the materials and hardware at a local home center. There's no router mounting plate to buy; the router attaches directly to the hinged top.

FEATURE-PACKED

Despite the low cost, this is no bare-bones router table. It's packed with great features: an easy-to-adjust zero-clearance fence with sacrificial faces, an offset router mounting that allows you to use more of the table for work support, table inserts

FEATURES

The cutout at the front of the support frame provides better access to the router when the top is down.

With the tabletop tilted up, it's easy to pop open the base clamp and pull the motor to change bits.

Dust collection is built into the fence and can be added under the table.

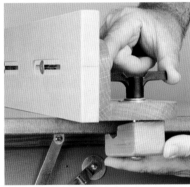

Integral clamps stay with the fence, yet allow it to be adjusted one end at a time. Big plastic wing nuts are easy on the fingers.

Adjustable fence faces are counterbored on both sides giving you four faces that can be turned over as the ends get chewed up.

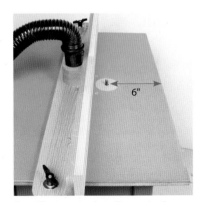

An offset router location puts the router close to you for the lion's share of router-table operations.

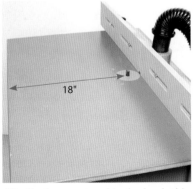

Flip the fence around to the back side of the top for a big offset. The extra support is ideal for panel raising.

Shop-made reducers improve the safety of your router table at virtually no cost.

to accommodate different bit sizes, a tilt-top for easy access to the router and quick bit changes (even with a plunge router), and built-in dust collection.

Of course there's a host of possible enhancements to the basic $100 router table including enhanced dust collection below the table, a front-mounted switch, and even bit storage. All these add-ons are covered at the end of the chapter.

BUILD THE BASE

1. Cut the leg blanks (E, Fig. A,) oversize from 2x6 lumber that's been seasoned in your shop for two weeks or more.

2. Cut 3-degree compound miters on the tops and bottoms of the legs. All the cuts are made with the head tilted 3-degrees. Divide the legs into 2-pairs consisting of one front and one back leg.

3. Cut the plywood panels (F-H). First, crosscut a 30-3/4-in. piece from a sheet of plywood. Rip it into a 19-in.-wide piece for the bottom, a 13-in.-wide piece for the back apron, and a 16-in.-wide piece for the side aprons. Crosscut the side-aprons piece in half.

4. Tilt the tablesaw blade 3-degrees and cut a bevel on all four edges of the bottom panel, reducing it to its final length and 1/8-in. shy of its final width.

5. Glue a strip of solid wood (J) to the front edge of the bottom panel. Trim flush after the glue's dried.

6. Return the tablesaw blade to 90-degrees and set the miter gauge to 3-degrees. Cut the tapered ends on the side and back panels.

7. Lay out marks for biscuit slots on the ends of the side and back aprons. Align the legs with the aprons and transfer the marks.

8. Lay out biscuit slots on the bottom shelf and transfer them to the bottom edge of the aprons.

9. Cut the biscuit slots. Set the joiner's fence to 87-degrees to slot the beveled edges of the bottom panel.

10. Glue and clamp the two side assemblies together (Photo 1) as well as the back and bottom panel assembly.

11. Join the two leg assemblies to the back and bottom panel assembly (Photo 2). Use masking tape to attach the tapered scraps from the panels to the legs so clamps will have parallel bearing surfaces.

BUILD THE TABLETOP

12. Cut the tabletop panel (A). Chamfer all four edges, top and bottom, to minimize chipping.

13. Lay out the bit hole location on the top (Fig. A.). Install a V-groove bit and park the router with the bit on the penciled crosshair. Orient the router exactly the way you want it—handles side-to-side, front-to-back, or on a diagonal. Mark the center points for the mounting screws (Photo 3).

14. Drill and countersink the mounting holes in the top. Mount the router to the tabletop.

15. Cut the support frame parts (B, C and D). Cut rabbets in the ends of the front and back pieces.

FIG. A: EXPLODED VIEW

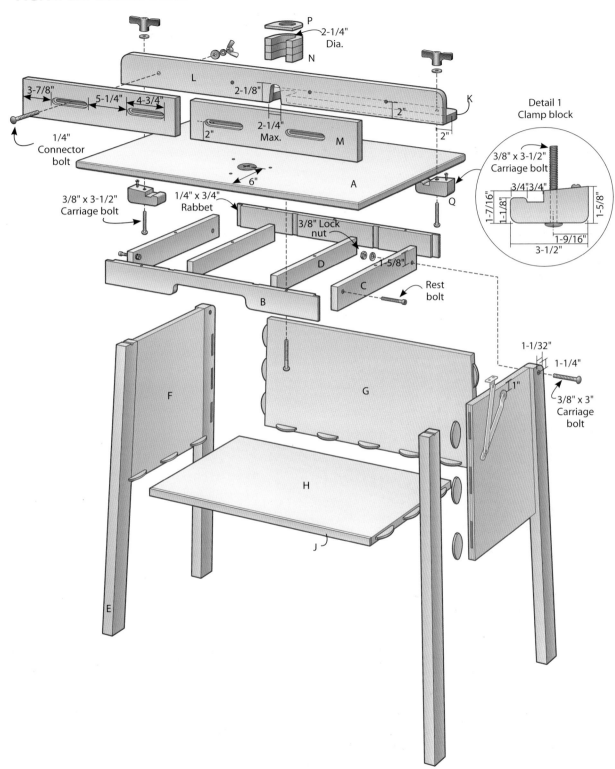

P
2-1/4" Dia.
N

L
2-1/8"

3-7/8"
5-1/4"
4-3/4"
1/4" Connector bolt

2"
2-1/4" Max.
M
K
2"
2"

Detail 1
Clamp block

3/8" x 3-1/2" Carriage bolt
3/4" 3/4"
1-7/16"
1-1/8"
1-5/8"
1-9/16"
3-1/2"

A
6"

3/8" x 3-1/2" Carriage bolt
1/4" x 3/4" Rabbet
3/8" Lock nut
Q

D
1-5/8"
C
Rest bolt
B

1-1/32"
1-1/4"
1"
3/8" x 3 Carriage bolt

F
G

H

E
J

Glue and clamp the two side assemblies. Use the offcuts from tapering the aprons as cauls so the clamps have parallel surfaces to address.

Glue and clamp the side assemblies to the back apron and bottom shelf. Use the tapered cauls to keep the clamps from slipping as they're tightened.

16. Dry assemble the frame on the tabletop. Use your router base to determine the spacing between the stretchers. Lay out the dadoes and rabbets in the front and back frame members as well as the cutout in the front.

17. Machine the front and back rails. Then assemble the frame on a surface you know is flat.

18. Drill 1/4-in. holes though the frame edges. Set the frame on the tabletop and transfer the hole locations to the tabletop (Photo 4).

19. Drill and tap stopped holes in the MDF for 1/4" - 20 machine screws (Photo 5). Threaded MDF has better holding power than wood screws driven into pilot holes.

20. Mount the tabletop to the frame (Photo 6). You could glue the frame, but if you ever changed routers, you'd need to build a new top.

21. Drill the holes for the hinge bolts in the frame (Photo 7, Fig. A). Cut threads in the rest of the bolt holes for 1/4" - 20 bolts.

22. Set the top on the stand. Use shims between the top edge of the stand and the MDF top. This keeps the top floating above the stand so all the weight from the top is carried by the framework underneath.

23. Transfer the hinge bolt holes from the top frame to the back legs of the stand. Drill the hinge-bolt holes through the back legs (Photo 8). Install the hinge bolts and rest bolts.

24. Mount the stay to hold the top open (Photo 9 and 10).

BUILD THE FENCE

25. Cut the fence base (K) and fixed face (L).

26. Cut the bit opening in the two fence pieces with a Forstner bit or a holesaw. From the near edge, saw into the hole, transforming it into a U-shaped notch.

27. Assemble the base and fence. Glue the edge of the base to the upright's face (Photo 11).

28. Round off the outside corners at the ends of the fence face and base on a bandsaw, then sand smooth.

29. Cut and glue-laminate scraps of hardwood to form the dust-pickup block (N).

30. Bore a 2-1/4-in. hole through the block (Photo 12).

31. On the bandsaw, cut a U-shaped hole and the outside profile of the block. Sand the sawed surface smooth.

32. Cut the dust pickup's cap (P). Bore a hole to fit your dust collector hose. Glue the cap to the dust pickup and the pickup to the fence (Photo 13).

33. Square the face of the fence to the base on a jointer (Photo 14).

34. Lay out the two clamp jaws on some scrap (Q) (Fig. A, Detail 1) and cut on the bandsaw. Sand the faces and edges.

35. Lay out and drill mounting bolt holes in the fence base and the clamp jaws (Fig. A).

36. Drive a round head or pan head screw into the clamp jaws near the bolt hole to act as an alignment screw. Drill oversize holes for the bolts in the fence base and add a shallow

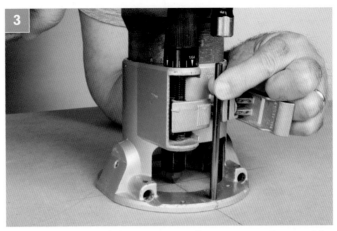

Mark the locations of the router mounting screws on the top with a transfer punch—a.k.a. a spotter.

Transfer the mounting-bolt holes in the framework to the MDF top using a transfer punch.

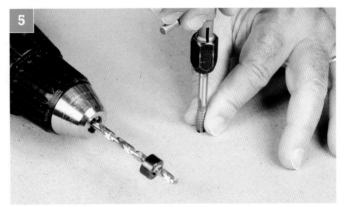

Cut threads in the top with a 1/4"-20 tap. Use a 13/64-in. bit to drill a 5/8-in. deep stopped hole at each mark, first. Make sure you clear all the chips from the holes. Then turn the tap into the hole until it bottoms out.

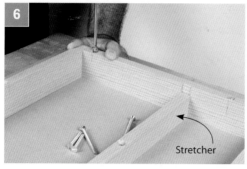

Reposition the frame on the tabletop and fasten it with 1/4"-20 flathead machine screws. I used seven 3-in.-long screws in the perimeter frame members and two 2-in.-long screws in the stretchers.

Lay out and drill the two 3/8-in. hinge-bolt holes in the frame. Clamp a backup scrap to the inside of the frame to prevent blowout.

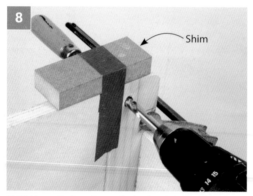

Drill hinge holes through the back legs. Tape 3/4-in. shims to the top edges of the stand and rest the tabletop on them. Use a transfer punch to mark the hinge-bolt hole locations on the back legs, then drill.

Mount the folding stay to the stand first. Measure down 1-in. from the stand's top edge and scribe a line. Hold the folded stay on the line so it clears the front leg and mark the screw location.

Attach the stay to the top. Hold the stay in position with a clamp. You decide the degree of tilt that suits you.

Glue and clamp the base and fixed face together.

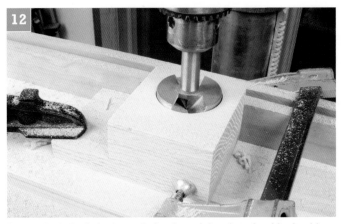

Bore a 2-1/4-in. hole through the dust pickup housing block with a Forstner bit or holesaw.

Glue and clamp the dust pickup to the fence. Tape scrap across the openings in the face to provide a bearing surface for the clamps.

Joint the glued-up fence to square the face to the base. Joint the base surface first to flatten it, then joint the fence face with the base against the jointer fence.

hole to house the alignment screw head (Photo 15).

37. Make the sliding facings (M) from pieces of leftover MDF. Cut faces to size, then use your new router table to rout stopped slots for the mounting bolts (Photo 16).

38. Drill mounting holes for the adjustable facings in the fence (Fig. A).

39. Use your largest bit to rout the opening in the tabletop. Cut a narrow rabbet around the opening, so its depth matches the thickness of the material you use for the inserts.

40. Cut one insert that fits nice and snug, and use it as a pattern for routing out a half-dozen more. When you put a hole in an insert, label its diameter.

Enhancement 1

BELOW-THE-TABLE DUST COLLECTION CAPTURES FUGITIVE DUST

Capturing all the chips and dust generated by router-table operations is a tough proposition. A fence-mounted pickup is important, but without a pickup under the table, a lot of the dust will escape capture.

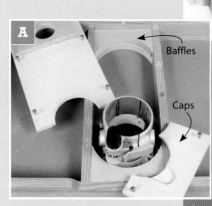

You can use the support frame's stretchers as the basis of a very effective dust chute. Make a two-piece cover from scraps of MDF or plywood. Insert rounded baffles to close off corners where dust gets trapped. Fit the caps as close as possible around the router base and drill a hole for a dust-hose connector (Photo A).

Extend a hose from this under-the-table channel and splice it into the hose from the fence-mounted pickup with a wye fitting. Leave enough slack in the hose to permit tilting the tabletop (Photo B).

Enhancement 2

EXTERNAL SWITCH ADDS SAFETY AND CONVENIENCE

Powering up a table-mounted router with the router switch is usually a nuisance. And many of us are uneasy about fumbling for an out-of-sight switch in an emergency. So a front-mounted switch is a worthwhile addition to any router table. I wired the switch to an extension cord. The cord wrap is made from hardwood scraps.

Enhancement 3

CONVENIENT ONBOARD BIT STORAGE

Bit storage is a practical addition to the table, and there's enough plywood left to construct a small box for two or three drawers. The drawer fronts require an additional 4-ft. piece of 1-in. x 4-in. oak. The drawer bottoms are 1/4-in. plywood and are cut wide enough to fit in slots cut in the box sides.

Two drawers have the bottoms drilled for 1/2-in. and 1/4-in. shank bits; together they'll accommodate about 80 bits. The top drawer holds wrenches, collets, bit-opening inserts, and other accessories. It is exposed when the tabletop is tilted up for easy access during bit changes.

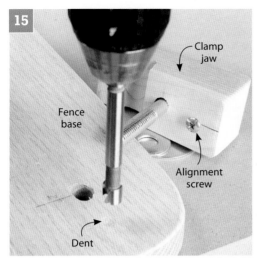

Drill a stopped hole in the fence base that will hold the alignment screwhead and keep the clamp block aligned perpendicular to the tabletop. To mark the hole, tighten the clamp block in place so the alignment screw-head dents the base.

Use the fence to cut the countersunk grooves in the adjustable faces.

Cutting List

Overall Dimensions: 24" D x 36" W x 34-1/2"H

	Part	Qty.	Dimensions	Material
A	Tabletop	1	3/4" x 24" x 36"	MDF
B	Frame front/back	2	3/4" x 2-1/2" x 27-1/2"	hardwood
C	Frame ends	2	3/4" x 2-1/2" x 17-1/8"	hardwood
D	Stretchers	2	3/4" x 1-3/4" x 17-1/8"	hardwood
E	Legs	4	1-1/4" x 2-1/4" x 33"	2 x 6
F	Side aprons	2	3/4" x 16" x 15-3/16"	plywood[1]
G	Back apron	1	3/4" x 13-1/8" x 29-3/16"	plywood[1]
H	Bottom	1	3/4" x 18-15/16" x 29-3/16"	plywood[2]
J	Edge band	1	3/4" x 1/4" x 29-3/16"	2 x 6[3]
K	Fence base	1	3/4" x 3-1/2" x 42"	hardwood
L	Fixed face	1	3/4" x 3-1/2" x 42"	hardwood
M	Sliding faces	2	3/4" x 4" x 24"	MDF
N	Dust pickup block	3	3/4" x 3-1/2" x 3-1/2"	hardwood[4]
P	Dust pickup cap	1	1/4" x 3-1/2" x 3-1/2"	1/4-in. MDF
Q	Clamp jaws	2	1-1/2" x 2-1/2" x 3-1/2"	2 x 63

[1] Miter ends at 87° [3] Cut from scrap
[2] Bevel edges at 3° [4] Stack and glue

by DAVE MUNKITTRICK

The American Woodworker Router Table

AS EASY TO USE AS IT IS TO BUILD

You won't find this router table in any store or catalog. But it incorporates all the best features found in those store-bought systems at half the cost!

At AW we've had the opportunity to study and use most of the router-table systems on the market. From that experience we've designed our own fully featured, easy-to-build router table. Commercial cabinet-based tables sell for several hundred dollars; ours can be built for about half that. You'll save enough to buy yourself a new router!

CHECK OUT THESE GREAT FEATURES

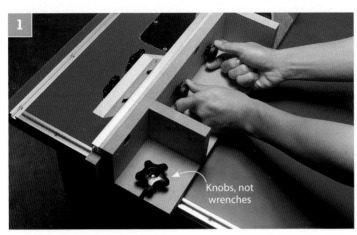

A totally tool-free fence. Forget about wrenches, screwdrivers, or clamps for fence adjustments.

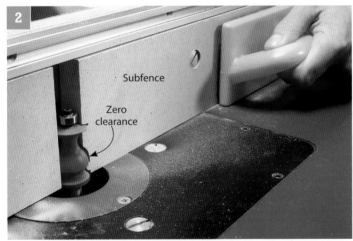

Easy-to-make, sacrificial subfences allow you to make a zero-clearance opening for super-clean, super-safe cuts. Simply slide the infeed fence slowly into the spinning bit.

THE ALL-IMPORTANT FENCE

At the heart of any great router-table system lies a well-designed fence. Ours offers all the best features identified in our router table tool test:

■ An easy-to-use, tool-free fence can be set and adjusted in an instant (Photo 1).

■ Easy-to-make sacrificial subfences can be adjusted for any size bit or used to create zero-clearance openings (Photo 2). They're easy to make from plain old 3/4-in. MDF.

■ Quick, rock-solid fence settings are made possible by T-tracks in the table (Photo 3). For fine adjustments, leave one hold-down tight to create a pivot point for the fence.

■ Fence-mounted T-track for attaching accessories (Photo 3, page 54).

■ A dust port for picking up the debris that routers kick out.

THE SAG-FREE TOP

In this article we'll show you how to build flatness into your top and keep it there. Our top's features include:

■ A dead-flat top that will never sag because it's supported by braces built into the cabinet (Fig. A).

■ A versatile offset router mount puts the router near the front edge for easy access and easy stock feeding. This is where you'll do 90 percent of your routing. The other 10 percent will be at the back of the table, which offers more table support for routing large stock, such as door panels (Photo 4).

■ Plastic laminate for a slick, durable top. We put the laminate on both surfaces to protect and stiffen the top.

■ Our Best Buy router-mounting plate allows easy removal of the router for bit changes and hand-held work.

A LARGE, EASY-TO-BUILD CABINET

Made from heavy, vibration-absorbing MDF, the cabinet goes together with butt joints and screws. There's plenty of storage plus the following features:

■ The capacity to handle the largest routers on the market for a router table that approaches the capabilities of a shaper.

■ A pair of doors on the front and back cut noise while giving you access to the router from either side of the table.

■ An external power switch (no wiring required) makes routing easier and safer. Easier because there's no fumbling under the table to turn on your router. Safer because who wants to be opening doors and groping for the power switch in an emergency?

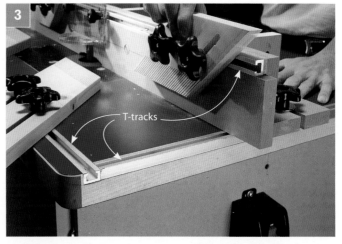

T-tracks provide slide-and-lock adjustments for maximum versatility. They make for super-smooth fence adjustments and convenient attachment points for accessories.

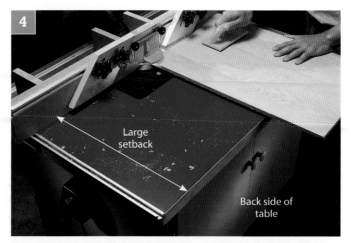

You can work at the back of the table to take advantage of the large setback to support big stock, like this door panel. That way you're not having to divide your attention between feeding the stock and keeping it from falling off the table.

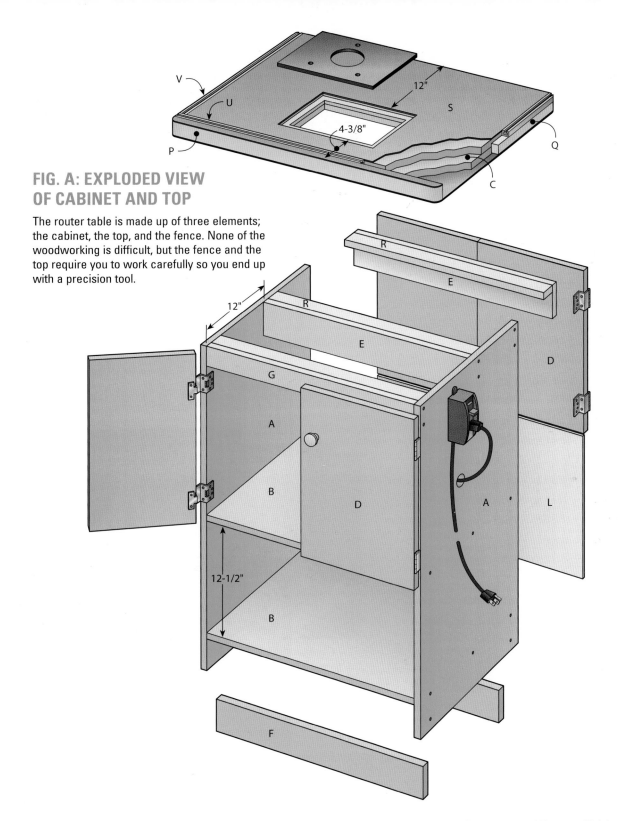

FIG. A: EXPLODED VIEW OF CABINET AND TOP

The router table is made up of three elements; the cabinet, the top, and the fence. None of the woodworking is difficult, but the fence and the top require you to work carefully so you end up with a precision tool.

BUILD THE BASE AND TOP

You'll need a tablesaw, router, jigsaw, belt sander, drill, and drill press to build this table.

We'll build from the bottom up, starting with the cabinet. It serves as a solid foundation for the working parts of our table. Ready? Here we go:

BUILD THE CABINET

1. Start by cutting the cabinet and top parts according to the Cutting List.

2. Assemble the cabinet with butt joints and screws (Fig. A). Use the toe-kick (F) as a spacer for setting the bottom shelf (Photo 1). Make a similar 12-1/2-in. spacer to set the middle shelf. Check for square as you build.

3. Add the braces (E and G) to support the top. The narrow brace (G) at the front of the cabinet makes it easier to adjust the router. Cleats (R) are glued at right angles to the support beams to provide a flange for screwing the top down onto the cabinet.

4. Hang the doors with self-closing, surface-mount hinges.

BUILD THE TOP

5. Glue together the two MDF pieces (C) that make up the top (Photo 2). Then, trim the substrate flush and square (Photo 3). Important: leave an extra 1/2 in. on the width to be trimmed after the hardwood edges are applied.

6. Glue on the two short pieces of hardwood edging (Q). Trim to finished width on the tablesaw leaving the hardwood flush with the front and back of the substrate (Photo 4).

Assemble the cabinet with butt joints and screws. Use the toe-kick as a spacer for locating the bottom shelf. Spring clamps are like having a third hand for supporting cabinet parts during assembly.

Glue together the two top pieces on a flat surface, such as your tablesaw. Sandbags (wrapped in plastic to avoid spills) provide the clamping pressure. Be sure to offset the two pieces by about 1/4 in. This will give you two clean edges to place against your tablesaw fence as you cut the top to final dimensions (see Photo 3).

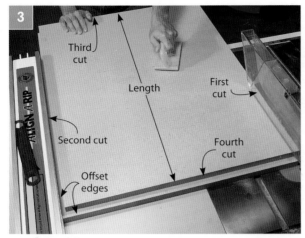

Trim the built-up top on the tablesaw using the two offset edges against the fence. You'll have to make four cuts to get the whole top square with flush edges. Leave an extra 1/2 in. on the width for trimming the hardwood edges (see Photo 4).

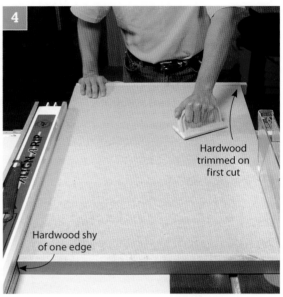

Cut the top to final width with the hardwood edging glued onto the sides. The hardwood is placed just shy of one edge on the MDF core. This leaves a clean edge to reference against the tablesaw fence for the first cut. The second cut is made to final width and leaves the hardwood perfectly flush with the edges of the MDF.

Apply the plastic laminate. Slip sticks prevent the plastic laminate from sticking to the top before you have it properly positioned. When the laminate evenly overlaps all four edges of the top, slip one stick out at a time and apply pressure to the laminate using a block of wood or a roller.

Rout the recess for your mounting plate. Build the template to fit snugly around your mounting plate. Use a top-bearing flush-trim bit to cut an exact-size opening. Make sure the template is deep enough to accommodate the bit length. Use a jigsaw to cut a hole in the center of the recess, leaving a 1/2-in. ledge for the mounting plate (Fig. A).

7. Glue the long hardwood edge (P) to the front and back of the top. Trim and sand the hardwood edges flush with the MDF. Then, round the corners with the belt sander. Now you're ready for the plastic laminate.

8. Glue the plastic laminate (S) to the top and bottom of the substrate with contact cement (Photo 5, page 57). Trim the laminate flush with the top using a flush-trim bit. File a slight bevel along the laminate edge to remove the sharp edge and prevent chipping.

9. Cut the recess for the mounting plate with a router (Photo 6, page 57). Cut the hole for the router with a jigsaw.

10. Rout the channels for the T-tracks (Photo 7).

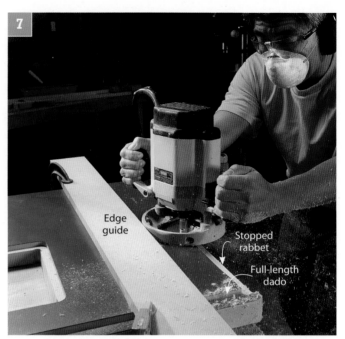

Rout channels for the T-track with a 3/4-in. straight cutter and an edge guide. Cut the full-length dado at the front of the table first; then cut the stopped rabbets on the two edges.

BUILD THE FENCE

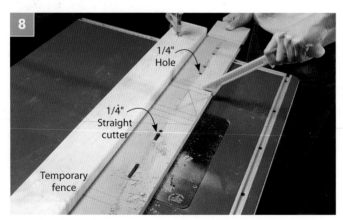

Rout slots in the fence parts using your newly built table and a temporary fence. Drill a 1/4-in. hole at the beginning and end of each slot. With the router turned off, set the blank against the fence so the 1/4-in. straight cutter protrudes through the first hole of the slot. Hold the blank firmly and turn on the router. Push the blank forward until the bit reaches the second hole.

BUILD THE FENCE

11. Cut the MDF parts for the fence (H through K). Carefully lay out the location of the supports, cutouts, and slots on the base and face pieces.

12. Rout the slots in the fence face (Photo 8) and at the ends of the base. The slots in the face allow the subfence to slide back and forth to create the adjustable opening. The slots in the base allow the fence to skew and pivot for fine adjustments. They also facilitate attaching and removing the fence from the top.

13. Cut out the bit opening in the face and base of the fence (Photo 9). A 45-degree bevel at the back of the cutout on the base (Fig. C) helps with dust collection.

14. Assemble the fence with screws (Photo 10). Drill your pilot holes a little deeper than the screws to prevent splitting the small support blocks.

15. Drill and countersink holes for each subfence.

Tip:

As long as you're making two subfences, you may as well make a dozen. That way you'll always have a fresh one when you need it and you won't be tempted to "make do."

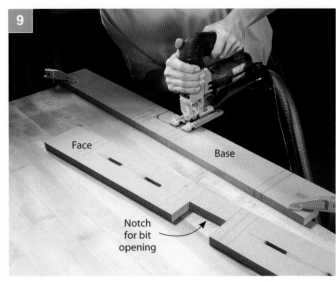

Face

Base

Notch for bit opening

Cut notches in the fence parts with a jigsaw. Once the fence is assembled, the notches form an opening in the fence to accommodate the router bit.

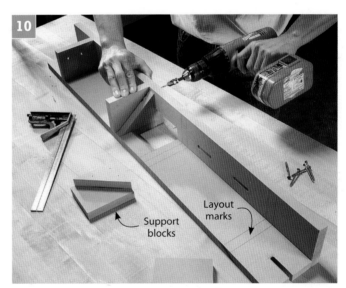

Support blocks

Layout marks

Assemble the fence with screws. Check each support block for square before you use it. Perfectly square support blocks ensure a perfectly square fence.

FIG. B: CUTTING DIAGRAM FOR BASE, TOP AND FENCE

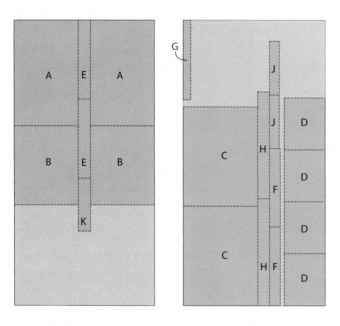

Special thanks to Richard Tendick for his help in engineering this router-table fence and accessories.

FIG. C: EXPLODED VIEW OF FENCE

Take the time to accurately lay out the position of each support block, slot, and screw hole on the fence base and face. Moving parts require precise construction.

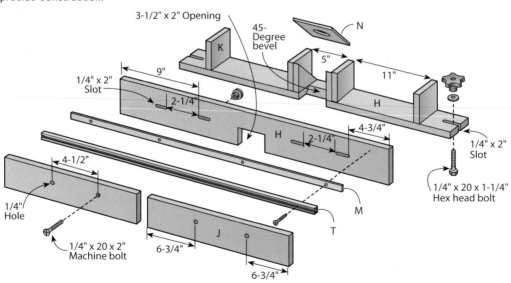

Cutting List

Overall Dimensions: 37-1/4"H x 34"W x 25-1/2"D

Part	Name	Qty.	Dimensions	Material	Notes
A *Base*	Sides	2	22" x 35-1/2"	3/4" MDF	
B *Base*	Shelves	2	22" x 26-1/2"	3/4" MDF	
C *Top*	Top	2	24" x 32-1/2"	3/4" MDF	Add 1" to length and width and trim to final size after lamination.
D *Base*	Doors	4	13-3/8" x 17-1/2"	3/4" MDF	
E *Base*	Top Brace	2	4" x 26-1/2"	3/4" MDF	
F *Base*	Toe-Kick	2	3-1/2" x 26-1/2"	3/4" MDF	
G *Base*	Top Brace	1	3" x 26-1/2"	3/4" MDF	
H *Fence*	Face & Base	2	4" x 36"	3/4" MDF	
J *Fence*	Subfence	2	3-3/16" x 18"	3/4" MDF	Make a dozen while you're at it.
K *Fence*	Support Blocks	5	3-1/4" x 4"	3/4" MDF	Cut one block in half diagonally to create supports for dust port.
L *Base*	Back	1	13-1/2" x 28"	1/4" Hardboard	
M *Fence*	Shim	1	3/4" x 36"	1/4" Hardboard	Use to shim out fence T-track.
N *Fence*	Dust Port	1	5" x 5-1/8"	1/4" Hardboard	
P *Top*	Maple Edging	2	1-1/2" x 34"	3/4" Solid Wood	Rough cut 1/16" over in width and 1" in length. Trim to final size after gluing to the top.
Q *Top*	Maple Edging	2	1-1/2" x 24"	3/4" Solid Wood	Rough cut 1/16" over in width and 1" in length. Trim to final size after gluing to the top.
R *Base*	Pine Cleats	3	1-1/2" x 26-1/2"	3/4" Solid Wood	Edge glue to top of each top brace.
S *Top*	Surface	2	25-1/2" x 34"	Plastic Laminate	Cut 1" oversize in all dimensions and flush trim to substrate after glue down.
T *Fence*	T-track	1	36"	T-track	Cut to fit from 48" stock.
U *Top*	T-track	1	34"	T-track	Cut to fit from 48" stock.
V *Top*	T-track	2	24"	T-track	Round the exposed ends with a file to eliminate catch points.

by JOHN ENGLISH

Next-Generation Router Table

MAKE MORE ACCURATE CUTS WITH A FLAT, SOLID-SURFACE TOP

This router table took thirty years to build. No kidding. I don't mean that it took me thirty years to actually make it, but it took me that long to figure out how to do it right.

I've used a lot of router tables over those years, and all have come up short. I've been frustrated with complicated fence locks, panels tipping because the fence wasn't tall enough, insert plates that were finicky to level, small worktops that don't support a door or drawer, inadequate dust collection, bad lighting, and on top of all that, having to kneel on the floor to change the depth of cut.

After all those disappointments, I finally built a router table that solved all these problems.

BUILD THE CASE

1. Glue two pieces of hardwood to create the four legs (A). Plane all four faces of each leg, and then trim them to length. Using a dado set or a router equipped with

9 Key Features

1. Hinged Top.

Bit changes are much easier.

2. Pivot Control.

Just loosen the fence's left side
for quick micro-adjustment.

3. Tall Fence.

There's plenty of support for
raised panel work

4. Solid-Surface Top.

It's slick, flat, and durable.

5. Fence T-slots.

Attach a light, stops, and
feather-boards.

6. Huge Work Surface.

It's 26" x 43".

7. Double Dust Collection.

There are ports top and
bottom.

8. Custom Sized Bit Opening.

Make it any diameter you need.

9. Storage.

There's lot's of room for bits, routers, and accessories.

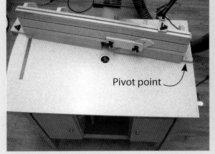

Pivot point

a straight bit and a fence, mill a stopped groove in two adjacent faces of each back leg and one face of each front leg (Fig. A). These grooves receive the side and back panels. Note that the front legs are not grooved to receive the face frame. Square the end of each groove with a chisel.

2. Clamp the four legs together and locate the screw holes in each groove. On the drill press, use a 3/32" bit to drill pilot holes through the legs. Counterbore the exit holes for plugs, using a 3/8" Forstner bit.

3. Cut the sides (B) and the back panel (C). Screw and glue the two back legs to the panel. Screw and glue the side panels to the back legs, then attach the two front legs. Keep the panels flush with the tops of the legs. Glue plugs in the legs to cover the screw holes.

4. Mark the locations of the two divider panels (J) on the inside face of the back panel (Fig. A). Drill five equally-spaced pilot holes along the center of each location. Cut the divider panels to size, and then glue and screw them to the back panel using screws driven through pre-drilled, countersunk pilot holes. Clamp the panels in place as you drive the screws.

5. Make the side stiles (D) and the top and bottom rails (E and F) of the cabinet's face frame. Drill and countersink pilot holes at the joints, then glue and screw the pieces together. Glue and screw the face frame between the front legs. Cut the two middle stiles (G) to size and install them with glue and finish nails (Photo 1). Run a couple of screws up through the bottom rail into the end of each stile.

6. Cut the sub-top (K) to size and install it with glue and thirty-two screws driven into the top edges of the sides, back and divider panels, and the top rail of the face frame (Photo 2). Pre-drill for the screws and countersink the heads.

7. Mark the opening in the top (Fig. C) and clamp four cleats to the cabinet to act as guides for your router (Photo 3). Their locations will depend on the size and shape of your router base. Chuck a 3/8" straight bit in the router and plunge through the top in four or five incremental passes in order to remove the waste from the opening. Glue and nail trim (L) to all four edges of the sub-top, mitering the corners. Screw and glue cleats (M and N) around the bottom edges of each of the two side compartments. Cut the two compartment bottoms (P) to size. Notch one

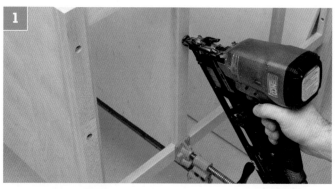

Begin building the router table by making the base. Construction is quite simple, using just screws, glue, and a nailed-on face frame in front.

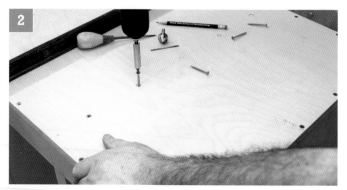

Attach a plywood sub-top to the base. The subtop prevents the base from racking. It also supports the working top which is made from 1/2" thick solid-surface material, such as Corian or Avonite.

Rout a rectangular hole in the center of the sub-top. Make a series of shallow passes until you've cut all the way through. Place the solid surface top on the sub-top.

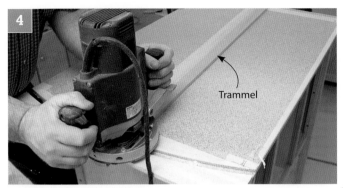

Rout an arc on one end of the solid-surface top using a trammel fastened to the router's base.

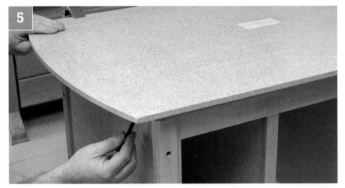

Clamp the top to the base and trace all the way around the top's underside. Turn the top over.

Build a frame to fit inside the rectangle you drew. Glue the frame to the top using silicone adhesive. Attach the top assembly to the case with a continuous hinge.

back corner of each using the bandsaw so they fit around the cabinet legs, and install them with screws driven up through the cleats into pre-drilled, countersunk holes. The doors (Q) are simply birch-veneered plywood panels with edge trim (R) that is mitered to length and applied with glue and finish nails. Install them with surface-mounted, self-closing hinges. Use a couple of drawer pulls for handles.

PREPARE THE TOP

8. On the tablesaw, cut Corian or Avonite solid surface material for the top (S) to 26" x 43" and belt sand the edges. Apply masking tape in the general vicinity of the pivot hole (Fig. B), and then mark the hole's exact location on the tape. Drill the hole. Make a trammel for your router by fastening the router to some 1/2"-thick hardwood or plywood stock that's at least 4" wide and 4 ft. long. Chuck a 1/2" dia. straight bit in the router. At the pivot end of the trammel, drill a 1/4" dia. hole 41-3/4" from the center of the bit. Loosely attach the end of the trammel to the top with a 1/4" bolt, two washers and a hand-tightened nut, and cut an arc across the left end of the top in several 1/8" deep passes (Photo 4). Once you've cut all the way through, gently sand all the top's edges.

9. Place the top on the cabinet flush with the back. The top's right edge (where the pivot hole is located) should overhang the cabinet by 2". Temporarily clamp the top in place and mark the cabinet's outline (Photo 5). Also mark the large, rectangular hole in the sub-top. Cut two stiles (T) and four rails (U) for the support frame (Photo 6). The inner rails should line up with the edges of the large hole in the sub-top. Assemble the support frame with biscuits and glue and attach it to the underside of the top with clear silicone adhesive. Apply weight (a sandbag works well) while the silicone cures. An overnight cure is good, but it's better to let it cure for a few days.

10. Connect the top and support-frame assembly to the cabinet with a continuous (piano) hinge. Use longer 1-5/8" bugle screws in the center and one near each end for strength.

THE TOP'S LIFT SUPPORT

11. When raised, the top is locked in the open position by a three-part mechanism: an arm with both top and bottom cleats (Photo 7). Make the top cleat (V, Fig. D). Attach it to the inside edge of the support frame's left-hand rail, using two screws and glue.

12. Make the bottom cleat (W). Cut it to size and then miter one end. Bore three holes for carriage bolts. Epoxy a bolt into the middle hole. Use a washer and nut to pull the bolt tight while the epoxy cures, and then locate the bottom cleat in the cabinet. Drill holes in the partition for the other two bolts, and install the cleat with washers and nuts.

13. Make the arm (X) and install it with two plastic tri-knobs.

Build an arm to prop the top. This makes it much easier to change bits because there will be plenty of elbowroom around the router. Plus, you don't have to bend over.

Drill a 3/4" dia. hole through the top, then remove the router's baseplate and mark the locations of its mounting holes onto the top. Drill the holes and lower the top.

Enlarge the opening by using a series of rabbeting bits and pattern bits. A rabbeting bit leaves a ledge around the hole making it perfect for fitting an insert.

Make a set of wooden zero-clearance inserts to fit the hole. Drill variously sized holes in the inserts to fit your bits.

Mark the length of the fence's bottom board. Cut the board 2" longer than the top.

Drill pilot holes in the fence using a drill press. This ensures that all the pieces of the fence are square when they're assembled.

MOUNT THE ROUTER

14. With the top closed, drill a 3/4" dia. hole where the center of the router will be located (Fig. B). Lock the top in the open position and use the hole to locate your router's baseplate on the underside (Photo 8). Mark and drill holes for mounting bolts using the baseplate as a pattern. Close the top and countersink the holes. Install the router base, minus the baseplate, with stove bolts, washers, and nuts.

15. Take a look at your router bit collection and decide how large you would like the hole in the top to be. (At my woodworking school, I strongly recommend limiting router bits to 2" dia.) To enlarge the hole, begin by using a rabbeting bit with a guide bearing that is slightly smaller than the hole (Photo 9). Follow up with a bearing-guided pattern bit, and then use these bits in sequence until the hole is as large as you wish. Make a final pass with the rabbeting bit to leave a ledge that will support hardwood inserts (Photo 10).

BUILD THE FENCE

16. Cut the fence base (F1) to size and use a miter saw to trim the pivot end at an angle (Fig. H). Drill the pivot hole at the location indicated. Lay the fence base on the top and secure the pivoting end with a bolt, two washers and a nut that is just finger tight. Mark the opposite end (Photo 11), then cut the base 2" longer than the top, using the offcut from the top as a guide to make a curved end. Mark and cut the circular bit opening in the fence base, then pre-drill some screw holes for assembling the frame (Photo 12).

17. Cut the fence back wall (F2) to size and bandsaw the opening in it for a dust collection port (Fig. H). Align the back wall along the front edge of the base and attach it with glue and screws. Cut the front wall (F3)

Cut T-slots in the fence's face pieces. This can't be done on a tablesaw, but you could borrow a friend's router table or use a handheld router and an edge guide.

Make the fence's clamping block. It contains a T-bolt that's trapped between two pieces of wood that are glued together. Attach a felt chair pad as a spacer.

Drill a hole through the fence for the clamping block's T-bolt.

Clamping block

Attach the clamping block to the fence with a plastic knob. To adjust the distance from any router bit to the face of the fence, loosen the knob and pivot the fence back and forth.

to size. Cut the sliding fences (F4 and F5) to size and mill one T-slot in each (Photo 13 and Fig. G). (It helps to mill each groove with a 1/4" straight bit first, and finish the cut with the T-slot bit.) Cut the top molding (F6) to size and plow a T-slot in that, also. Glue and clamp the front and back walls together. When the glue has dried, trim the top molding to length with a short 45° miter on each end (that is, leave about 1/3 square and miter the rest), and then attach it with glue and clamps. Cut the four fence braces (F7) to size and shape, and install each with glue and screws. Drill four holes for the T-bolts that lock the sliding fences in place.

18. Build the fence-clamping block (Photo 14 and Fig. E). Nibble a small dado on the bottom section (F9), and install a T-bolt before gluing both sections together (Photo 15). Attach a self-adhesive felt chair pad to the top of the lock, then add a little sandpaper or grip tape to the top of the rabbet. Mark and drill a hole in the fence base to align with the T-bolt, and install the lock with a tri-knob (Photo 16). Screw the dust port in place behind the fence and you're ready to add some handy accessories (see page 69).

Accessories

FEATHERBOARD

Make one or two adjustable featherboards to fit the fence's T-slots (Fig. F). A featherboard increases the accuracy and consistency of your cut by holding your workpiece firmly down on the tabletop.

SWITCH

Add an aftermarket switch to the table to make it easier to turn the router on and off. If you're right-handed, mount the switch on the right side of the cabinet, near the front and up high.

DUST HOOD

Install a 12" plastic dust hood to keep dust away from your router's motor. Mount the hood on a plywood frame attached to cleats. The gap between the bottom of the router and the hood should be about 2".

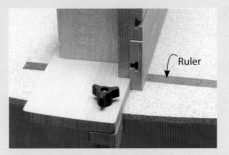

Ruler

FENCE POSITION RULER

Epoxy a 12" metal ruler into the top for fine-tuning a setup. The distance you move the fence from the bit is half the distance shown on the ruler. Use a plunge router to create a shallow mortise for the ruler.

LAMP SUPPORT

Good light is always an issue, isn't it? You can use the T-slot in the top of the fence to support a bracket for an adjustable lamp. It's easy to move the lamp anywhere you want.

GUARD

Protect your fingers by covering the bit with an adjustable plastic shield that fits in the fence's T-slot.

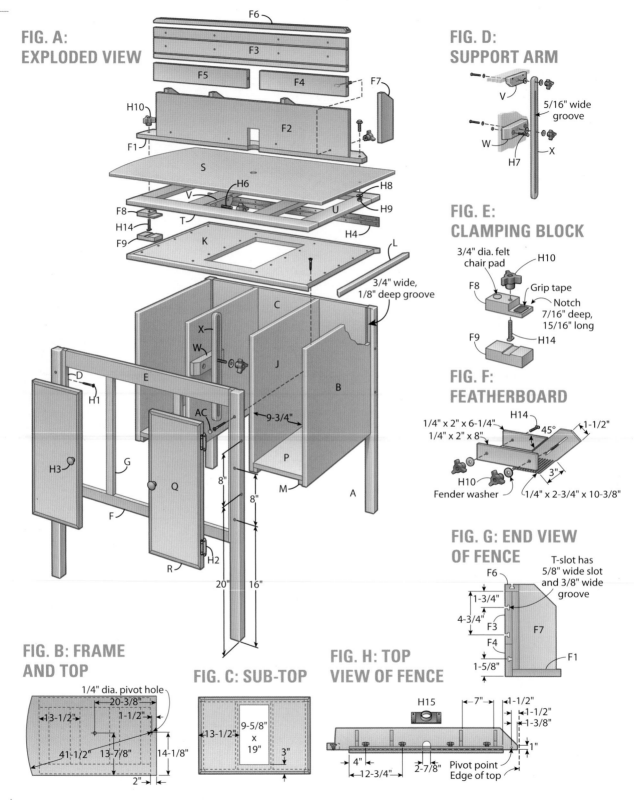

FIG. A:
EXPLODED VIEW

F6

F3

F5   F4

F7

H10

F2

F1

S

H6

H8

V   U   H9

F8

T   H4

H14

F9   K   L

3/4" wide,
1/8" deep groove

C

X

W   J

B

D

E   9-3/4"

H1

AC

H3   G   P

Q   M   A

F   8"   8"

R   H2

20"   16"

FIG. D:
SUPPORT ARM

V   5/16" wide
groove

W   X

H7

FIG. E:
CLAMPING BLOCK

3/4" dia. felt
chair pad   H10

F8   Grip tape

Notch
7/16" deep,
15/16" long

F9   H14

FIG. F:
FEATHERBOARD

H14   45°   1-1/2"

1/4" x 2" x 6-1/4"
1/4" x 2" x 8"

H10
Fender washer   3"

1/4" x 2-3/4" x 10-3/8"

FIG. G: END VIEW
OF FENCE

T-slot has
5/8" wide slot
and 3/8" wide
groove

F6

1-3/4"

4-3/4"   F3

F7

F4

F1

1-5/8"

FIG. B: FRAME
AND TOP

1/4" dia. pivot hole

20-3/8"

13-1/2"   1-1/2"

41-1/2"   13-7/8"   14-1/8"

2"

FIG. C: SUB-TOP

13-1/2"   9-5/8"
x
19"

3"

FIG. H: TOP
VIEW OF FENCE

H15   7"   1-1/2"

1-1/2"
1-3/8"

13-1/2"

1"

4"   Pivot point
Edge of top

12-3/4"   2-7/8"

Cutting List

Overall Dimension: 37-1/4" H x 43" W x 26" D

Part	Name	Qty.	Material	Dimension
A	Leg	4	Hardwood	1-1/2" x 1-1/2" x 35-1/4"
B	Cabinet side	2	Plywood	3/4" x 22" x 22"
C	Cabinet back	1	Plywood	3/4" x 33-1/2" x 22"
D	Face frame outer stile	2	Hardwood	3/4" x 3/4" x 22"
E	Face frame top rail	1	Hardwood	3/4" x 2-1/2" x 31-1/2"
F	Face frame bottom rail	1	Hardwood	3/4" x 1-1/2" x 31-1/2"
G	Face frame middle stile	2	Hardwood	3/4" x 1-1/4" x 18"
J	Divider Panel	2	Plywood	3/4" x 22" x 22"
K	Sub-top	1	Plywood	3/4" x 23-1/2" x 35-1/4"
L	Sub-top trim	1	Hardwood	3/4" x 3/4" x 117-1/2" (a)
M	Compartment long cleat	4	Hardwood	3/4" x 3/4" x 22"
N	Compartment short cleat	4	Hardwood	3/4" x 3/4" x 8-1/4"
P	Compartment bottom	2	Plywood	3/4" x 9-3/4" x 22"
Q	Cabinet door	2	Plywood	3/4" x 8-1/2" x 18-1/4"
R	Door trim	1	Hardwood	1/4" x 3/4" x 111" (a)
S	Top	1	Solid Surface	1/2" x 26" x 43" (b)
T	Frame stile	2	Hardwood	3/4" x 3-1/4" x 36-3/4"
U	Frame rail	4	Hardwood	3/4" x 3-1/4" x 18-1/2"
V	Arm top cleat	1	Hardwood	3/4" x 1-7/8" x 7"
W	Arm bottom cleat	1	Hardwood	1-3/8" x 2-1/8" x 8" (c)
X	Arm	1	Hardwood	1/2" x 1-3/4" x 24-3/4"
Y	Router table insert	3	Hardwood	1/4" thick, custom dia.
Z	Dust hood plate	1	Plywood	3/4" x 13-1/8" x 14"
AA	Dust hood plate trim	1	Hardwood	1/4" x 3/4" x 13-1/8"
AB	Dust hood cleats	2	Hardwood	3/4" x 3/4" x 14"
AC	Decorative plug	20	Hardwood	3/8" dia.
Fence				
F1	Base	1	Hardwood	3/4" x 5-1/4" x 45" (d)
F2	Back wall	1	Hardwood	3/4" x 8-1/2" x 38"
F3	Front wall	1	Hardwood	3/4" x 5-3/4" x 38"
F4	Sliding fence - right	1	Hardwood	3/4" x 3-1/4" x 16-3/4"
F5	Sliding fence - left	1	Hardwood	3/4" x 3-1/4" x 19-1/4"
F6	Top molding	1	Hardwood	3/4" x 1-1/2" x 38"
F7	Brace	4	Hardwood	3/4" x 4" x 9-1/4"
F8	Clamp block top	1	Hardwood	3/4" x 1-1/2" x 3"
F9	Clamp block bottom	1	Hardwood	3/4" x 1-1/2" x 3"
F10	Lamp base		Hardwood	3/4" x 1-1/2" x 4"

Hardware

Part	Name	Qty.	Dimension
H1	Screw	176	1-5/8" Bugle
H2	Cabinet hinge, pair	2	Overlay, surface mount
H3	Cabinet pull	2	Knob
H4	Continuous hinge	1	1-1/2" x 36"
H5	Machine bolt	1	1/4" x 2"
H6	Carriage bolt	1	1/4"-20 x 2"
H7	Carriage bolt	3	1/4"-20 x 3"
H8	Washer	4	1/4" ID
H9	Nut	3	1/4" nylon locking
H10	Tri-knob	10	1/4"-20, plastic
H11	Router mounting bolt	3	To fit, countersink stove
H12	Stove bolt washer	3	Locking or spring washer
H13	Stove bolt nut	3	To fit
H14	T-bolt	8	1/4"-20 x 2-1/4" toilet bolts
H15	Dust port	1	To fit your hose

(a) Cut to length as needed

(b) You may use Corian, Avonite, or another synthetic countertop material

(c) Make the cleat from 3 pieces of 3/4" x 1-3/8" stock.

(d) Rough cut at 47" long, then cut to fit

by JOHN ENGLISH

Mobile Router Center

THIS ROLLING ROUTER UNIT HAS STORAGE FOR ALL YOUR ROUTER COMPONENTS

Without question, a router table is one of the most versatile tools you can add to any shop. Whether you're making doors or moldings, router tables are do-it-all tools. This shop-made unit is a fully featured router table with portability, versatility, and compactness. And you can build the whole thing for less than $260. It's perfect for any shop in which floor space is precious. The top has as much real estate as a full-size router table but, like a benchtop unit, the router center can easily be stowed when you're done.

The key to a flat, rigid table is the torsion-box design. A torsion box is nothing more than a crisscross frame captured in a top and bottom. It's easy to build, dead flat, and solid as a rock.

Move it!

Use it!

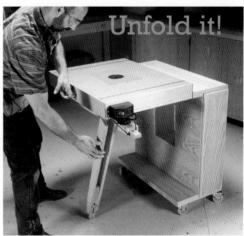

Unfold it!

Store it!

Organize it!

EDITOR: RANDY JOHNSON • ART DIRECTION: VERN JOHNSON • PHOTOGRAPHY: RAMON MORENO • ILLUSTRATION: FRANK ROHRBACH

FIG. A: EXPLODED VIEW

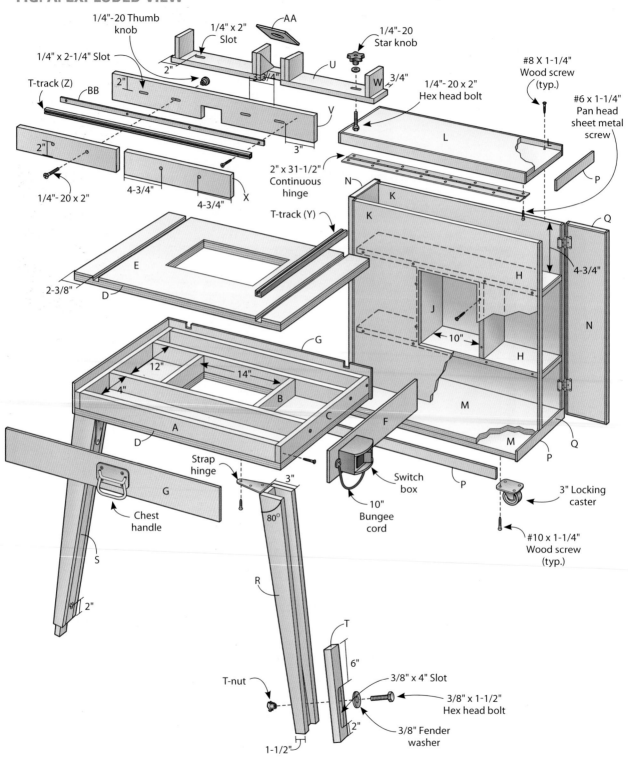

1/4"-20 Thumb knob

1/4" x 2" Slot

AA

1/4"-20 Star knob

1/4" x 2-1/4" Slot

2"

T-track (Z)

BB

2"

U

W

3/4"

1/4"-20 x 2" Hex head bolt

#8 X 1-1/4" Wood screw (typ.)

#6 x 1-1/4" Pan head sheet metal screw

2"

3"

V

L

L

P

1/4"-20 x 2"

4-3/4"

4-3/4"

X

2" x 31-1/2" Continuous hinge

N

K

K

Q

T-track (Y)

N

E

H

4-3/4"

2-3/8"

D

J

10"

H

N

G

12"

14"

4"

B

C

H

M

A

D

F

M

Q

G

3"

Switch box

M

P

Strap hinge

80°

10" Bungee cord

3" Locking caster

Chest handle

S

R

#10 x 1-1/4" Wood screw (typ.)

2"

T

6"

T-nut

3/8" x 4" Slot

3/8" x 1-1/2" Hex head bolt

2"

3/8" Fender washer

1-1/2"

The router table top is a torsion box, which guarantees a stiff, flat surface. Assemble it with glue and screws, holding the edges flush. Brad-nail the parts first to hold them in place while you drill and drive the screws.

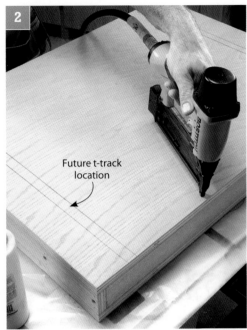

Future t-track location

Pin the top and bottom skins to the torsion box so they don't shift during clamping. Avoid the T-track locations so you don't rout into a brad later. It only takes a few brads to hold the parts in place.

BUILD THE TOP

Crosscut both sheets of plywood required for this project into 32-in.-long slabs (see Cutting Diagram, page 80).

1. Cut to size the ribs (A, B), ends (C) and top and bottom skins (D). Cut the hardboard top (E) 1 in. larger than the top skin.

2. Glue and screw the torsion-box ribs together (Photo 1). Pin the top and bottom skins to the torsion box (Photo 2). Assemble the torsion box on your tablesaw (Photo 3).

3. After the glue is dry, rough out the cavity in the bottom of the torsion box and trim it flush with a router (Photo 4). Use a 1/4-in. round-over bit to ease the sharp corners. Flip the torsion box and flush-trim the hardboard top to match the box's top skin (D).

BUILD THE CASE

The assembly of the case is very similar to that of the torsion-box top, with internal ribs that create the compartments in the case.

4. Assemble the case ribs (H, J).

5. Glue and screw the case skins (K) to the ribs (Photo 5).

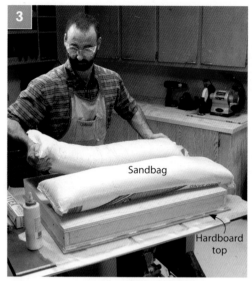

Sandbag

Hardboard top

Glue the torsion-box on your tablesaw. The surface of the saw virtually guarantees a flat top. Place the hardboard face down on the saw, spread a uniform film of glue on the hardboard and lay the torsion box on it. Weight the sandwich with sandbags.

Bottom side of table

Flush-trim the cavity in the bottom of the torsion-box assembly. Use a jigsaw to remove most of the waste first.

Inner case ribs

Assemble the case using glue and screws. Use layout lines to correctly locate the skins on the ribs.

Tapering jig

Taper the sides of the legs using a taper jig on the tablesaw. The leg sides must be cut to final length before you taper them.

Screw the leg hinges to the bottom of the router table top. The legs should bypass each other when they're folded.

Attach the top assembly to the case using a continuous hinge. Use a pair of 2-1/4-in. spacers under the case to make it level with the top.

6. Rough-out and flush-trim the router cavity on the inside of the case. Use a 1/4-in. round-over bit to ease the corners.

7. Screw and glue the top (L) and bottom (M) to the case. Attach one layer first. Then add the second piece of plywood by screwing from below so no screws show on the top side of the double panels.

8. Cut the door panels (N) to size.

ADD EDGE BANDING

Make all the edge banding 1/32 in. oversize in width. After you glue it on, sand it flush to the plywood.

9. Make the banding for the case and door (Q), the double-thickness top and bottom (P) and the torsion-box top (F, G).

10. Cut, fit, and glue the narrow banding to the remaining edges of the case and the doors and the wide banding to the top and bottom of the case.

11. Cut, fit, and glue the extra-wide banding to the torsion box's sides and long back edge. You don't band the long front edge until after you install the T-track (see Step 13).

FINISH THE TOP

12. Use your router to cut the dado for the T-track (Y) in the top. Cut the T-track to length, file the sawn edges to remove burrs, and screw it in place.

13. Cut, fit, and glue the final edge banding to the front of the top.

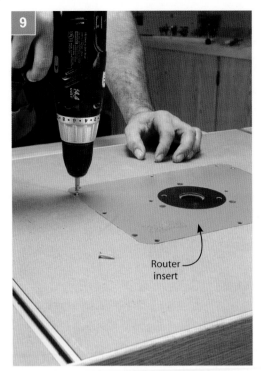

Router insert

Self-closing hinge

Drill and countersink eight holes through the table insert, and fasten it to the top with flat-head sheet-metal screws. This ensures your router won't tumble out when you fold the table top down.

Screw the self-closing hinges to the door and fasten the door to the case. It's easier to drive the screws if you first prick the plywood using a scratch awl.

14. Round all the edge-banded corners by hand-sanding or using a 1/8-in. round-over bit.

15. Center the router plate on the top and rout the recess for it according to the manufacturer's instructions.

MAKE THE LEGS

16. Prepare the leg material from solid wood. Cut the parts to final length with a 10-degree angle on the top ends of the box parts (R, S) and the bottom end of the adjustable foot (T).

17. Cut the leg tapers (Photo 6).

18. Cut the slot in the adjustable foot.

19. Install the T-nut in the leg. Glue and clamp the leg boxes together.

20. Bolt the adjustable foot to the leg box.

PUT IT ALL TOGETHER

21. First, screw the hinges to the legs. Then, with the legs in place, screw the hinges to the bottom of the top (Photo 7).

22. Flip the case upside down onto a pair of spacers and install the casters and continuous hinge (Photo 8). The casters we've specified are double locking, so they don't roll or swivel when locked.

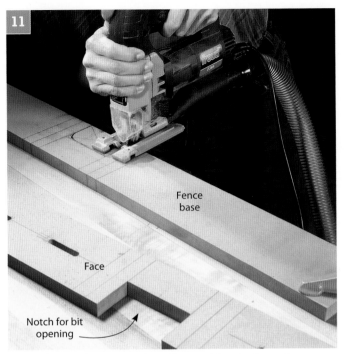

Cut notches in the fence using a jigsaw. After the fence is assembled, the notches provide clearance for router bits.

Assemble the fence with glue and screws. Make sure the face and base are dead square to each other.

23. Fold the top and case together. Get some help and flip the case and top assembly upright.

24. Open the top and level it using the adjustable feet.

25. Drill and countersink the table insert and screw it to the opening in the top (Photo 9).

26. Screw the hinges to the door, and fasten the door to the case (Photo 10).

27. Attach the router table switch and chest handle to the folding top.

28. Using the same screws that hold the switch, fasten a bungee cord to the top. This acts as a retainer for one leg when you're folding and unfolding the table. The other leg swings free so it drops into place when you unfold the table.

MAKE THE FENCE

29. Cut all the fence pieces (U, V, W, X, AA, BB) to size. Tip: Make a handful of subfences so you have extras.

30. Rout the slots in the fence base and face and cut out the bit clearance notches (Photo 11). Long slots in the base allow the fence to skew on the table as you're making adjustments. Slots in the face allow you to slide the subfences for the adjustable opening in the fence.

31. Glue and screw the face to the base and attach the support blocks and dust port (AA, Photo 12).

32. Cut the T-track and spacer (BB) to length and screw it into the face.

FINISH IT

33. There's plenty of plywood and hardboard left to make drawers, trays, hooks and racks. Outfit your table to hold all your goodies.

34. Most routers can remain fastened to the top when the table is folded, and they'll swing right into the cavity in the case. If your router bumps the back of the cavity, just cut that side out, as in Step 6, to provide clearance.

35. Apply a coat of finish to all the wooden parts. It's not a must to seal the hardboard top, but a coat of paste wax will help your material slide across it better.

Materials List
- Taper jig
- 4-in. guard
- Two sheets 3/4-in. x 48-in. x 96-in. oak plywood
- One sheet of 1/4-in. x 48-in. x 96-in. tempered hardboard
- Two pair 1/2-in. overlay self-closing hinges
- One 48-in. continuous hinge
- One 3-1/2-in. chest handle
- Two 6-in. strap hinges
- Miscellaneous hardware
- Four casters
- 24-in. T-track with knobs and bolts
- 48-in. T-track with knobs and bolts

PLYWOOD CUTTING DIAGRAM

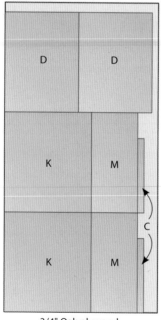

3/4" Oak plywood

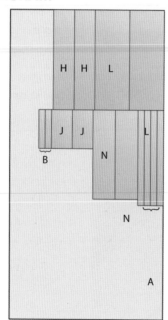

3/4" Oak plywood

PROJECT REQUIREMENTS AT A GLANCE

Materials:
- Two sheets of 3/4-in. oak plywood
- One sheet 1/4-in. tempered hardboard
- 8 bd. ft. of oak

Cost:
- Less than $260

Hardware:
- Strap hinges
- Chest handle
- Switch box
- T-track
- Casters
- Router table insert

Tools:
- Tablesaw
- Router
- Jigsaw
- Taper jig
- Planer

Cutting List

Overall Dimensions: 35-1/2"D x 41"W x 40-3/8"H open w/fence (16"D x 39"W x 34"H closed)

Part	Section	Name	Qty.	Dimensions	Material	Notes
A	Torsion box	Long ribs	4	2" x 29-1/2"	3/4" oak plywood	
B	Torsion box	Short ribs	2	2" x 12"	3/4" oak plywood	
C	Torsion box	Ends	2	2" x 23"	3/4" oak plywood	
D	Torsion box	Skins	2	23" x 31"	3/4" oak plywood	
E	Torsion box	Top	1	24" x 32"	1/4" tempered hardboard	Flush-trim after gluing on.
F	Torsion box	Banding	2	3-3/4" x 23"	1/4" oak	
G	Torsion box	Banding	2	3-3/4" x 31-1/2"	1/4" oak	
H	Case	Long ribs	2	6-1/2" x 31"	3/4" oak plywood	
J	Case	Short ribs	2	6-1/2" x 12"	3/4" oak plywood	
K	Case	Skins	2	27-1/8" x 31"	3/4" oak plywood	
L	Case	Top	2	10-3/4" x 31"	3/4" oak plywood	
M	Case	Bottom	2	14-1/2" x 31"	3/4" oak plywood	
N	Case	Doors	2	7" x 27-5/8"	3/4" oak plywood	
P	Case	Banding	8	1-1/2" x various lengths	1/4" solid oak	
Q	Case	Banding	12	3/4" x various lengths	1/4" solid oak	
R	Legs	Sides	4	3" x 31"	3/4" solid oak	Cut 10-degree angle on top end. Cut taper.
S	Legs	Backs	2	1-1/2" x 31"	3/4" solid oak	Cut 10-degree angle on top end.
T	Legs	Adjustable foot	2	1-1/2" x 12"	3/4" solid oak	Cut 10-degree angle on bottom end.
U	Fence	Base	1	4" x 31-1/2"	3/4" MDF	
V	Fence	Face	1	4" x 31-1/2"	3/4" MDF	
W	Fence	Support blocks	5	3-1/4" x 4"	3/4" MDF	Cut one block in half diagonally to create supports for dust port.
X	Fence	Subfence	2	3-1/4" x 15-3/4"	3/4" MDF	Make a bunch while you're at it.
Y	Top	T-track	2	23-1/4"	T-track	Cut to fit from 24" lengths.
Z	Fence	T-track	1	31-1/2"	T-track	Cut to fit from 48" length.
AA	Fence	Dust port	1	5" x 5-1/8"	1/4" tempered hardboard	Drill a 2-1/4"-dia. hole.
BB	Fence	Spacer	1	3/4" x 31-1/2"	1/4" tempered hardboard	

by JENNIFER FEIST

Hang a Router... Perfectly

SURE-FIRE ROUTER PLATE INSTALLATION

Are you tempted by the benefits of owning a router table plate but hesitate to take the plunge because of the hassles involved in mounting it in your table? That's understandable because a poorly fit router table plate leads to endless frustration. A loose fit makes it impossible to maintain a consistent distance between your bit and fence. A plate that's set too high or too low in the rabbet creates catch points for stock and makes depth-of-cut settings difficult. Fortunately, you don't have to put up with these headaches. Here's how to correctly install the plate for peak performance.

If you're still worried about approaching your immaculate tabletop with a screaming router, do what I did and practice the procedure on a piece of scrap first. You'll need a pattern bit (Photo 1), a jigsaw, a drill, double-stick tape, and some 1-in.-thick stock. (The 1-in. material can be made from built-up sheet stock.)

Top-bearing pattern bit

Choose a pattern bit with the same radius as the corners on your router table plate.

EDITOR: DAVE MUNKITTRICK • ART DIRECTION: PATRICK HUNTER AND BARBARA PEDERSON • PHOTOGRAPHY: RAMON MORENO

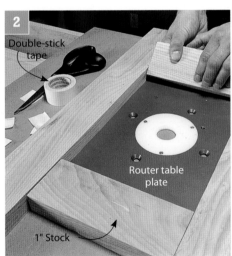

2

Double-stick tape

Router table plate

1" Stock

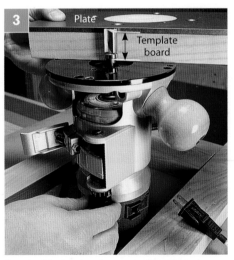

3

Plate

Template board

Make an exact template using your plate as a guide. We used 1-in.-thick stock to accommodate the depth of the bit and the bearing (Photo 3). Double-stick tape works great for holding the boards in place without making holes in your router table top.

Set the bit depth using a template board and your plate as a guide. The depth-of-cut equals the thickness of the template boards plus the thickness of the plate.

Rout the rabbet after adding support boards for the router base to the middle of the cutout.

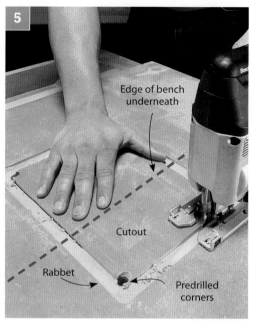

Rough cut the opening with a jigsaw. Be sure to support the cutout so it can't break off before the cut is finished. Predrilling the corners helps start the cut and makes cutting the corners easier.

Accurately Centering the Router on the Plate

If you want to use template guide bushings with your router table plate, the router must be mounted dead-on center, and that's not easy.

Rousseau has developed a baseplate mounting system that's simple and accurate. The bit includes a centering disc, alignment pin, longer mounting screws, and pointed tapping screws that accurately mark where to drill your plate. This system works with any plate that accepts 1-3/16-in. guide bushings.

PHOTO COURTESY OF ROUSSEAU

ART DIRECTION: VERN JOHNSON · PHOTOGRAPHY: BILL ZUEHLKE · ILLUSTRATION: FRANK ROHRBACH · CONSULTANT: RICHARD TENDICK

by DAVE MUNKITTRICK

Soup Up Your Router Table

YOUR ROUTER TABLE WILL REALLY SING WITH THESE GREAT ACCESSORIES

Like all good tools, our accessories will increase safety and improve results. They're easily adapted to use on almost any router-table system.

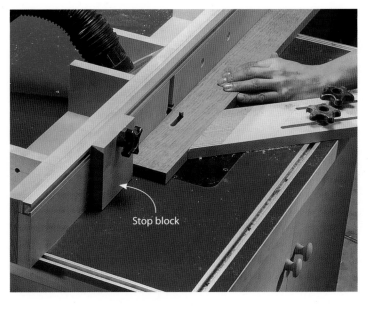

Stop block

STOP BLOCKS

A stop block is indispensable for cuts that don't go the entire length of the board. Ours mounts on the fence T-track for quick settings that won't budge.

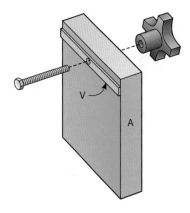

Cut hardwood runners (V) wide enough to just fit into the T-track slot, but not as deep. Glue the strips on the blocks, and drill out for the 1-1/4-in.1/4-20 hex bolt.

FEATHERBOARDS

Featherboards make routing safer and better. Safer because they hold the work against the table and fence instead of your hands. Better because the constant pressure holds the piece on both sides of the bit for smooth, washboard-free profiles.

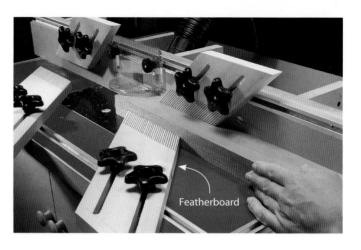

Featherboard

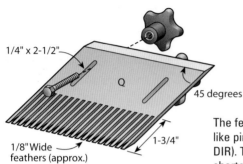

1/4" x 2-1/2"

Q

45 degrees

1/8" Wide feathers (approx.)

1-3/4"

The featherboards are made from clear, solid-wood stock like pine or poplar. There are two sizes (see Cutting List, DIR). The longer ones are mounted on the table and the shorter ones on the fence. Cut the 45-degree angles first. The 1/4-in. slots can be cut on the router table and the feathers are cut using a bandsaw.

Freehand guard

Starting pin

FREEHAND GUARD

A freehand guard and a starting pin are a must for routing curved profiles, such as this arch-topped door panel. Dust collection isn't perfect, but it keeps the bit area clear.

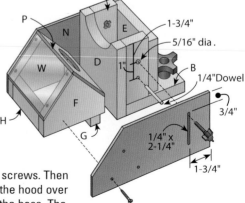

P

N

E

1-3/4"

5/16" dia.

W

D

1"

B

1/4" Dowel

H

F

3/4"

G

1/4" x 2-1/4"

1-3/4"

Assemble the base (parts B, C and D) with glue and screws. Then build the hood (parts E through H, N, P and W). Slip the hood over the base and glue the two 1/4-in. guide dowels into the base. The winged bolts allow you to adjust the height of the hood. Drill *two* 1/4-in. holes at the back of the base for the hold-down knobs.

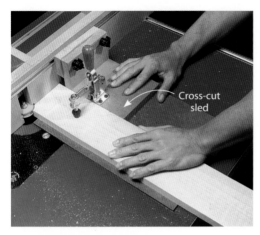

Cross-cut sled

ROUTER-TABLE SLED

A router-table sled replaces the miter slot found on many commercial tables. It allows you to safely perform end-grain cutting, such as the cope cut on this rail, without having to set your fence perfectly parallel to a miter slot.

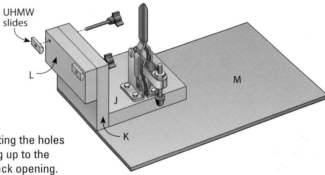

UHMW slides

L

J

K

M

The only tricky part to making this accessory is getting the holes for the bolts just right. Simply hold the completed jig up to the fence with the base on the table and mark the T-track opening. Then, drill your holes in the center of the marked opening. UHMW T-track slides guide the sled along the fence.

TALL FENCE

A tall fence makes vertical routing safe and accurate. It provides plenty of support for work that must be stood on end to rout, such as drawer joints, lock-miter joints, and vertical panel raising.

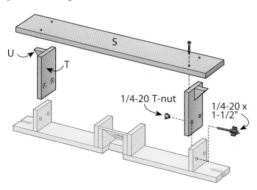

U

T

S

1/4-20 T-nut

1/4-20 x 1-1/2"

Tall fence attachment

The tall fence fits between the two outside supports of the main fence. Build the two supports (U and T) and attach them to the main fence. Use a square to align the top (S) with the face of the main fence and secure with screws or winged bolts.

by DAVE MUNKITTRICK

See-Through Router Base

SEE WHERE YOU'RE GOING ON A DOVETAIL JIG

Why are so many router bases solid black? I hate peering through those little holes to align my router on a workpiece. The problem is worse on a dovetail jig, where you must blindly feel your way around the template's fingers. I managed to nick my template a few times before I discovered router expert Bill Hylton's technique for making a see-through base. It eliminates all that hesitation and anxiety.

This new clear base is designed to accept Porter-Cable-style guide bushings. If your old base doesn't accept guide bushings or they're hard to find, making this new base and adding guide bushings will allow you to do more things with your router. The trick to making this base is getting the guide bushing centered on the router's axis. Just follow these steps and you'll be routing in the clear in no time.

MATERIALS AND TOOLS

Make your base from 1/4-in.-thick acrylic or polycarbonate plastic. Acrylic is available at most hardware stores and home centers. Polycarbonate is more shatter-resistant, although it's less stiff, harder to find and more expensive. Either plastic can be machined like any hardwood using standard woodworking equipment. Leave the protective film on to protect the plastic from scratches during machining.

To make your clear base, you'll need these items: a drill press, router table, bandsaw or jigsaw, flush-trim bit, 1-1/4-in. and 1-3/8-in. Forstner bits, a countersink bit, a centering bit for your router and double-stick tape. You may need longer screws to fasten this new thicker base to your router.

DRILL MOUNTING HOLES

Use the manufacturer-supplied base as a template for your clear base. Secure the original base to the plastic blank with double-stick tape. Cut and shape the blank on your bandsaw and router table (Photo 1). Keep the blank moving at about the speed of a clock's second hand to prevent the plastic from melting. On the drill press, mark the centers for the mounting screws (Photo 2).

Gently pry the original base off the blank using a putty knife. Select a twist bit just large enough to let the mounting screw shank easily pass through the hole. Drill the mounting holes all the way through the base (Photo 3). Friction from a spinning drill bit can easily melt plastic. When drilling plastic, use a quick, repetitive in-and-out action. Pause for a second between strokes to allow the bit and plastic to cool.

Drill countersinks for flat-head screws (Photo 4). I use flat-head screws to mount a base, because the tapered heads automatically draw the base into the exact location each time it's fastened. A countersink bit has the same profile as a flat-head screw. Don't use a large twist bit to drill the countersinks; the profiles don't match.

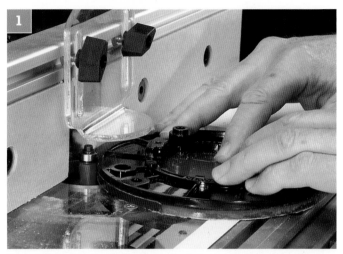

Shape a rough-cut clear plastic blank on the router table using a flush-trim bit. Secure the original base to the blank using double-stick tape.

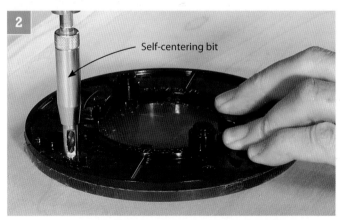

Self-centering bit

Mark the mounting screw locations using a self-centering bit mounted in a drill press. All you need is a slight dimple on the surface. Don't drill all the way through the blank, because the centering bit is not the final diameter.

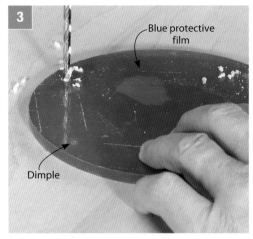

Drill the mounting screw holes using the dimple marks to center the bit. Center the dimpled hole under the bit with the power off. Secure the blank firmly with your hand, raise the bit, turn on the drill press and drill the hole.

Countersink the mounting screw holes. Center the bit by lowering it into the hole with the power off, as in Photo 4. Set the depth of cut so the screw heads will be sunk slightly below the base's surface.

DRILL CENTER HOLES

After the base has been shaped and the mounting screw holes completed, fasten the base to your router. Chuck a centering bit or a V-groove bit with a sharp point into your router. With the new base in place, gently lower it onto the router until it barely touches the plastic surface. Lock the router base assembly tightly to the router. Take a small hammer and lightly tap the plastic over the centering bit (Photo 5). Use the resulting mark to center the base under a 1-1/4-in. Forstner bit. Clamp the base to the drill press table. Check to make sure the bit is still in line with the mark. Drill the center hole through the base (Photo 6).

Flip the base so the countersinks face up (Photo 7). Center the base on the table using the same Forstner bit that drilled the hole and clamp the base down to the drill press table.

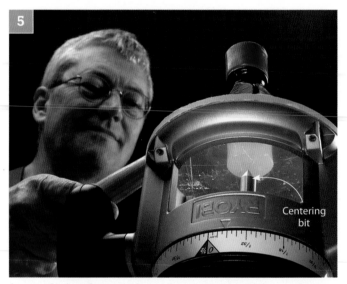

Locate the base's center by putting a centering bit in your router, lowering the baseplate onto it, and tapping the plastic with a hammer. The resulting mark will be dead center.

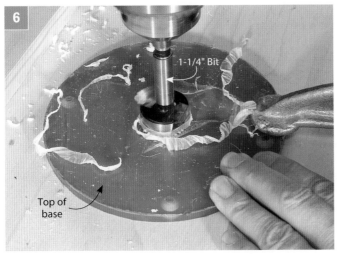

6

1-1/4" Bit

Top of
base

Drill out the center hole. Center the plate on the bit and clamp
it down. Use an in-out feed action to keep the bit cool and the
plastic from melting. You should get wispy curls of plastic, not
molten mounds.

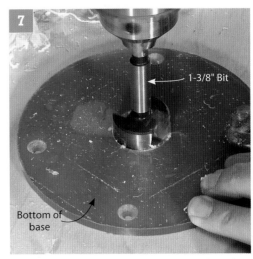

7

1-3/8" Bit

Bottom of
base

Flip the plate and drill the larger counterbore
hole. Center the plate using the smaller bit and
clamp. Change to the larger bit
and drill.

8

Routed
surface

Clear finish

A flame finish adds just the right touch. It turns the hazy, machined
edges crystal clear. Just wave the flame from a blowtorch back
and forth until you see the haze disappear. Be careful not to
overheat the plastic or it will bubble.

Change to a larger 1-3/8-in. Forstner bit. Now,
before you get too excited about drilling from
a smaller hole to a larger one, let me explain:
Typically, you would drill a large counterbore
first, followed by the smaller through hole.
In this case, the mark from the centering bit
is on the wrong side of the base for the large
counterbore hole. I use Forstner bits because
they are rim-guided. They can cut a larger
hole over a smaller one without trouble.

After all the machining is done, remove the
protective film and use sandpaper to lightly
round-over the bottom edge. You can clean
up machine marks and scratches by carefully
using a blowtorch (Photo 8). The result is a
crystal-clear finish that's not really necessary,
but it sure looks good.

by BRUCE KIEFFER & RICHARD TENDICK

Shop-Made Router Lift

FEATURES YOU CAN'T BUY AT A PRICE YOU WON'T BELIEVE

Router lifts are hot items these days and for good reason. Veteran router table users love their ability to make super-fine micro adjustments or rapidly raise the bit right from the tabletop. No more fumbling under the table like a contortionist.

The only drawback is the price: several hundred dollars. Ouch! That's why we were so thrilled when Richard Tendick walked into our offices with his idea for a shop-made router lift. Not only does Richard's lift offer above-the-table height adjustment but it costs around $100. Plus, unlike the expensive commercial lifts, this lift allows you to change bits without cranking the router all the way up. It also features effective below-the-table dust collection. When combined with dust collection in the fence it results in near-perfect dust collection. This design also isolates the exhaust end of the router in the cavity. That leaves the router air intake sucking only clean, dust-free air. And,

unlike all the other mechanical lifts on the market, Richard's lift hangs off the back of the router table, not on the top where the excess weight can lead to sagging.

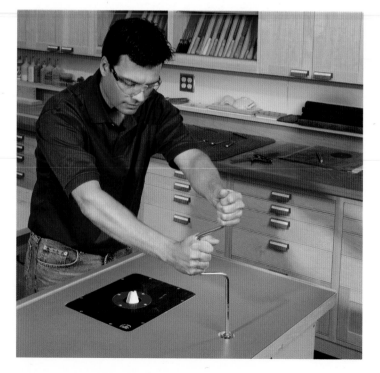

EDITOR: DAVE MUNKITTRICK • ART DIRECTION: VERN JOHNSON • PHOTOGRAPHY: MIKE HABERMANN • ILLUSTRATION: BRUCE KIEFFER

BENEFITS OF THE ROUTER LIFT

Bit height changes are quick and precise. A speed wrench allows you to raise the router bit to any height in seconds. For fine adjustments, a one-quarter turn of the wrench equals a mere 1/64-in. change in bit height.

Changing router bits is fast and easy. The lift is mounted to the cabinet, not the top. This allows you to hinge the top for easy access to the router. It makes bit changes a snap.

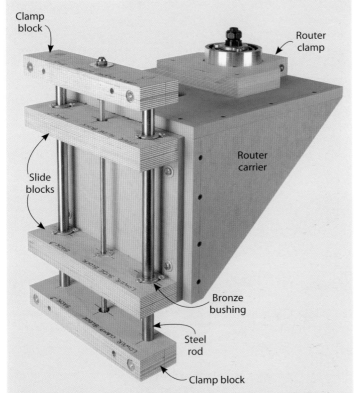

Router table dust collection that really works! Two side boards mounted alongside the lift create a cavity like an elevator shaft. Wood dust is captured in the cavity and vented out a dust port in the router carrier.

Our router lift consists of two components: the lift mechanism and the router carrier. The lift mechanism uses finely machined steel rods that slide through oil-impregnated bronze bushings set in upper and lower slide blocks. Upper and lower clamp blocks capture the ends of the steel rods and provide attachment points for securing the lift to the router table back. The router carrier attaches to the lift mechanism. A plywood router clamp holds the router motor in the carrier. Adjusting the height is as simple as turning the acorn nut on top of a threaded rod.

FIG. A: EXPLODED VIEW

The lift mechanism is universal and you should build it just as we show here. You may need to adjust the lengths of the router carrier top (F) and sides (G) to get the router centered under the mounting plate in your table. 13-ply birch plywood is used for all the parts that require strength and stability. The router carrier is made primarily of MDF or other sheet stock.

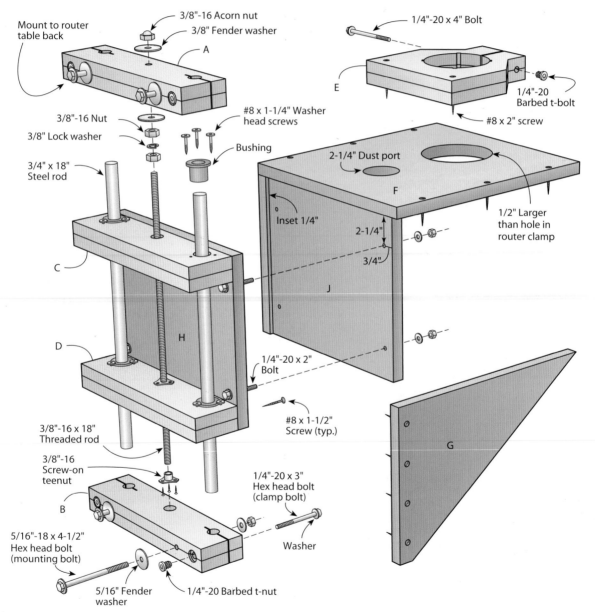

Mount to router table back

3/8"-16 Acorn nut

3/8" Fender washer

A

1/4"-20 x 4" Bolt

E

1/4"-20 Barbed t-bolt

#8 x 2" screw

3/8"-16 Nut

3/8" Lock washer

#8 x 1-1/4" Washer head screws

Bushing

2-1/4" Dust port

F

1/2" Larger than hole in router clamp

3/4" x 18" Steel rod

C

Inset 1/4"

2-1/4"

3/4"

J

D

H

1/4"-20 x 2" Bolt

#8 x 1-1/2" Screw (typ.)

3/8"-16 x 18" Threaded rod

3/8"-16 Screw-on teenut

B

1/4"-20 x 3" Hex head bolt (clamp bolt)

G

5/16"-18 x 4-1/2" Hex head bolt (mounting bolt)

5/16" Fender washer

1/4"-20 Barbed t-nut

Washer

Build the slide and clamp blocks by gluing up plywood blanks in pairs. Keep the edges as flush as possible. Trim to finish size after the glue dries.

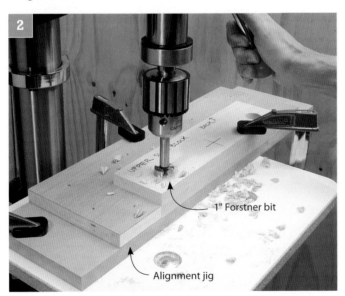

Drill holes for the bushings, steel rods and threaded rod on the drill press. A simple jig registers each blank so each set of holes is drilled in exactly the same spot. Important: Clearly label each block and mark the back edge to prevent mix-ups.

If you're groaning because this sounds like one of those tedious projects that require machinist-level tolerances, stop fretting. This project is really dirt simple. We'll show you a few simple tricks, like fine-tuning your drill press (see "Super-Tune Your Drill Press," page 97) that guarantee a smooth-running lift.

WILL IT FIT MY ROUTER TABLE?

If you already own a full-size router table don't sweat. A few simple modifications allow you to mount this lift into most commercial tables.

WHAT YOU'LL NEED

This project requires some specialized hardware unfamiliar to most woodworkers, like bronze bearings and steel rod. We recommend you buy your lifter parts from the mail order sources we used. We know all of these parts work in harmony with each other. Plus, our source for the steel rods will cut them to length for no charge and that'll save you a lot of work.

Besides the hardware, you'll need a tablesaw, bandsaw, drill press, heavy-duty circle cutter, and 3/4- and 1-in. Forstner bits.

BUILD THE LIFT MECHANISM

1. Cut and assemble the slide and clamp-block blanks (A–D) (Photo 1).

2. Lay out the holes on the clamp and slide blocks as shown in Figs. B through E, page 103. Be sure to mark the back edge of each blank.

3. Make a jig to register the clamp and slide blocks on the drill press (Photo 2). The jig is simply a board onto which pieces of wood are nailed to form a cradle around the

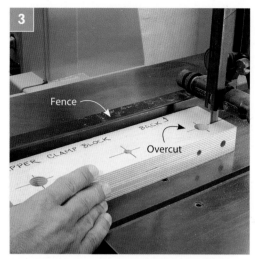

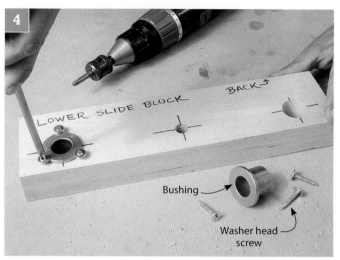

Cut relief slots in the clamping blocks on the bandsaw. Cut each slot 1/4-in. past the hole so the clamping blocks can squeeze tightly on the steel rods.

Screw in three washer head screws around each bushing. Place these screws about 1/16 in. away from the bushing edges. Don't over tighten; you want the bushings to turn freely in their holes.

plywood blanks. This guarantees perfect hole alignment from block to block, which is critical to the smooth operation of the lift mechanism.

4. With the jig and a blank in place, set the table height on your drill press low enough to allow the longest bit to be taken in and out without moving the table.

5. Clamp the upper slide block in the drilling jig. Insert a 1-in. Forstner bit in the drill press and align its point with a bushing hole center point. Clamp the drilling jig to the drill press table and drill this hole. Don't move the drilling jig! Pull the upper slide block out of the jig, clean the jig if necessary, and insert the lower slide block, clamp, and drill.

6. Switch to a 3/4-in.-diameter Forstner bit and drill the clamp holes in the upper and lower clamp blocks.

7. Now position the drilling jig to drill the opposite side holes following the same drilling sequence. Don't be tempted to

just flip the blanks over to drill the second set of outside holes. Any error in the perpendicularity of the holes will get magnified.

8. Move the drilling jig and drill the center holes for the threaded rod and the screw on teenuts.

9. Lay out and drill the counterbore holes (Figs. B and E) for the barbed T-nuts on the upper and lower clamp blocks.

10. Drill the through-holes for the clamp bolts and mounting bolts.

11. Saw relief slots in the clamp blocks (Photo 3).

12. Hammer the barbed T-nuts into the clamping hole recesses.

13. Mount the bronze bushings in the upper and lower slide blocks with washer head screws (Photo 4). Washer heads are screws with a built-in flat washer under the head.

Super-Tune
Your Drill Press

Before you start building, make sure your drill press will drill holes that are perfectly perpendicular. That's the key to a smooth operating lift mechanism. We found that just checking the table with a square is not enough. Here's how to super-tune your drill press:

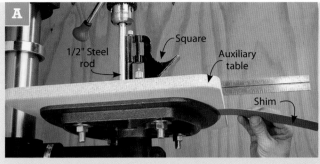

Adjust your drill press table to 90 degrees as best you can with a square and a 1/2-in. steel rod chucked into the drill press. All drill press tables can be adjusted side-to-side but few can be adjusted front-to-back. Chances are your table is slightly off. Make adjustments by inserting paper shims between the drill press table and an auxiliary table.

Drill a 3/4-in.-diameter x 2-1/2 in.-deep hole in a test block. The test block is just a four-piece stack of 3/4-in. MDF glued together. Label the front of the test block for reference so you know where to shim your table if necessary.

Check the drilled hole for square using one of the 3/4-in.-diameter steel rods for the lift mechanism. Label the bad holes and keep shimming the table until you get a drilled hole that's perfectly perpendicular.

The edge of the washer head catches the flange of the bushing. Tip: A self-centering bit held next to the bushing flange provides the perfect setback.

14. Attach the top screw-on teenut to the lower slide block and run the threaded rod through.

15. Attach the bottom teenut (Photo 5). The double teenut system eliminates backlash (that annoying free-spin you get when changing direction on the lift mechanism)

because the threads of the rod are always in tight contact with the threads of the screw-on teenuts.

16. Remove the threaded rod.

17. Cut the lift and carrier back plates (H and J) to size. Clamp these two pieces flush together and drill the four 1/4-in.-diameter holes through them for joining the router carrier to the lift mechanism (Fig. A).

18. Drill four countersunk pilot holes near the bottom edge of the lift back plate for

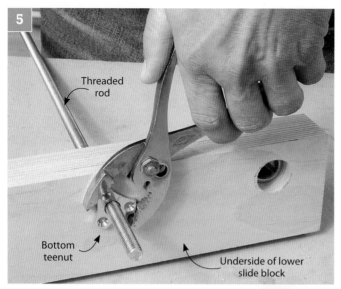

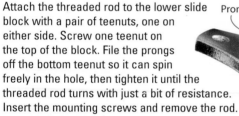

Attach the threaded rod to the lower slide block with a pair of teenuts, one on either side. Screw one teenut on the top of the block. File the prongs off the bottom teenut so it can spin freely in the hole, then tighten it until the threaded rod turns with just a bit of resistance. Insert the mounting screws and remove the rod.

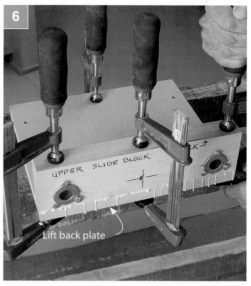

Glue the upper slide block to the lift back plate. Make sure the side and top edges are flush with each other.

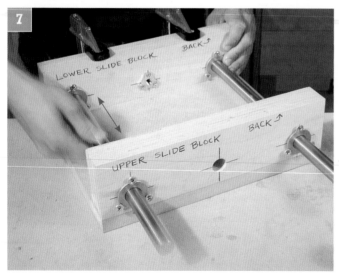

Clamp the lower slide block in place and check its alignment. The steel rods should slide smoothly. If they bind, give the lower slide block a tap with a mallet to the left or right until the rods move freely. Then secure the lower slide block with screws.

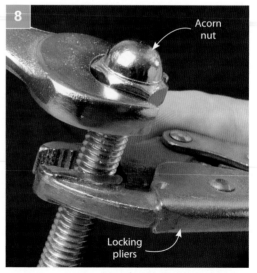

Lock an acorn nut onto the top of the threaded rod. Really jam it on! You want the nut locked on the rod so it can be turned in both directions without coming undone. Clamp the locking pliers close to the nut so any damaged threads get buried in the upper clamp block.

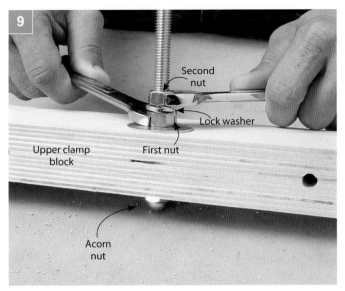

9

Second
nut

Lock washer

Upper clamp
block

First nut

Acorn
nut

Attach the threaded rod to the upper clamp block by locking two nuts together. Finger-tighten the first nut against the block so the rod turns with just a slight amount of resistance. Then add a lock washer and tighten the second nut against the first.

10

Clamping
bolts

Tighten the clamp blocks on the steel rods. Make sure the tops of the rods are flush with the surface of the clamp block.

mounting the lower slide block. Make sure the pilot holes are positioned so the screws won't run into the bushings or threaded rod.

19. Glue the upper slide block to the lift back plate (Photo 6).

20. Grind or file a slight chamfer on the ends of the 3/4-in.-diameter steel rods. Smooth away any remaining burrs using a fine emery cloth.

21. Clamp (no glue) the lower slide block to the bottom edge of the lift back plate. Insert the steel rods through the bushings. Adjust the position of the lower slide block so both steel rods slide smoothly through the bushings (Photo 7), and attach with screws.

22. Attach the acorn nut to the top of the threaded rod (Photo 8).

23. Attach the threaded rod to the upper clamp block (Fig. A and Photo 9).

24. Slide the threaded rod with the upper clamp block attached through the hole in the upper slide block and into the screw-on teenuts mounted in the lower slide block.

25. Slide the steel rods up through the holes in the upper clamp block and tighten the clamping bolts (Photo 10).

26. Slide the lower clamp block over the steel rods and clamp it in place. The lift mechanism is now complete.

INSTALLING THE LIFT

27. Alter your router table to accept the lift mechanism. Most tables will only require a 3/4-in. back added to the cabinet (see "Fitting the AW Lift to Your Router Table," page 102).

28. Locate the mounting bolt holes in the back of the cabinet by clamping the lift about

3/4 in. down from the top edge of the back.

29. Use the mounting holes in the clamp blocks as guides to drill through the back panel.

30. Insert the mounting bolts through the back and mount the lift mechanism (Photo 11).

BUILD THE ROUTER CARRIER

31. Glue up and cut the router clamp blank (E). Then lay out the pattern for the router clamp (Fig. F).

32. Cut the hole for the router (Photo 12). You'll need some scrap to make test holes until you get a snug fit.

33. Cut off the side waste pieces, then lay out and drill the countersunk hole for the T-nut and the through-hole for the clamp bolt. Secure the router clamp in a vise for easier drilling.

34. Cut the router clamp relief slot on the bandsaw. Some routers have locating pins on their sides that require notches (Photo 14) to be cut inside the opening. This can also be done with the bandsaw.

35. Assemble the router carrier (F, G, and J, Fig. A). Don't use glue for the carrier top (F). Be sure to keep a 1/4-in. inset on the carrier back. This creates the lip to hang the carrier onto the lift mechanism.

36. To locate the hole in the router carrier top, temporarily mount the carrier on the lift with a couple of bolts. Close the router tabletop and crank the lift all the way up. Scribe the bit opening in the tabletop onto the carrier top.

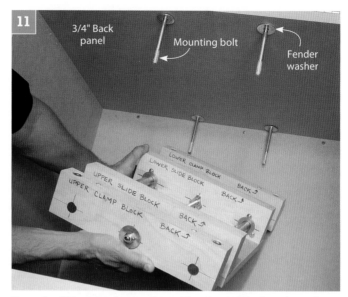

Hang the lift mechanism on the cabinet back. Washers keep the moving parts of the lift clear of the back. Note: The cabinet back must be 3/4-in. thick to support the lift.

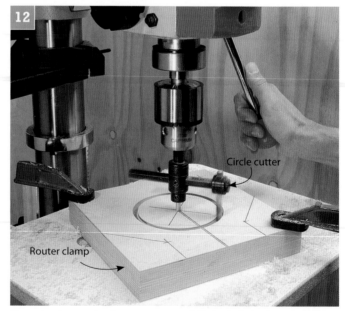

To make the carrier for your router, drill the hole in the router clamp using a heavy-duty circle cutter. Make test cuts to ensure a snug fit on the router motor body.

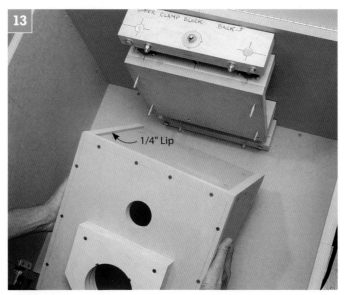

13

1/4" Lip

Bolt the router carrier to the lift mechanism. The lip around the back edge of the router carrier makes it very easy to align the two components.

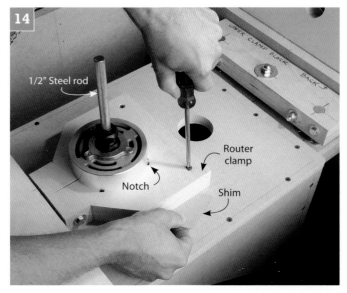

14

1/2" Steel rod

Router clamp

Notch

Shim

Mount the router in the clamp. Chuck the 1/2-in.-diameter steel rod in the router and check that it's square to the table. If you find the router is not perfectly perpendicular to the table, shim the router clamp.

Note the notches cut in the clamp to accommodate pins on the motor housing.

37. Remove the router carrier from the lift. Remove the carrier top and router clamp.

38. Drill a hole in the router carrier top using the bit opening as a center point. Make the hole 1/2-in. larger than the hole you drilled in the router clamp.

39. Adjust the circle cutter and cut the hole for the vacuum hose.

40. Reattach the carrier top. Set the router with the clamp attached in the hole. Close the top and center the router in the opening. Open the top and screw down the router clamp.

41. Remount the router carrier to the lift mechanism using bolts (Photo 13).

42. Mount your router in the router clamp and tighten the clamp bolt. The router should protrude out of the router clamp an inch or so (Photo 14).

43. Add a couple of 6-in.-wide sidepieces to enclose the router lift for more effective dust collection.

44. That's it! You're ready to rout!

Fitting the Lift to Your Router Table

Our router lift will fit any router table, whether it's an enclosed cabinet or an open stand. No matter what style cabinet you have, you'll want to make these alterations: 1. Add a stiff back (Photo 1). 2. Hinge the top to the back (Photo 2). 3. Add a lock- down bracket on both sides of the top. These brackets hold down the top and stop it from racking side-to-side (Photo 3). 4. Drill a 1-1/4-in.-diameter access hole through the tabletop so you can get at the height adjusting acorn nut.

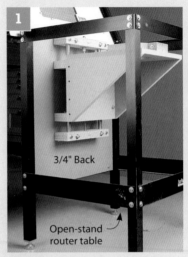

3/4" Back

Open-stand router table

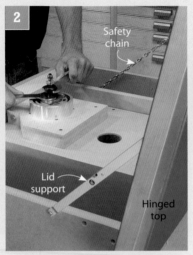

Safety chain

Lid support

Hinged top

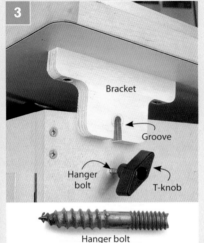

Bracket

Groove

Hanger bolt

T-knob

Hanger bolt

A stiff back is a must for mounting the router lift. No matter what style router table you own—open-stand or cabinet—you'll need to have a 3/4-in.-thick back.

Add a continuous hinge and a lid support to the top. The lid support prevents the top from closing accidentally. The safety chain prevents the heavy top from opening too hard and stressing the hinges or lid support.

Secure the hinged top with a pair of locking brackets. Screw in hanger bolts centered in the bracket grooves, and lock down the top with plastic T-knobs.

Materials List

- One 3/4" x 24" x 48" MDF
- Four 5/16"-18 x 4-1/2" Hex Head Machine Bolts, Fender Washers, Washers, and Lock Nuts
- Four 1/4"-20 x 3" Hex Head Machine Bolts and Washers
- Two 3/8" Fender Washers
- One 3/8"-16 Acorn Nut and Lock Washer
- Two 3/8"-16 Hex Nuts
- Four 1/4"-20 x 2" Hex Head Machine Bolts, Lock Nuts and Washers

- One 1/4"-20 x 4" Hex Head Machine Bolt and Washer, One 3/8"-16 x 18" Threaded Rod
- Two 3/4" dia. x 18" round ground shafting 1045
- Four 3/4" ID x 1" OD bronze "Oilite" bushings
- One 3/4" x 24" x 30" Finnish Birch, 13-ply Plywood
- 1" Forstner Drill Bit
- 3/4" Forstner Drill Bit
- Heavy-Duty Circle Cutter
- Five 1/4"-20 Barbed T-Nuts

- Two 3/8"-16 Screw-On Teenuts
- Two 1/4"-20 x 1-1/2" Hanger Bolts
- Two 1/4"-20 x 2" Plastic T-Knobs
- Twelve #8 x 1-1/4" Washer Head Face Frame Screws

FIG. B: UPPER CLAMP BLOCK

1"
1-1/2"
3/4" Dia.
3/8" Dia.
Back edge
6"
7/8"
A
3/4" Dia. 1/8" deep
counterbore,
3/8" dia. hole
5/16" Dia.
2-1/2"
Relief
slot

FIG. C: UPPER SLIDE BLOCK

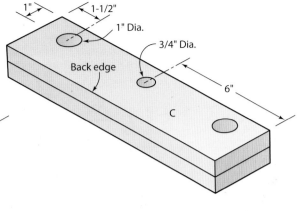

1"
1-1/2"
1" Dia.
3/4" Dia.
Back edge
6"
C

FIG. D: LOWER SLIDE BLOCK

1"
1-1/2"
1" Dia.
1/2" Dia.
Back edge
6"
D

FIG. E: LOWER CLAMP BLOCK

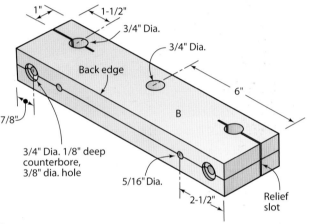

1"
1-1/2"
3/4" Dia.
3/4" Dia.
Back edge
6"
7/8"
B
3/4" Dia. 1/8" deep
counterbore,
3/8" dia. hole
5/16" Dia.
2-1/2"
Relief
slot

Cutting List
Overall Dimension 13-1/2"W x 18"T x 18-1/2"D

Part	Name	Qty.	Dimensions	Notes
3/4" 13 ply Birch Plywood				
A	Upper Clamp Block	2	3" x 12"	Cut 1/4" oversize; face glue to form one, 1-1/2"thick block; trim to finish size
B	Lower Clamp Block	2	3" x 12"	
C	Upper Slide Block	2	3" x 12"	
D	Lower Slide Block	2	3" x 12"	
E	Router Clamp	2	8" x 8"	
3/4" MDF				
F	Carrier Top	1	13-1/2" x 15"	Length determined by your setup
G	Carrier Sides	2	10-1/2" x 15"	
H	Lift Back Plate	1	10-1/2" x 12"	
J	Carrier Back Plate	1	10-1/2" x 12"	

FIG. F: ROUTER CLAMP

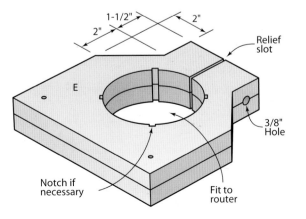

1-1/2"
2"
2"
Relief
slot
E
3/8"
Hole
Notch if
necessary
Fit to
router

by GEORGE VONDRISKA

Feature-Filled Router Table Fence

THIS FENCE CAN MAKE YOUR ROUTER TABLE SING

You can build this completely tricked-out router table fence in an afternoon, using easily available parts. Here's what you get:

■ Flexibility. Tall or short, it's easy to swap between the faces of this fence, so you always have the right one for the job.

■ Adjustability. It's a breeze to adjust the faces to surround the bit and make a tear-out-limiting, zero-clearance fence.

■ Interchangeable fences. The left and right faces can be swapped. If you need a fresh end for a zero-clearance fence, just trade left for right. The faces are so easy to make, you can have plenty of replacements ready to go.

■ Offset outfeed fence. Use your router table as a jointer by adding a simple shim to the outfeed fence.

■ Dust collection. Just hook up to a standard 2-in. hose.

■ Safety. The guard is easy to make and easy to use.

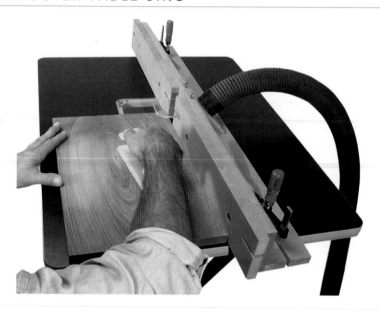

■ Easy clamping. Two simple clamps hold the fence to the table, making fence adjustments simple. Plus, you won't have any trouble clamping featherboards to this fence.

The fence we show here works for router tables from 28- to 34-in. long. For longer tables, simply cut the fence parts 4-in. longer than the length of your table.

FEATURES

THE WHOLE PACKAGE

Here's the fence with all its options.

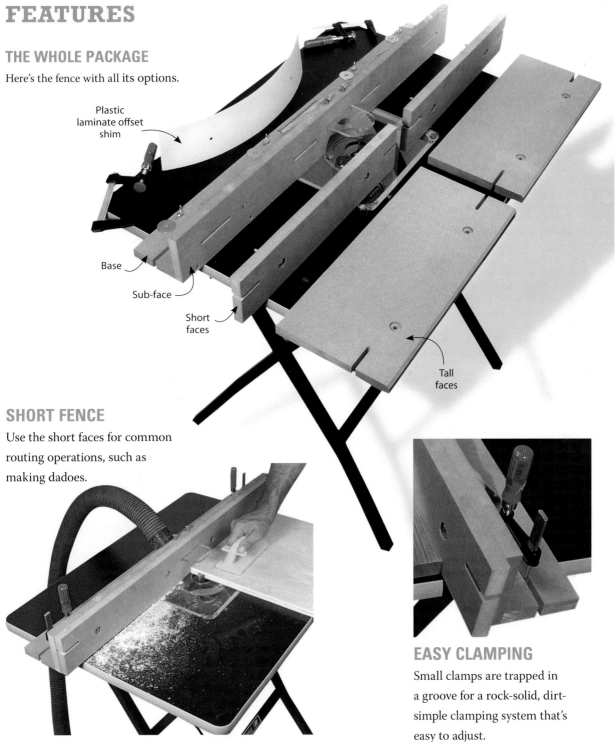

Plastic laminate offset shim

Base

Sub-face

Short faces

Tall faces

SHORT FENCE

Use the short faces for common routing operations, such as making dadoes.

EASY CLAMPING

Small clamps are trapped in a groove for a rock-solid, dirt-simple clamping system that's easy to adjust.

FEATURES

TALL FENCE

Use the tall faces for routing pieces on edge, such as vertical raised panels, lock miters, or lock-rabbet drawers.

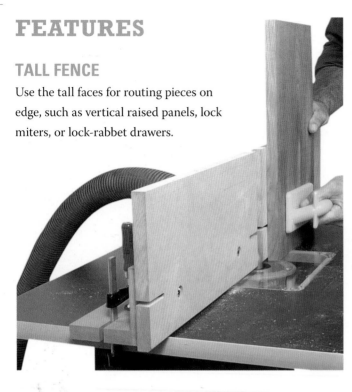

JOINTING

Slip a shim between the outfeed face and the fence. This offset allows you to joint edges. Joint with a straight bit by aligning the cutting edge with the face of the outfeed fence.

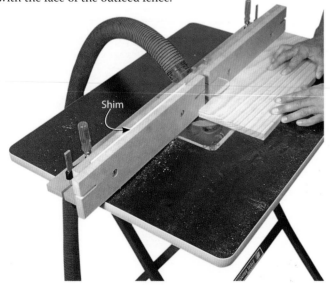

Shim

Removable pins

GUARD

This polycarbonate guard keeps your fingers away from the bit when edge routing, but is easily removed when necessary—simply pull up on the pins.

Chamfer

ZERO CLEARANCE

Reduce tear-out by adjusting the infeed face so the bit cuts into it, eliminating the clearance around the bit. Each face slides sideways in slots to permit this. The chamfer on the bottom edge of the face creates a dust relief so your material can ride tight to the face of the fence.

BUILD THIS FENCE

CONSTRUCTION TIPS

1

Cut these supports dead square. If they're off, the fence will be, too.

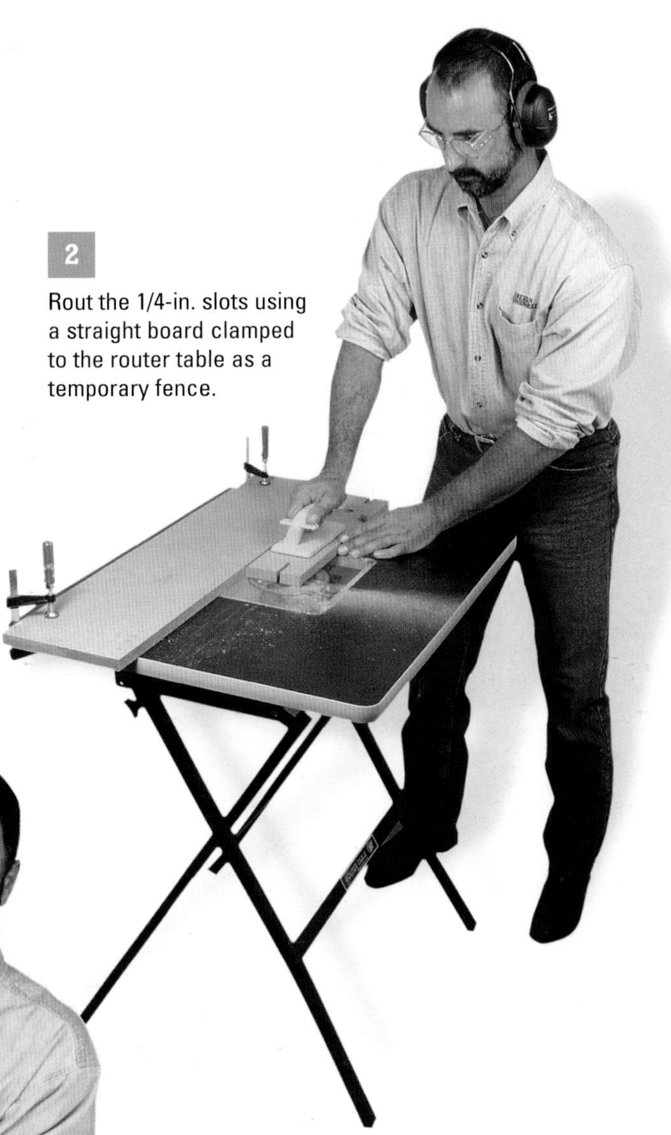

2

Rout the 1/4-in. slots using a straight board clamped to the router table as a temporary fence.

3

Create clearance for the bits in the fence base by drilling a 3-1/2-in. hole in the center of an 8 x 36-in. piece of MDF. Then rip the fence bottom and front from this piece.

3-1/2" Wide base

4" Wide sub-face

Forget fancy tracks and hardware! This fence uses common hardware-store parts.

TOOLS AND MATERIALS

The fence is made from medium-density fiberboard (MDF). MDF is dense, hard and flat, which makes it a great choice for this fence and other shop-made jigs. It's also darn heavy, at almost 100 pounds per 4x8-ft. sheet. You'll need help handling it. The fence requires about a half sheet, so you could share a sheet with a fellow woodworker.

To make this fence you need a tablesaw and a router table equipped with a carbide-tipped 1/4-in. straight bit. The routing required to make the fence is simple. A straight board clamped to the table is all it takes. You don't need to have a good router table fence already in order to make one!

Cutting List				
Part	Name	Qty.	Dimensions	Material
A	Base	1	3/4 x 3-1/2 x 36	MDF
B	Sub-Face	1	3/4 x 4 x 36	MDF
C	Faces	2	3/4 x 4 x 18	MDF
D	Tall Faces	2	3/4 x 8 x 18	MDF
E	Corner Blocks	4	3/4 x 2-3/4 x 2-3/4	MDF
F	Guard	1	1/4 x 3-1/4 x 3-1/4	Polycarb.
G	Dust Shroud	1	1/4 x 5 x 4	Plywood

FIG. A: EXPLODED VIEW

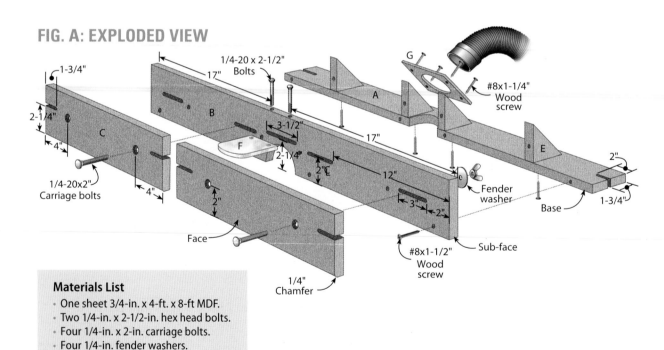

Materials List
- One sheet 3/4-in. x 4-ft. x 8-ft MDF.
- Two 1/4-in. x 2-1/2-in. hex head bolts.
- Four 1/4-in. x 2-in. carriage bolts.
- Four 1/4-in. fender washers.
- Four 1/4-in. wing nuts.
- 1/4-in. router bit.
- Two clamps.
- One 1/4-in. x 12-in. x 12-in. polycarbonate plastic.

1. Rough-cut the MDF into manageable pieces, 1-in. larger than the finished sizes.

2. Rip and crosscut a piece to 8 in. x 36 in. for the fence base (A) and sub-face (B).

3. Use a hole saw to bore a 3-1/2-in. hole in the center of this piece (Photo 3).

4. Rip a 4-in.-wide sub-face and 3-1/2-in.-wide base from this piece, cutting through the hole.

5. Cut all interchangeable faces (C and D) to finished size. Take advantage of your tablesaw setups to make extra faces.

6. Rout a 1/4-in. slot in the sub-face for the guard.

7. Rout slots in the interchangeable faces so they can slip over the guard ("Guard" photo page 106).

8. Rout 1/4-in. slots in the sub-face for the carriage bolts.

9. Rout 1/4-in. slots in the base for the clamps. If the fence is 4-in. longer than your table, the slot length is 2-in.

10. Screw and glue the sub-face to the base using #8 x 1-1/2-in. wood screws. Predrill for the screws so you don't split the MDF.

11. Cut the corner blocks (E), being very careful to make them square (Photo 1).

12. Screw and glue the corner blocks to the fence. The corner blocks are small pieces, so use #8 x 1-1/4-in. screws to prevent splitting.

13. Bore 3/4-in. holes to a depth of 1/4 in. in the interchangeable faces (for the carriage-bolt heads).

14. Bore 1/4-in. holes through the interchangeable faces (for the carriage bolts).

15. Rout a 1/4-in. chamfer for dust relief on the bottom corner of each interchangeable face.

16. Cut the polycarbonate guard to size using a fine-tooth blade on the tablesaw or bandsaw.

17. Cut a 1-in. radius on the front corners of the guard using a bandsaw or jigsaw. Use a felt-tip marker to lay out the radius on the plastic.

18. Bore 1/4-in. x 2-in.-deep holes for the guard pins in the fence sub-face.

19. Place the guard in its slot and use a felt-tip marker to transfer the locations of the guard-pin holes to the guard.

20. Bore 1/4-in. holes in the guard. It's best to use a twist bit on polycarbonate.

21. Cut a piece of 1/4-in. plywood or hardboard for the dust collection shroud. Don't worry about beveling the edges to match the corner blocks; you can fix that with caulk later.

22. Bore a 2-1/4-in. hole in the center of the dust collection shroud.

23. Screw and glue the dust collection shroud to the corner blocks. Use silicone caulk to seal the dust collection box where it doesn't fit perfectly around the fence.

24. Bolt a pair of faces to the fence, hook up the dust collection, clamp the fence to your table, and you're ready to rout!

Router Table Jointer Fence

EDGE JOINT LONG STOCK, THICK STOCK, WIDE STOCK, OR MAN-MADE MATERIALS

Is your shop too small to even think about squeezing in a jointer? Then do we have a project for you! And even if you already own a jointer, there are some things this fence can actually do better:

■ Drop-in shims adjust the fence offset to accommodate the depth-of-cut (Photo 1).

■ Carbide router bits allow you to edge joint man-made materials like particleboard or melamine without sentencing yourself to hard time replacing dull knives (Photo 2).

■ An oversize table lets you edge joint wide stock flat, rather than balancing it on edge against a jointer's narrow fence (Photo 3).

■ The fence is a cinch to build particularly if you've got any scrap laying around. That shouldn't set your shop-tool savings plan back much!

Submitted by Rick McKee,
Woodbury, MN.

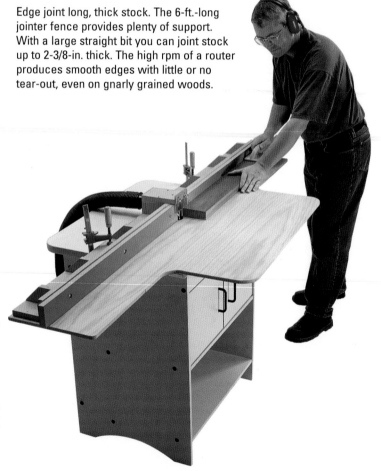

Edge joint long, thick stock. The 6-ft.-long jointer fence provides plenty of support. With a large straight bit you can joint stock up to 2-3/8-in. thick. The high rpm of a router produces smooth edges with little or no tear-out, even on gnarly grained woods.

EDITOR: DAVE MUNKITTRICK • ART DIRECTION: VERN JOHNSON • PHOTOGRAPHY: RAMON MORENO AND MIKE HABERMANN • ILLUSTRATION: DON MANNES

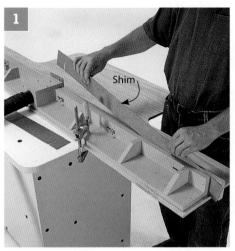

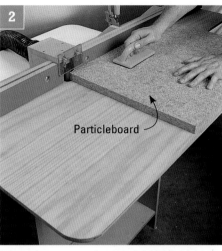

Drop-in shims offset the fence equal to the depth-of-cut you want to make. Use plastic laminate shims for heavier cuts and construction paper for very light cuts, such as cleaning up.

Edge joint man-made material. With this fence you can edge joint particleboard without dulling the cutters. Carbide router bits can take it, unlike the softer steel of jointer knives.

Tip:

Avoid glue! It's better to assemble shop jigs and fixtures with screws only. It makes future modifications and alterations possible without having to bust things apart.

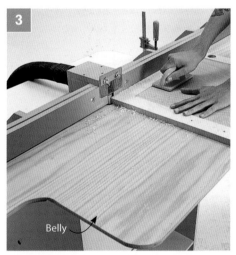

Support for wide stock. This jointer fence is excellent for trimming doors and drawer fronts for a perfect fit. The belly of the table provides extra support when jointing wide stock like this panel saw marks.

EXPLODED VIEW

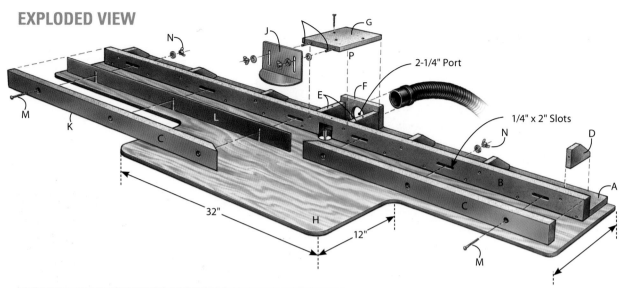

2-1/4" Port

1/4" x 2" Slots

32"

12"

CUTTING LIST				
Part	**Name**	**Qty.**	**Dimensions**	**Material**
A	Fence Base	1	4" x 72"	3/4" Mdf
B	Fixed Fence	1	3" x 72"	3/4" Mdf
C	Adj. Fence	2	2-7/8" x 36"	3/4" Mdf
D	Braces	6	2-1/4" x 4"	3/4" Mdf
E	Dust Port Sides	2	2-1/4" x 3-1/4"	3/4" Mdf
F	Dust Port Back	1	3" x 4"	3/4" Mdf
G	Dust Port Top	1	4" x 5"	3/4" Mdf
H	Base	1	24" x 74"	1/2" Plywood
J	Guard	1	2-3/4" x 4"	1/4" Lexan
K	Fence Face	2	2-7/8" x 36"	Plastic Laminate
L	Shims	2	3" x 36"	Plastic Laminate
M	Carriage Bolts	6	1/4" x 2"	
N	Wing Nuts & Washers	8	1/4"	
P	Hanger Bolts	2	1/4" x 1-1/2"	
Q	Wood Screws	30	#8 x 1-1/4"	

ROUTER TABLE JOINTER FENCE

We used plywood for the base (H) to conserve weight. Slots cut in the fixed fence (B) allow the adjustable fences (C) to slide back and forth to safely accommodate different bit sizes.

The adjustable fences are raised up from the base by 1/8-in. to keep sawdust and shavings from interfering with feeding stock. Without the shim (L) the fence can be used like any standard router table fence.

Materials List
- 1/4" thick x 12" wide x 12" long Lexan
- 1/4"-20" x 1-1/2" hanger bolts

by BILL HYLTON

5 Router Jigs

IMPROVE YOUR ACCURACY AND CONTROL

Why buy a commercial jig when making one yourself will triple your enjoyment? First, you'll experience the joy of building a useful shop fixture from nothing more than some scrap wood and a good idea. Second, you'll enjoy the money you'll save. And finally, as all woodworkers understand, you'll have the satisfaction that comes with saying, "I made it myself." The five jigs described here are all designed to deliver improved accuracy, control, and adjustability for a lifetime of better routing.

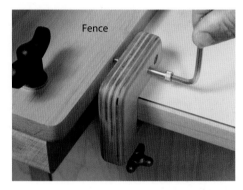
Fence

FENCE MICRO-ADJUSTER

This jig enables you to make tiny, accurate adjustments in positioning a router table fence. A pair of jigs clamp to the tabletop, one at each end of the fence. Each jig has a stop that extends to meet the back of the fence. The stop is a simple cap screw that you turn with an Allen wrench (see photo, right). The two screws, in 3/8-in.-16 and 3/8-in.-20 sizes, have different thread pitches that produce different rates of adjustment. An L-shaped Allen wrench makes it easy to track the amount of adjustment, for example, a quarter turn or half turn. By retracting the cap screw in small increments, you move the fence backward to slowly reveal more of the cutter or forward to reduce bit exposure. By moving only one end of the fence, you can make some incredibly small adjustments. For example, if one end of the fence is moved back 1/64 in. (a quarter turn of the 3/8-in.-16 bolt) and the other end remains stationary, the router bit will make a 1/128 in. deeper cut.

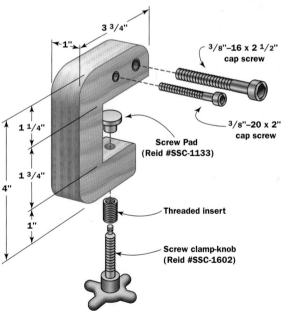

3 3/4"
1"
3/8"–16 x 2 1/2" cap screw
1 1/4"
3/8"–20 x 2" cap screw
Screw Pad (Reid #SSC-1133)
1 3/4"
4"
Threaded insert
1"
Screw clamp-knob (Reid #SSC-1602)

Face-glue two layers of 1/2-in. multi-ply plywood to create a blank for the jig body. Adjust the opening and overall dimensions as needed to match your router table.

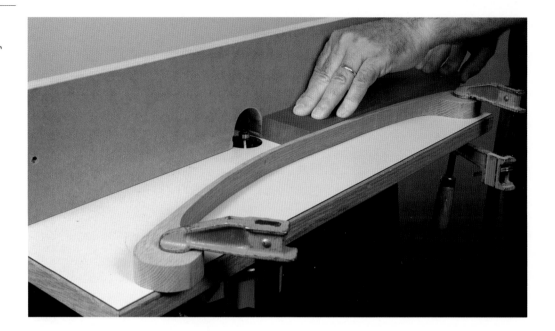

SPRINGBOARD

This unusual jig—a bow-like affair with a clamp pad on each end—can be secured to the fence or tabletop and employed in place of a featherboard.

Making the jig is a straightforward bandsaw project (see the pattern). The jig's length can be adjusted to suit any router table. Species with natural resilience, such as oak, ash, or hickory, make the best springboards.

To use the springboard, clamp one end in place, flex the jig to create pressure against the workpiece and then clamp the other end in place. Two springboards can be used simultaneously to hold a workpiece against the fence and the table as it passes by the bit.

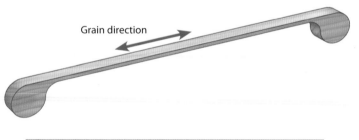

Grain direction

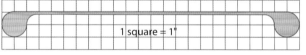

1 square = 1"

Select a straight-grained board and lay out the springboard so its thin middle section follows the grain direction exactly. Avoid any grain run-out because it could result in a weak point that might fracture under tension. After you cut the springboard from the blank, sand it smooth to reduce friction where it contacts the stock.

DEPTH GAUGE

Setting bit height is either a hit-or-miss proposition based on eyeballing or a simple measuring task featuring a depth gauge jig (see photo, right). The latter approach is faster and more accurate. Plus, it saves aging knees by eliminating that awkward hunkering-down motion to reach bit level. With a depth gauge, you simply set the desired bit height and then raise the bit until it hits the bottom of the slide bar. With a piloted bit, make sure the slide clears the bearing and touches the cutter.

Built from multi-ply for strength and stability, this depth-gauge jig requires a short length of self-stick measuring tape with large numbers, a thumbscrew, and a little piece of clear acrylic.

Lay out the depth-gauge body on some plywood. Drill the hole for the nickel 1/16-in. deeper than the T-slot using a 7/8-in. Forstner bit. Plow the T-slot with a T-slot router bit before shaping the body. The slide is a simple T-molding made by cutting two rabbets on the edge of a board and then ripping the molding free. Apply the self-stick tape rule at the bottom. Secure the acrylic plate with a couple of screws.

Zero the gauge by setting it on a flat surface, for example, your tablesaw. Let the slide drop to the table and lock. Score a line on the face of the acrylic over the 0-in. mark on the tape. Drill the holes slightly oversize in the acrylic plate to allow some minute adjustment, if necessary.

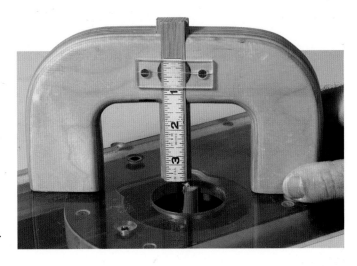

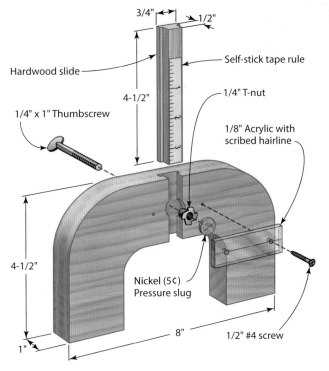

3/4"
1/2"
Hardwood slide
Self-stick tape rule
4-1/2"
1/4" T-nut
1/4" x 1" Thumbscrew
1/8" Acrylic with scribed hairline
4-1/2"
Nickel (5¢) Pressure slug
1"
8"
1/2" #4 screw

EDITORS: JOHN ENGLISH AND DAVE MUNKITTRICK · ART DIRECTION: GEORGE MCKEON AND VERN JOHNSON · PHOTOGRAPHY: DONNA CHIARELLI · ILLUSTRATION: FRANK ROHRBACH

Tip:

If you don't have a trammel and want to cut a small hole or disc, drill a small hole in the router baseplate and drop it onto a headless nail driven partway into the workpiece. Doing so makes the base a very short-armed trammel.

ADJUSTABLE TRAMMEL

This trammel uses interchangeable arms to create circles and arcs of different diameters. It can handle jobs as varied in size as the small plug you see in the photo and the broad arc on the base of a wide cabinet. The short arm has two pivot holes and three mounting holes. You can reverse the arm and use different pivot-mounting hole combinations to cut 1-1/2-in. to 16-in. diameters. The longer arm creates diameters up to 36 in. A small plunge router works best with the trammel because it has the ability to both initiate a cut and extend its depth quite easily.

Lay out the trammel's base on a blank of 3/4-in. sheet stock—multi-ply works best. Make the blank extra long so the pivot block can be cut from it later. Rout the two-step groove while the blank is still a rectangle.

Cut the pivot block from the blank. Drill the bit opening with a Forstner bit. Then cut the baseplate profile on a bandsaw and sand the edges.

Each arm is a simple T-shaped molding made to fit the stepped groove in the base and pivot block. To machine the arms, rout two rabbets on the edge of a wide board and rip it to thickness. Cut the T-shaped molding to the desired lengths. Drill and countersink holes for adjustment bolts. Then tap holes for a pivot screw.

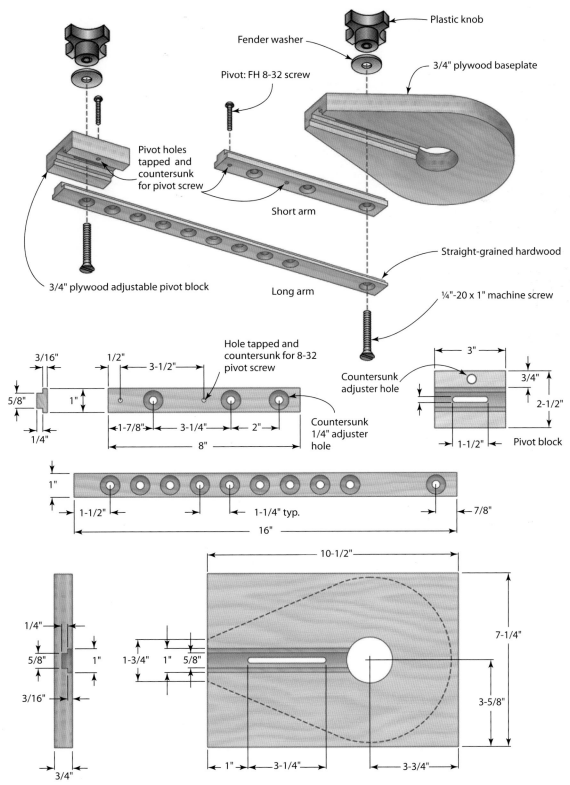

Plastic knob

Fender washer

3/4" plywood baseplate

Pivot: FH 8-32 screw

Pivot holes tapped and countersunk for pivot screw

Short arm

Straight-grained hardwood

3/4" plywood adjustable pivot block

Long arm

¼"-20 x 1" machine screw

3/16"

1/2"

3-1/2"

Hole tapped and countersunk for 8-32 pivot screw

5/8"

1"

Countersunk adjuster hole

3"

3/4"

2-1/2"

1/4"

1-7/8"

3-1/4"

2"

Countersunk 1/4" adjuster hole

1-1/2"

Pivot block

8"

1"

1-1/2"

1-1/4" typ.

7/8"

16"

1/4"

5/8"

1"

3/16"

1-3/4"

1"

5/8"

10-1/2"

7-1/4"

3-5/8"

3/4"

1"

3-1/4"

3-3/4"

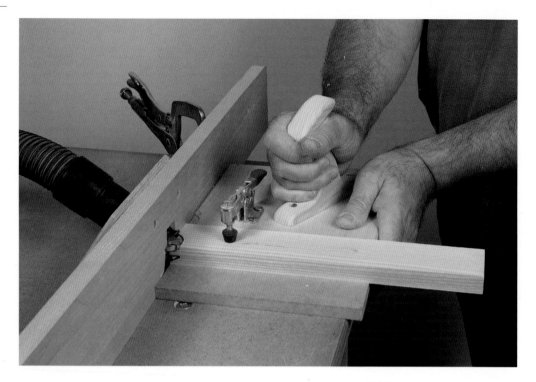

COPING SLED

End-grain milling can be difficult. The stock tends to walk, angling forward or backward instead of staying at right angles to the fence. In addition, the leading corner can dip into the bit opening in the fence.

A coping sled solves these problems. It holds a rail securely during a cut and backs the cut to protect against tearout. The sled doesn't rely on a miter-gauge groove, and it is large enough to bridge the opening in the fence. The comfortable handle provides a sure grip on the sled and keeps your hands out of harm's way.

The router bit mills the sled's fence. This isn't a problem as long as you use the same sled with the same bit and height every time. In fact, it helps set the bit height. Because these sleds are easily made from materials in your scrap bin, you could have a number of

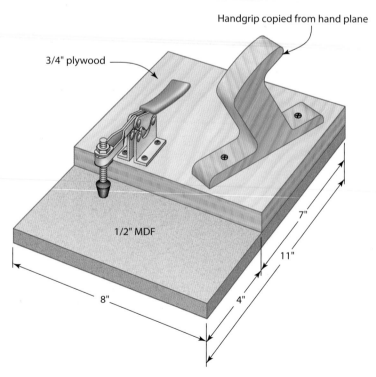

Handgrip copied from hand plane

3/4" plywood

1/2" MDF

7"

11"

8"

4"

sleds on hand for various bits. An alternative is to install a strip of scrap wood—3/4-in. square pine would work nicely—between the fence and the workpiece and let the router chew it up. Or simply replace or rotate the 3/4-in. plywood fence.

To use the jig, make sure your fence is set flush with the cutter bearing. Position the workpiece on the sled. For incremental cuts, hold the piece slightly back from the edge of the sled for the first cut. Then reposition the piece flush with the sled base. Hold the sled firmly against the fence while you make the cut.

Use 1/2-in. stock for the base so the toggle clamp's force won't distort it. Make the handle from doubled up 1/2-in. birch multi-ply or from maple. If you use maple, pay attention to the grain direction; it should move diagonally across the handle profile to minimize short-grain weaknesses. Trace the profile of a bench plane handle onto the handle blank. Cut out the handle on the bandsaw and file and sand it smooth. Install the handle at an angle so that during operation the pressure is naturally applied into the fence as well as down on the sled.

Apply a thin coat of paste wax or shoe polish to the bottom of the sled. Let it dry and then buff it to a high shine. This will virtually eliminate friction between the sled and the tabletop.

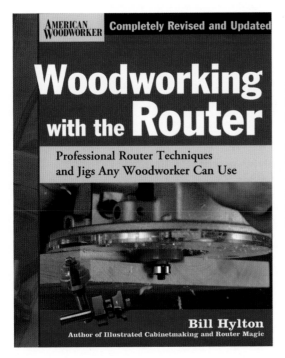

Bill Hylton has been writing about woodworking for more than 20 years. All the jigs in this story are taken from his newly revised book, *Woodworking with the Router*. He has written dozens of books on the topic, including the best-selling *Router Magic* and *Illustrated Cabinetmaking*.

Source: Fox Chapel Publishing, www.FoxChapelPublishing.com 800-457-9112

by JERRY SPRUIELL

"Two-Cent" Micro Adjuster

THIS FENCE CAN MAKE YOUR ROUTER TABLE SING

"I f I could just open that sliding dovetail by 1/128", I thought while staring at my router table setup, "choirs of angels would sing!" Sure, I could buy a micro-adjuster for the fence, but that would mean I'd have to leave the sanctuary of my shop and spend money. So, I dug in my heels, got a fresh cup of coffee, and started scratching my head. Using left over hardware and scraps from my offcut pile, I eventually came up with this micro adjuster. It works great and has a nifty on-board clamping system that makes it easy to install and remove on any router table top (with or without T-track).

The best way to create the small pieces that comprise this jig (see Fig. A) is to start with blanks that are oversize in length. Drill the holes and cut the grooves and tenons first. Then cut each piece to final length. To start, you'll need some hardwood scraps to make the jig's body and post. To make the top piece, start with a blank that's 7/8" x 3" x 12" long. Cut a 1/8" x 3/4" groove on one side and a 1/2" x 1-3/8" notch in one end. The post's tenon will go in the notch.

Centered in the top's groove and 7/8" from each end, drill 1/16" x 3/4" counterbores with a Forstner bit, to hold two pennies (Photo 1). Next, drill holes all the way through, centered in the counterbores, using the correct size bit for the threaded inserts you're using. Flip the top over and thread in the inserts until they're flush. Cut the top to its final 4" length, and put one penny in each of the counterbores.

Mill a strip of springy hardwood, such as oak or birch, to fit flush in the groove, minus the thickness of the PSA sandpaper that you'll adhere to the surface. After applying the sandpaper, drill two countersunk holes in the center of the spring strip and pilot holes in the groove. Install the pennies and attach the spring strip (Photo 2). Thread the clamp bolts into the threaded inserts (Photo 3). The pennies evenly distribute the pressure.

The height of the jig's side piece is the thickness of your router table plus a strong 7/8". Pre-drill and countersink holes for the screws, and fasten the side piece to the top piece.

The width of the jig's bottom piece depends on the overhang of your router table's top. Drill a hole in this piece, positioned so that you can access the screws that hold the spring strip in the top piece, just in case you ever need to replace

it. Glue and screw the bottom piece to the side piece.

To make the post, start with a 7/8" x 1-3/4" x 12" blank. Bandsaw a tenon to fit the notch in the jig's top. Next, cut the post's profile (Photo 4). Drill a hole through the post and install the coupler nut, using epoxy (Photo 5). Take care not to get epoxy on the threads. Glue the post to the top piece.

To make the T-bolt bar, cut a short piece of aluminum bar stock. Epoxy two wood blocks on each end of the bar, leaving a space for a lock nut. When the epoxy

has cured, drill three holes, one through the center of the bar and one through the center of each block.

Next, cut a length of threaded rod. I cut mine at 9"; you may have to adjust the length to fit your setup. Lock nuts and washers hold the T-bolt bar on the rod. The first nut has to thread almost the entire length of the rod, so chuck the rod in your drill and spin it while holding the nut with a wrench. Stop about 5/8" from the end, and install a nylon washer.

Next, slip on the T-bolt bar assembly, with its flat side against the nylon washer. Install a second nylon washer and the second lock nut to secure the assembly (Photo 6). It should be just tight enough so there's no slop. Thread the rod through the post's coupler nut from front to back. Screw on the knob and secure it with a jam nut.

Cut a 3" section of mini T-track and fasten it to the bar assembly, using T- bolts and knurled knobs (Photo 7). Install the jig on the router table. Slide the fence against the jig and mark the location of the T-track on the fence's back. (Photo 8). Back off the jig, remove the T-track and screw it in place on the fence (Photo 9).

To use the jig, remove the T-bolts and install them in the T-track. Position the fence approximately where you need it, slide the jig onto the table's edge, and attach the T-bolts to the T-bolt bar. Tighten the jig's spring clamp and you're ready to micro adjust!

An ingenious clamp mechanism secures this jig to the router table. Pennies recessed in a groove in the jig's top transfer clamping pressure applied by threaded-in bolts.

Here's the heart of the clamping mechanism. The pennies bear against an abrasive-covered wooden strip that fits in the groove and is attached at its center, so it acts as a spring.

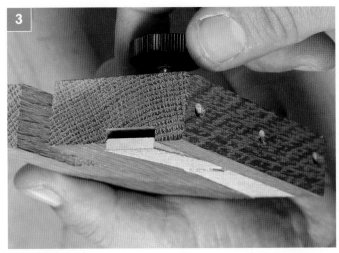

Tightening the clamp bolts pushes down the pennies, and flexes the spring. This locks the completed adjuster to the router table.

Create the post on the bandsaw. Use the fence to cut the tenon. Then saw the profile.

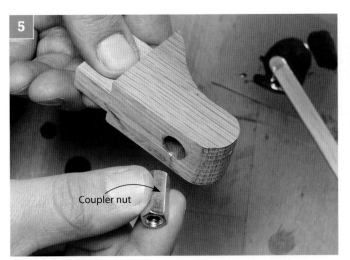

Epoxy a coupler nut in a hole drilled through the post. The jig's adjustment rod threads through this nut. Glue the post in the top's notch. Then attach the jig's side and bottom pieces.

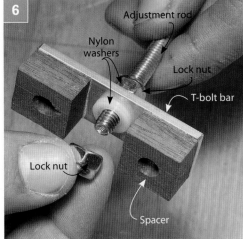

Fasten the T-bolt bar to the end of the adjustment rod. Epoxied-on wooden spacers house the lock nut and provide clearance for the T-bolts that connect the jig to the router table fence.

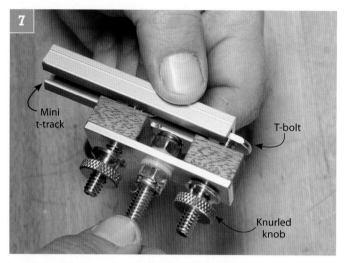

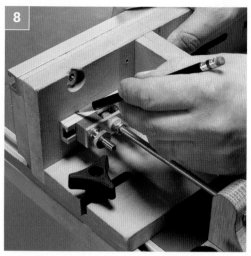

Install the T-bolts and a length of mini T-track on the bar. This allows using the jig to position the T-track on the router table's fence in the next step. Install the adjustment rod in the jig and attach the knob.

Mark the T-track's location after installing the jig, locking it in place and sliding the fence against it.

Remove the T-track from the jig and fasten it to the fence, using the marks you've made. To attach the jig, transfer the T-bolts to the T-track and then reattach them to the jig's T-bolt bar.

FIG. A: "TWO-CENT" MICRO ADJUSTER

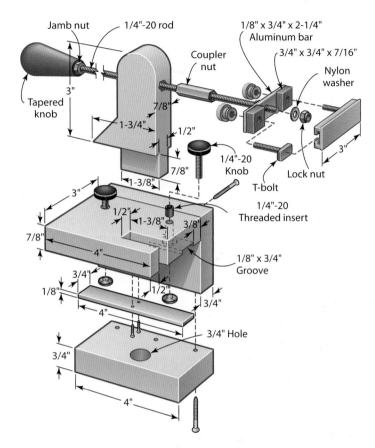

You don't need extra clamps to install this micro-adjust, because it has a nifty integral clamp mechanism.

by JOHN ENGLISH

Router Bit Caddy

SEPARATE, SORT, AND SEE YOUR COLLECTION

With just five different parts to make, this easy-to-build caddy accommodates bits with both 1/2" and 1/4" shafts. It can be customized to handle just about any collection. The caddy stands solidly on its wide base, stores easily on a shelf or in a cabinet, and is light enough to tote around the shop or take to a jobsite.

CUT SLIDING DOVETAILS

1. Cut the sides and shelves to size. Cut two 1/4" wide dadoes on the inside face of each side piece (Photo 1). Set up the router table with a 1/2" dovetail bit, raise the bit 1/2" high, and enlarge the four dadoes, making sliding-dovetail sockets (Photo 2). Joint the edges of these pieces to remove any tear-out.

2. Use a scrap piece exactly the same thickness as the two shelves to set up the router table for cutting tails (Photo 3). Use the same dovetail bit and leave it at the same height. Adjust the fence so the dovetails are loose enough to slide in the sockets without using any force. Once you've achieved the correct fence setting, mill the tails on the real shelves. Glue and clamp the shelves to the sides.

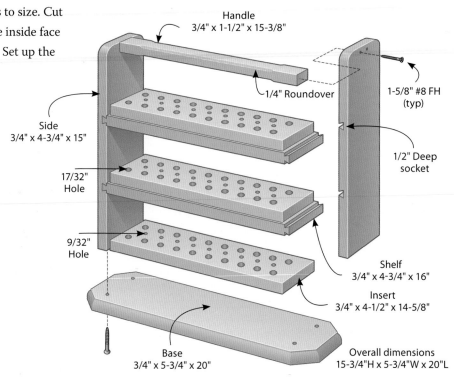

Handle
3/4" x 1-1/2" x 15-3/8"

1/4" Roundover

1-5/8" #8 FH (typ)

1/2" Deep socket

Side
3/4" x 4-3/4" x 15"

17/32" Hole

9/32" Hole

Shelf
3/4" x 4-3/4" x 16"

Insert
3/4" x 4-1/2" x 14-5/8"

Base
3/4" x 5-3/4" x 20"

Overall dimensions
15-3/4"H x 5-3/4"W x 20"L

The caddy is held together with sliding-dovetail joints. Start by cutting dadoes in the sides to remove most of the waste.

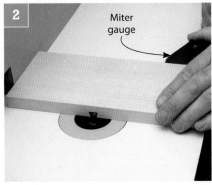

Widen the dadoes into dovetail sockets using a router table. Steady the workpiece with a miter gauge.

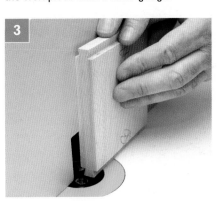

Using the same bit, make test cuts on a piece of scrap until it slides easily into the sockets. Then cut the real shelves.

MAKE SHELF INSERTS

3. Cut the shelf inserts 5" extra-long, to avoid splitting their ends when you drill holes. On each insert, lay out the holes according to your needs, staying at least 3" from each end. Use a sharp 17/32" bit for 1/2" shafts and a 9/32" bit for 1/4" shafts. These oversize holes make it easier to remove or replace the router bits. Drill all the way through each insert.

4. Run the inserts through a planer or across a jointer to remove any tear-out from the drilling. Trim the inserts to fit on the shelves. I left a 3/8" gap on each end for aesthetics.

ASSEMBLE THE CADDY

5. Cut the handle to size and use a 1/4" roundover bit to ease all four edges. Stop the cut 3" from each end. Install the handle with glue and screws.

6. Cut the base to size and saw the corners. Rout a decorative profile along the top edge, then ease the edges with sandpaper. Center the carcass on the base and attach it with glue and screws.

7. Glue and clamp the inserts onto the base and shelves (Photo 4). Apply a finish, and load it up!

Glue the inserts onto the shelves. This two-piece construction creates deep holes for the bits, so they won't tip over when you tote the caddy around.

Router Techniques

R outers are truly some of the most versatile tools that a woodworker can own. The proof is in the variety of ways they are used, which include cutting, profiling, panel raising, grooving, joining, trimming, dovetailing, and even carving. Each application, however, presents its share of challenges, such as preventing chipping, setting up jigs, and ensuring safety. Like most woodworking techniques, mastering your router is mainly a matter of understanding where things can go wrong and knowing how best to avoid pitfalls.

For example, grain tear-out is one of the most common problems woodworkers face when routing. This chapter provides sure-fire ways to avoid tear-out. If you've ever wanted to build raised-panel doors but were concerned about working safely with such large bits, the section on raised-panel jigs should inspire your confidence. To expand the use of your router even further, you should explore the many options available through template routing, which enables you to accurately create multiple parts of almost any shape, including precise joinery and complex curves. We show you many ways to take advantage of the benefits of template routers.

《 The versatility of a router allows craftsmen to design beautiful pieces such as this oval inlay.

by ERIC SMITH

9 Tips for Beating Router Tear-out

STOP ROUTER DISASTERS BEFORE THEY START

Snap, crackle, crunch!

No, it's not your breakfast cereal. That's the sound of router tear-out.

Aaargh!

And that's the sound of a woodworker facing a do-over or repair.

Tear-out can happen cutting across or against the grain, cutting too deeply, using a dull bit or just running into a hidden flaw. One thing's for sure: It'll always happen at the worst possible time. Although it can't completely be avoided, you can definitely minimize the chances of tear-out by following some simple techniques and precautions—without adding a lot of time or expense to your projects.

EDITOR: DAVE MUNKITTRICK · ART DIRECTION: VERN JOHNSON · PHOTOGRAPHY: STAFF

1 PAY ATTENTION TO GRAIN DIRECTION

Visualize a feather cut by a router. It would be a mess, of course, but the point is that when you rout against the grain (see photo, left), the wood reacts just like a feather. The grain is running right into the bit rotation. The wood's fibers are likely to catch and break apart ahead of the cut, producing tear-out. But when you run the router with the grain, you get a smooth cut.

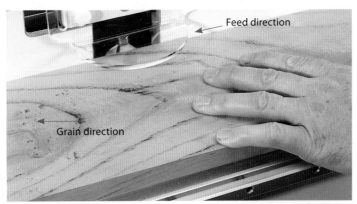

Feeding your stock so the grain direction crashes head on into the bit rotation is like running your finger the wrong way on a feather. Nasty tear-out is almost a sure thing.

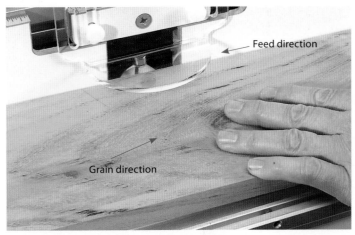

Flip a board end for end to change the direction from which the grain meets the cutter. Now the grain flows in the same direction as the bit rotation. The result will be a smooth cut with little or no tear-out worries.

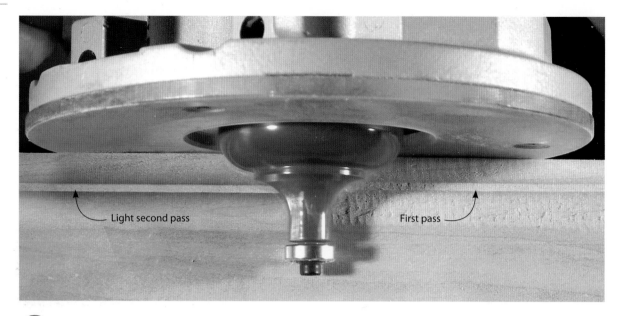

Light second pass — First pass

2 MAKE A VERY LIGHT FINAL PASS

Trying to hog out a clean edge in one pass is asking for tear-out trouble. Instead of gambling with an expensive piece of wood, take the time to make at least two passes: one heavy pass and a very light final pass. Because the final pass is just a shaving cut, the bit is a lot less likely to catch and tear the wood fibers. You'll get a smooth surface, even if the grain is going the wrong way.

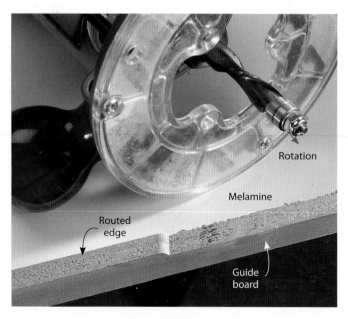

Rotation

Melamine

Routed edge

Guide board

3 USE A DOWN-CUTTING SPIRAL BIT FOR FLUSH TRIMMING

Down-cutting spiral bits push down on the wood's surface. The result is a clean, tear-out-free shearing cut. Down-cutting spiral bits work especially well for trimming or cutting through delicate veneers, melamine, laminates, and highly figured woods.

4 USE A ZERO-CLEARANCE FENCE

A zero-clearance fence backs up the wood as it's fed into the router bit, making it difficult for the wood to chip.

To make a zero-clearance fence, set the router bit at the height and depth you want. If you have removable subfences, turn the router on and slowly slide the infeed side of the fence into the bit. If your fence has a fixed face, clamp temporary subfences on both sides. With the router running, loosen the clamps on the infeed fence enough to slowly slide the subfences into the spinning bit.

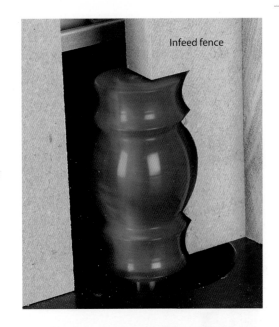

Infeed fence

5 RIP AND START OVER

Sometimes you have no choice but to cut your loss and make a new piece. Other times, you can afford to trim the piece and start over. Just rip a bit off the damaged edge and then rout it again.

When I'm working with wood that looks likely to tear out, I try to give myself some wiggle room by cutting a wider piece than I need, then ripping it to size after I've successfully routed the edge. the spinning bit.

Torn-out edge

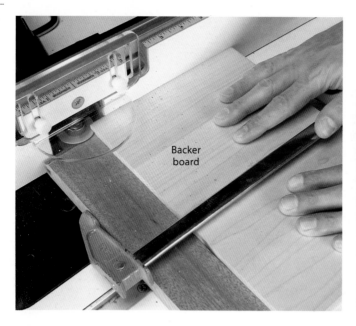

Backer board

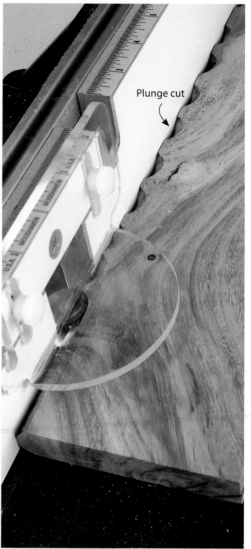

Plunge cut

6 STOP END-GRAIN BLOWOUTS WITH A BACKER BOARD

Rout the end grain first and use a backer board. That's the best way to reduce your chances of blowing out a corner. The backer board supports the cut so the corner has no chance to tear away. Make sure the backer piece is at least as thick as the piece you're routing. Clamp the pieces together for rock-solid support.

7 MAKE SOME PLUNGE CUTS

Routing against the grain may be unavoidable. On some edges, the grain reverses direction, so you can't win. If you're getting tear-out along an edge—or even if it looks like you might—make a series of plunge cuts every inch or two. This will cause the splinters to break off at the cutout before they can ruin your profile.

The best way to make plunge cuts is to hold one end of the board tightly against the outfeed fence and the other end away from the spinning bit. Push the board against the fence, then pull it out. Move the board forward an inch or two and repeat.

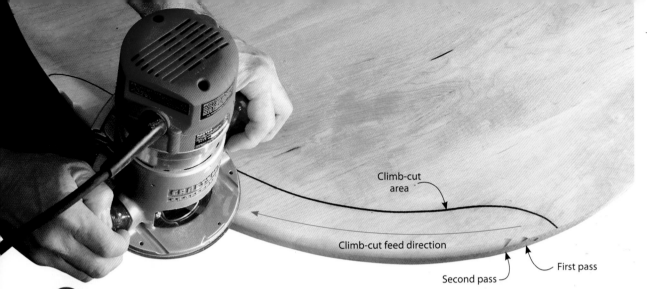

Climb-cut area

Climb-cut feed direction

First pass

Second pass

8 MAKE SHALLOW CLIMB CUTS

Reversing the normal direction of the router feed is called climb-cutting. Climb-cutting can involve either moving clockwise with a handheld router or pushing wood from left to right on a router table. Climb-cutting almost always eliminates tear-out, but it also makes the router more difficult to control. That's because the stock is fed in the same direction as the bit is spinning, so the bit wants to grab the wood and pull. This makes climb-cutting potentially dangerous. It's not recommended for most routing. If you follow a few rules, though, climb-cutting is a great way to get yourself over those pesky areas where tear-out is almost a sure thing.

Play it safe:

■ Always make very shallow, light passes, especially when using a big bit.

■ Secure the wood and/or router very firmly.

■ Make sure the bit is sharp. A dull bit grabs and pulls, but a sharp bit cuts with less effort.

■ On a router table, use featherboards whenever possible to hold the board and keep it from running away.

■ When using a handheld router, firmly clamp down the stock. If the workpiece is narrow, add support so the router won't tip.

■ Never climb-cut small or narrow pieces on the router table. It's better to cut the profile on a large piece and trim it to the size you want later.

9 MAKE A SCORING CUT ON DOVETAIL JIGS

Face grain can splinter when you run a bit in and out of a board in a dovetail jig. Instead of having wood filler at the ready, start by making a light scoring pass along the entire edge of the board. Gently move the router in and out of the template fingers. Make the cuts about a 1/8 in. deep. Then go back and finish.

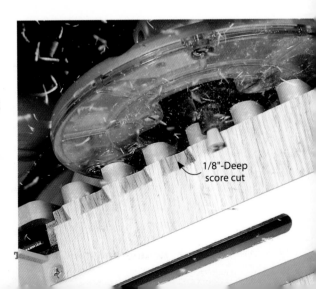

1/8"-Deep score cut

by TIM JOHNSON

Raise Panels Safely with Your Router

BUILD THREE FIXTURES THAT WILL GIVE YOU MORE CONTROL AND PROTECT YOUR FINGERS

Scary. That's what most woodworkers think about raising panels with a router. The idea of that big hunk of sharpened steel spinning around near your fingers is frightening. But what are the options? Raising panels by hand is time consuming and raising them on the tablesaw is just as scary.

Give your router a chance. I'll show you three different fixtures designed to tame those scary bits. When properly set up and used, they will make panel raising with your router safe and easy. Instead of feeling scared, you'll feel confident.

THOSE BIG BITS

There are two types of panel-raising router bits. Either the panel is laid flat on the work surface and fed past a horizontally oriented bit, or the panel is tipped on its edge and fed past a vertically oriented bit. Each type has advantages.

Because they are fitted with a bearing, horizontal bits can raise panels with either straight or curved edges. If you want to raise arched-top panels, a horizontal bit is your only choice. The bit's massive cutting surfaces and weight require a powerful router and its large diameter requires one with variable-speed capability. The combination of a horizontal bit with a 3-hp, variable-speed router is hard to beat. The bit gives you versatility and the router lets you adjust the speed for the best cut. However, these bits are costly—$100 or above—and if you don't own a compatible router, the total expense could be prohibitive.

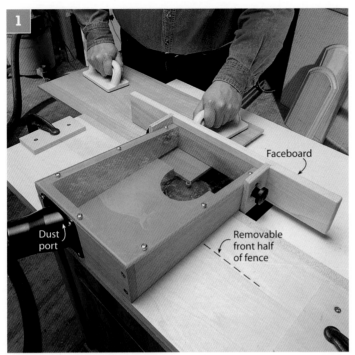

The box fence keeps your fingers well away from the router bit, and has an adjustable faceboard to hold the panel tight against the table. The box makes dust collection very effective and visibility through its polycarbonate top is excellent.

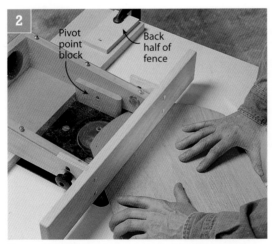

For arched panels, the front half of the base is removed, allowing you to swing the work past the bit. A pivot-point block, attached to the infeed side of the box, keeps the panel from kicking back when you feed it into the bit. The fixture is positioned to locate the pivot point close to the bit.

If straight-edged panels are all you anticipate making, vertical bits will serve you well. Because of their vertical orientation, they are smaller in diameter than their cousins, so they're less expensive and require a less powerful router to operate. Variable-speed control is less of an issue, as the smaller bits (1-in. diameter) can be used with single-speed, high-rpm routers.

The key to being comfortable using either of these bits is to protect yourself from them. Two accessories listed in the "Four Rules for Safe Operation" (page 139) help you do just that. Featherboards do double duty. They protect against kickback and also effectively block the bit and keep your fingers out of harm's way. Push blocks keep a firm grip on the workpiece and protect your hands in more ways than one. Keeping them away from the bit is obvious, but you'll find that gripping the push blocks is much less fatiguing for your hands than holding and manipulating the panel without them. Use these tools without fail—you'll be glad you did.

THE BOX FENCE: SAFE HOUSING FOR HORIZONTAL BITS

This fixture, consisting of a box and a base, surrounds a horizontal bit. The box has an adjustable faceboard at its front to bear on the panel, a polycarbonate top for visibility, and a dust collection port at its rear.

The box is attached to a split base. Aligned with the bit's pilot bearing, the front half of this base acts as a fence for

ART DIRECTION • MELANIE HAUBRICH; PHOTOGRAPHY • ZUEHLKE PHOTOGRAPHY; ILLUSTRATIONS • FRANK ROHRBACH straight-edged panels (Photo 1). Remove the front half of the base, add the pivot-point block, and the fixture accommodates curved-edge panels, or other operations run off the pilot bearing (Photo 2).

This fixture is effective because it offers versatility, excellent visibility, and great protection. If you can justify the expense of the horizontal bit and 3-hp., variable- speed router, read no further.

A SAFE FENCE FOR VERTICAL BITS

Safely using the vertical bit requires a fence with a tall face. This idea has been around for a long time, and is usually associated with the tablesaw. This fixture is the easiest of the three to build. Its face is 10-in. tall, high enough to support most panels (Photo 3 and inset). It must be firmly supported and built

square so that it clamps perpendicular to the router table.

The key to making this fixture work safely is a featherboard mounted on a block so that it presses the panel against the fence above the cut of the bit. It is positioned over the bit and clamped securely to the table.

When used with a push block, this fixture keeps your hands clear and eases the job of running panels on edge. Unfortunately, using it makes you stand in a twisted position, and that's a big shortcoming. With extensive use, this fixture can be tiring.

MAKE VERTICAL BITS WORK HORIZONTALLY

If you're set on using vertical bits, consider mounting the router horizontally on the end of your tablesaw. Then you can lay the panels flat and raise them without contorting

Types of Panel-Raising Router Bits

PANEL-RAISING BITS OPERATE HORIZONTALLY OR VERTICALLY.

Horizontal bit

Pros
- Most versatile; can cut straight or curved edges

Cons
- Expensive
- Requires a powerful (3 hp) router with variable speeds
- Large diameter cutter looks scary

Vertical bits

Pros
- Cheaper
- May be compatible with your old router because they require less power and small diameter bits (1-in.) can operate in single-speed routers

Cons
- Can't do curved edge
- Running lots of panels on edge can be tiring

FIG. A: THE BOX FENCE

For safe use of large, horizontal bits.

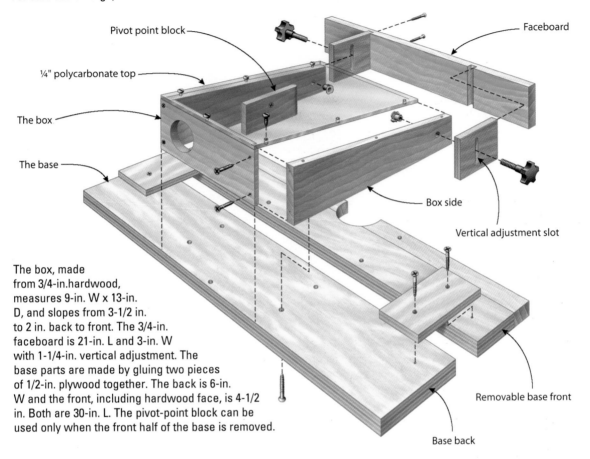

Pivot point block

¼" polycarbonate top

The box

The base

Faceboard

Box side

Vertical adjustment slot

Removable base front

Base back

The box, made from 3/4-in. hardwood, measures 9-in. W x 13-in. D, and slopes from 3-1/2 in. to 2 in. back to front. The 3/4-in. faceboard is 21-in. L and 3-in. W with 1-1/4-in. vertical adjustment. The base parts are made by gluing two pieces of 1/2-in. plywood together. The back is 6-in. W and the front, including hardwood face, is 4-1/2 in. Both are 30-in. L. The pivot-point block can be used only when the front half of the base is removed.

Four Rules for Safe Operation

These guidelines must be followed when using panel-raising bits:

1. Slow the router's speed according to the bit manufacturer's specifications. The larger the bit, the slower the speed.

2. Use a slow, steady feed rate and make several shallow passes. Listen to the motor, don't bog it down, and use common sense.

3. Make cross-grain cuts first.

4. Use appropriate safety gear:

   Eye and ear protection

   Featherboards

   Push blocks

your body. The fixture is complex and will take time to build, but its benefits will be noticeable if you have large panels or a large number of panels to raise. Although shown dedicated to a tablesaw, it could be adapted to a router table as well.

This fixture consists of a piece of plywood fastened perpendicular to the saw and an arm, housing the router, fastened to it. The arm pivots to raise the router and bit into position (Photo 5) and, when locked, acts as a bearing fence for the panel (Photo 4). Again, a block-mounted featherboard must be employed to bear on the panel beyond the top of the bit's cut. Positioned over the bit and clamped to the pivot arm, the featherboard effectively blocks your hands while guarding against kickback.

Once built, this fixture is effective because, with the panels on their faces and gravity as your ally, you can address them straight-on. Push blocks work great with this set-up.

You will find this fixture useful for any other operation where you would normally run the workpiece on its edge: Wide molding profiles or tenons, for example.

A tall fence, a featherboard, and a push block help to advance a panel, tipped on its edge, past the vertical bit.

The high face on this fence provides ample support for panels. Its hardwood top surface is smooth and splinter-free. Dust collection is effective because of the point-of-discharge port. The fence swivels on a threaded lock knob on its infeed end, and when used with a clamped block on the other end, makes minor adjustments easy.

FIG. B: THE TALL FENCE FOR VERTICAL BITS

This fixture, made from 3/4-in. plywood, consists of a plastic-laminate covered, 10-in. high fence edged on top with hardwood. It is mounted to a 5-1/2-in. wide base and held perpendicular to it by buttresses. It pivots around a hole drilled through the infeed side of the base and router tabletop and is fixed by a threaded lock knob.

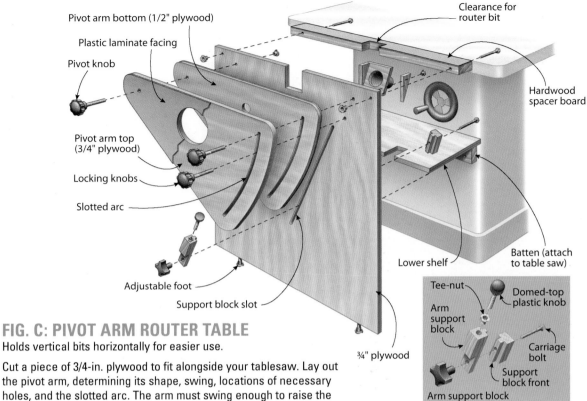

Clearance for router bit

Pivot arm bottom (1/2" plywood)

Plastic laminate facing

Pivot knob

Pivot arm top (3/4" plywood)

Locking knobs

Slotted arc

Adjustable foot

Support block slot

Hardwood spacer board

Lower shelf

Batten (attach to table saw)

¾" plywood

Tee-nut

Arm support block

Domed-top plastic knob

Carriage bolt

Support block front

Arm support block

FIG. C: PIVOT ARM ROUTER TABLE

Holds vertical bits horizontally for easier use.

Cut a piece of 3/4-in. plywood to fit alongside your tablesaw. Lay out the pivot arm, determining its shape, swing, locations of necessary holes, and the slotted arc. The arm must swing enough to raise the router bit above the saw table and the support block must support the arm through the length of its swing. The spacer board and the lower shelf hold the fixture properly at the side of the table.

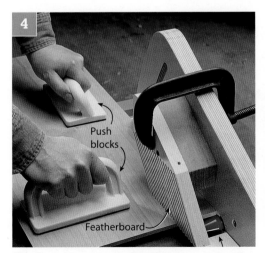

Push blocks

Featherboard

This fixture mounts to your tablesaw or other flat surface. It allows you to place the panel on its face, making it easy to control. The featherboard keeps the panel from kicking back and blocks your hands from the bit.

Height adjustment is precise: one complete turn of the knob moves the bit one-sixteenth of an inch. Make test cuts on scrap stock to dial in the exact position. A white line painted on the edge of the knob serves as a reference point.

Reed Molding with Your Router

MIRROR-IMAGE MOLDINGS TURN AN ORDINARY CABINET INTO A REAL EYE-CATCHER

Want to dress up a plain-looking cabinet? Add reeded moldings. The ones shown here are unusual because the reeding is diagonal, creating the look of turned spirals. All you need to make them is a point-cutting round-over bit for your router and a jig to hold the stock while you rout it. The jig (Fig. A), which was designed by Rick Christopherson, holds pieces up to 6-in. wide for cutting moldings with either left- or right-hand diagonals. Aluminum rails fixed at 45 degrees to the workpiece guide the router as it cuts the profile. You can make this jig in an afternoon and spend the evening reeding.

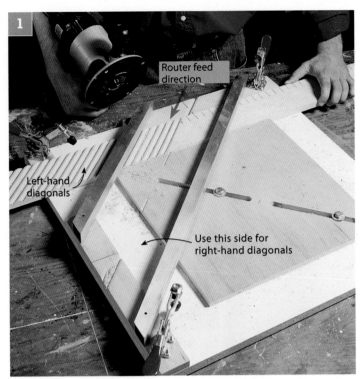

Using the jig. After each router pass, release the toggle clamps, advance the workpiece to the next index line, reclamp and make another pass. Rout from the outside of the jig across the workpiece.

This point-cutting round-over bit makes the half-round reeds. It takes two passes with the router to make each one.

MAKE THE JIG

Draw a line on the base (A) from corner to corner. On this line, mark and drill the two holes for fastening the backstop (B) and attach tee-nuts from the bottom. Glue and screw the fence block (C) to the front corner and the fence rails (D) to the sides of the base. Be sure to align the edges. Then cut the two slots in the backstop and fasten it loosely to the base so it slides in and out.

The alignment and spacing of the two diagonally fastened guides is important for making smooth router passes. Square aluminum tubing is rigid, durable, and dimensionally stable, making it a good choice for repeated use. Mark points on each fence rail 10 1/4-in. from the front corner. Clamp the front guide (E) to the base assembly at these two points and drill holes for screws through both the guide and base. Mark the guide with a felt-tip pen where it overhangs the base and miter it to fit before fastening. Washers raise the guides slightly so the workpiece can slide easily underneath. Fit and attach the back guide (F) the same way. It must be parallel to the front guide. Use an 18-in.-long scrap cut the same width as your router base plate to ensure proper spacing.

Draw an index line on each side fence rail between the guides and slightly offset from center so it's out of the path of the router cut.

PREPARE THE WORKPIECE

Make blanks from 5/8-in. stock, allowing an extra 6 in. in length and an extra 1/2 in. in width for cleanup after routing. Mark index lines along the length of each blank. Use these lines to position the piece for each cut (Photo 3 and Fig. B).

MAKE AND INSTALL THE MOLDING

Slide the blank in the jig, align the index marks, and snug the backstop up to it. Lock the blank in place with the clamps. Make the molding with repetitive cuts (Photo 1). Clean up the molding after routing by cutting it to final size and sanding (Photo 4). Then mount it, either recessed into the cabinet or on the surface, with trim molding (opening photo).

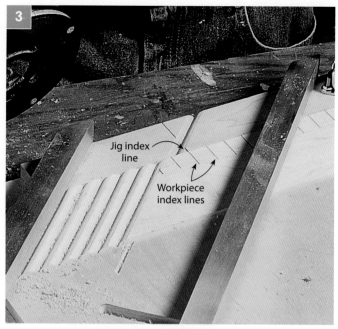

The radius of the router bit you use determines the distance between the index lines on the workpiece (see Fig. B). The bigger the radius, the larger the bead, and the farther apart the index lines. I used a 1/4-in.-radius bit (for a 1/2-in.-wide bead) so my index lines are 11/16 in. apart.

Sanding is necessary to smooth ridges and rough grain left by the router bit. A detail sander is perfect for this job.

FIG. A: JIG FOR DIAGONAL ROUTING

This jig can accommodate routers with base plates up to 6-in. dia. For larger routers, use a slightly larger piece for the base (A) so there's room for the outboard toggle clamps.

FIG. B: SPACE BETWEEN INDEX LINES ON WORKPIECE

Bit Radius	Index Lines
1/8"	3/8"
1/4"	11/16"
3/8"	11/16"
1/2"	13/8"

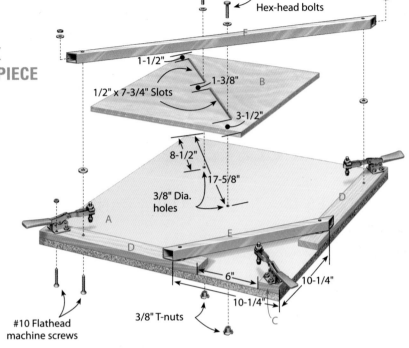

3/8" x 1-1/4"
Hex-head bolts

1-1/2"

1-3/8"

1/2" x 7-3/4" Slots

3-1/2"

8-1/2"

17-5/8"

3/8" Dia. holes

A

B

D

E

C

F

D

6"

10-1/4"

10-1/4"

#10 Flathead machine screws

3/8" T-nuts

Materials List
- Point-cutting round-over bits
- Toggle clamps
- 1-in. square aluminum tubing

Cutting List
Overall dimensions: 31/2" x 24" x 24"

Part	Name	Dimensions	Material
A	Base	3/4" x 24" x 24"	melamine or MDF
B	Backstop	1/2" x 15 1/2" x 15 1/2"	plywood
C	Fence Block	5/8" x 2 1/2" x 2 1/2"	hardwood
D	Fence Rails (2)	5/8" x 2 1/2" x 15 1/2"	hardwood
E	Front Guide	1" x 1" x 18"	square aluminum tubing, cut to size
F	Back Guide	1" x 1" x 32"	square aluminum tubing, cut to size

by DAVE EKLUND

Shop-Made Arts & Crafts Knobs

ALL IT TAKES IS A ROUTER AND A BANDSAW

You'll only need two machines to make these Arts & Crafts-style knobs: a bandsaw and a router table. Although the saw cuts can be done on a tablesaw, the bandsaw keeps the operation safe and simple. The router table work requires two bits: a 5/8-in. round nose bit and a straight bit.

Shop-made knobs may not save you a lot of money, but they offer a wealth of advantages over the store bought variety. For starters, the knobs will better match the project, because the wood comes from the project's scrap. In addition, you can customize the knob's size to fit the scale of the piece. Plus, making your own knobs is a satisfying project by itself.

Start by ripping 1-1/2-in. strips of wood from 1-1/4-in. thick quartersawn stock. The blanks can be any length, although a minimum length of 8-in. is best for machining. Cut enough blanks to make a

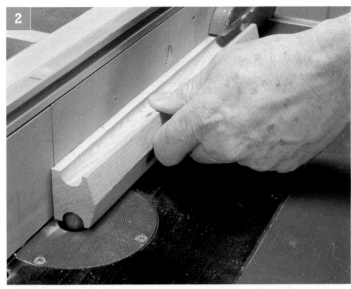

Start the knobs by cutting a pair of 15-degree bevels on the face of the blank. Set the fence so the bandsaw blade exits just above the marked centerline.

Rout finger grooves along both sides of the blank. Make one heavy pass then a light clean-up pass to avoid tearout.

few extra knobs; you're bound to loose a few to test cuts along the way.

Lay out a centerline on the face of the blank. Then head to the bandsaw and tilt the table 15-degrees. Set the fence and cut the bevels in two passes (Photo 1).

Take the beveled blank to the router table. Chuck a 5/8-in. core box or round nose bit in the router. Set the bit's height just shy of 3/8-in. for the first pass. Position the fence to leave a 3/16-in. edge below the bevel (Fig. A). Rout a groove along each edge (Photo 2). Head back to the bandsaw and crosscut the blank into 1-1/2-in. squares (Photo 3).

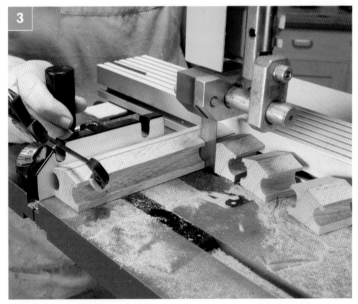

Crosscut the blank into 1-1/2-in. squares. A miter gauge insures a square cut. There's no risk of a kickback when you make this cut on the bandsaw.

Machining the remaining bevels and grooves on short little pieces, of course, is a bad idea. The solution is to reassemble the knobs in a line as before, but with their grain running in the opposite direction (Photo 4). Make a sled to hold the knobs from a piece of 2x4 squared up and ripped to the same width as the knobs. Make sure the knobs line up perfectly flush with each other. Mark the center of each knob face again to help set the bandsaw fence. Cut the bevels and grooves as before (Photos 5 & 6). Cut the knobs free of the sled (Photo 7).

The knobs look their best when the base is smaller than the face. Trim back the base on the router table (Photo 8). A notched 2x4 that's been jointed flat makes the perfect guide block. Blowing out the back edge is a real issue on these cuts. Start with an end grain cut. Then, rotate the knob 90-degrees clockwise, and cut the first long grain edge.

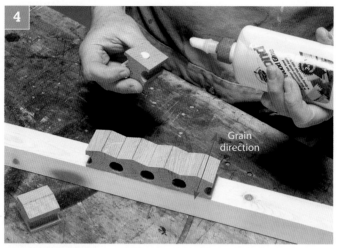

Glue the knobs onto a milled sled to machine the end-grain faces. Rotate each knob 90-degrees from its original orientation and use a small dab of glue.

Keep rotating the knob 90-degrees clockwise after each cut. If tearout is still a problem, make smaller incremental cuts.

Finally, sand the knobs, starting with 120-grit paper. Round the corners and soften the sharp edges until the knob feels comfortable.

FIG. A

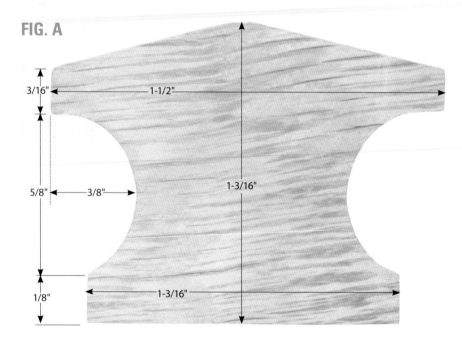

3/16"
1-1/2"
5/8"
3/8"
1-3/16"
1/8"
1-3/16"

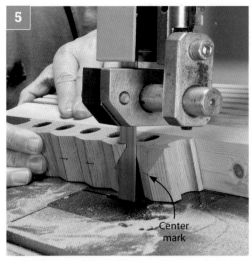

Cut the remaining two bevels on the knob faces. Once again, position the fence so the blade just misses the center mark.

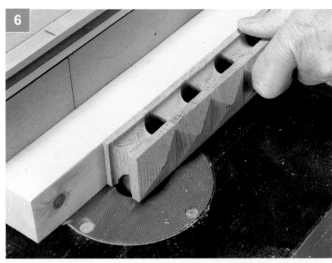

Rout the remaining grooves in the knobs. Take light passes and use a slow feed-rate to avoid tearout as the bit enters and exits the cavities between the knobs.

Slice the knobs free of the sled. Set the fence so the blade is centered on the glue line.

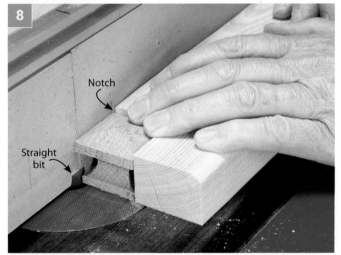

Trim down the base with a straight bit and a zero-clearance fence. A block of wood with a notch slightly smaller than the knob guides the knob safely through the cut.

by TOM CASPAR

Routing for Oval Inlay

GET A PERFECT FIT USING A SHOP-MADE JIG

Inlaying oval and circular designs is a time-honored method for adding class to a project, such as a jewelry box. Making your own inlay is an interesting challenge, but it's far easier to select one from a wide range of ready-made designs.Here's the $64,000 question, though: How are you going to create a perfectly-sized recess for the inlay? There's really no room for error on a prominent detail like this—you wouldn't want to ruin an inlay, or your project, using an imprecise technique. Not to worry: the following method for routing the recess ensures a good fit.

PREPARE THE INLAY

All inlays come with a layer of tape on one side, which helps keep together the various parts of the design. The tape is always placed on the good, or top, side of the inlay. Draw centerlines for the oval or circle on the tape using a combination square.

Some oval and circular inlays are made with a rectangular or square border which protects the edges of the design.

If your inlay has a border, the first step is to remove it (Photo 1). All the parts of the inlay are glued together, including the border, so the border must be cut off with a very sharp knife. A breakaway utility knife works well as long as you start with a fresh edge. Guide the cuts with a metal straightedge, such as the blade from a combination square. Avoid cutting into the oval border. Make a series of straight cuts—it's OK if small pieces of the border veneer remain.

Make a small station for sanding the inlay's edges (Photo 2). First, tape a piece of 150-grit sandpaper to a thick block. Clamp the block to a piece of plywood (melamine works well, because it's slippery). Sand the inlay by rotating it with your hands—the goal is to make a perfect oval.

MAKE THE TEMPLATE

MDF is ideal for making a template because it's uniform and easy to sand. It can be any thickness. (I'm using 1/2" material). Cut the MDF the same size as the piece of wood that you'll be routing for the inlay.

Draw centerlines on the template. The oval won't be perfectly symmetrical, so mark one portion of the inlay with an "X", and make the same mark on the template. Align the centerlines of the oval and template and trace around the inlay with a sharp, soft-leaded pencil (Photo 3). Widen the line with a dull pencil.

Some inlays have a rectangular border which must be removed. Cut off the border using a sharp knife guided by a metal straightedge.

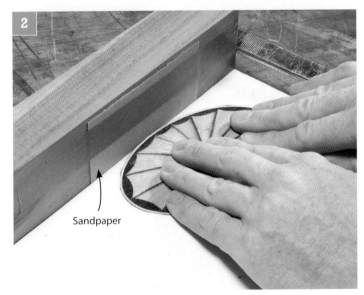

Sandpaper

Remove remaining bits of border material by sanding the oval on a right-angled block. This ensures that the oval's edges are square.

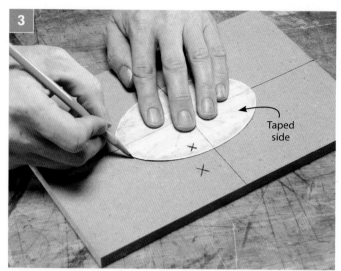

Make a router template from MDF. Turn over the inlay, taped side up (this is the show side), and trace around it.

Remove most of the waste inside the oval using a Forstner bit in the drill press.

Remove most of the waste by drilling (Photo 4). Keep the bit at least 1/32" away from the pencil line. Use a Forstner bit so you can overlap the holes.

Now for the picky part. Sand right up to the line–but don't remove any of the line (Photo 5). Take it easy and frequently check your progress (Photo 6). If you sand too far into the line, it's probably best to start over with a new template.

ROUT THE RECESS

You'll be routing the recess for the inlay with a top-bearing flush-trim bit. Your template will probably have to be shimmed to raise it high enough above the workpiece so the bit can create a shallow recess. I chose a bit with 9/16" long flutes and made a shim from 1/4" hardboard (Photo 7), but many combinations of bits and shims will work. Make the shim piece the same size as the template, to help with alignment when clamping the template to the workpiece.

If your router has a small-diameter base, you may have to replace the sub-base with a larger, shop-made sub-base to prevent the router from tipping into the template, and to enable it to reach the middle of the recess.

Install the bit in your router. I unplug the router and turn it upside down to initially set the bit's height (Photo 8). Place cutoffs from the template and the shim next to the bit to represent their combined thickness. Add two playing cards on top–they're just a hair thinner than the inlay.

Rout a piece of scrap wood to test the bit's depth of cut. Clamp the template at all four corners to the scrap piece. This ensures that the recess is an even depth. Place the inlay, or an offcut from the border, in the recess. The inlay (not including the tape) should stand proud of the recess by about the thickness of a sheet of paper. Adjust the bit if necessary, then mark the actual workpiece with an "X" (corresponding to the "X" on the template), and rout the real recess (Photo 9).

GLUE THE INLAY

Align the two "X" marks and test the inlay's fit into the recess (Photo 10). If the inlay is too large, remove a bit from its edges using the sanding station. Again, take it easy—the goal is for the inlay to drop into the recess using very little pressure.

Make a clamping block that's about 1/32" smaller than the inlay all around. Spread a thin coat of yellow glue in the recess—but not on the inlay—and position the inlay in the recess, tape side up. Make sure that the inlay is properly seated all around, then place the block on the inlay and clamp (Photo 11). Remove any glue squeeze-out and let the glue dry overnight.

Remove the tape by slightly moistening it with water (Photo 12). Sand the inlay flush with fine paper (Photo 13).

Sand up to the pencil line using an oscillating spindle sander or a sanding drum in your drill press.

Check your progress by placing the oval in the template's window. Aim for a snug fit, with no gaps.

Fasten a shim piece to the template's bottom side. The thickness of this piece is determined by the length of your router bit's cutting flutes.

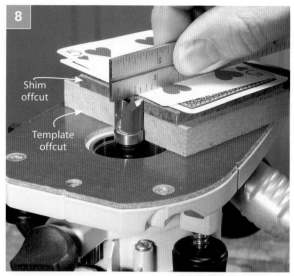

Adjust the height of a top-bearing flush-trim router bit. Use scrap pieces, plus a couple of playing cards, to represent the thickness of the template, shim and inlay.

Clamp the template to the workpiece and rout a recess for the inlay. Using this bit, the recess will be exactly the same size as the template's window.

Test the fit of the inlay in the recess. If the inlay is too large in spots, sand those areas using the right-angle sanding block.

Glue the inlay. Apply even pressure by using a thick block that's just a bit smaller than the inlay.

Remove the tape by moistening it with a sponge. Wait a minute or two, then scrape off the tape using a dull putty knife.

Sand the inlay flush with the surrounding wood. Use 220 grit paper wrapped around a cork-backed block.

by LONNIE BIRD

Template Routing

SIMPLE TO ADVANCED METHODS FOR PRECISELY DUPLICATING PARTS

No other method for shaping is as fast or efficient as template routing. It works like this: the part to be shaped is fastened to the template; the router follows the template as it is guided around the template's perimeter (Photo 1).

Template routing ensures that each part is identical; whether you're shaping six parts or sixty, each one matches the template (Photo 2).

Template routing is versatile, too. You can use this method for shaping almost any part, large or small. It works for making straight cuts, curved cuts, and even for moldings. The part can be as ordinary as a straight-sided shelf for a corner cabinet or as complicated as a serpentine drawer front, which has a convex section between two concave ones.

There are many methods of template routing, which I'll explain below. They range from simple techniques, such as routing that corner cabinet shelf, to advanced setups, such as shaping a complex S-curve molding.

Template routing is a method for guiding a router bit with a shop-made pattern, or template. Here, the bearing on a flush-trim bit follows a plywood template.

Identical parts with smooth, uniform surfaces are easy to make using a template.

Template routing is not just for production work. In fact, there are some cuts, such as shaping the entire edge of a curved tabletop or cutting a curved groove, that cannot be routed any other way. Once you understand this technique and use it a few times, you'll begin to imagine other possibilities for its use. I even use a template for routing some joints (Photo 3).

STRAIGHT-SIDED PARTS

Even though most straight-sided work is crosscut or ripped on a tablesaw, there are times when the tablesaw is not as practical as using the router and a template. For example, the diamond-shaped shelves of a corner cabinet have straight sides, but most of them are not parallel. Odd shapes such as these are quickly and easily shaped with a router, a template, and a flush-trim bit (Photo 4).

CURVED PARTS

Curves can add a lot of interest to a piece of furniture. Routing these curves, following a template, is one of the best ways to ensure that the curves are uniform. Curved legs and drawer fronts, for example, are easy to duplicate (Photo 5). All you have to do is to make one perfectly shaped template, and the router bit will do the rest of the work for you.

Seemingly difficult curves, such as a gooseneck molding, can be easily shaped with a template. After the rough shape of the molding is created with a bandsaw, a template and a flush-trim bit can be used to smooth away the bandsaw marks and fair the curves. Afterwards, the molding profiles can be shaped using an overarm guide at the router table—more about that later.

ROUTING GROOVES AND DADOS

Although there are a number of ways to cut grooves and dados with a router, using a template is among the most accurate methods—and in some cases the only choice available. When constructing fine casework, a template ensures accurate alignment of dividers and partitions (Photo 6). Instead of measuring and marking the location of the dados, a graduated set of templates, which register to the side of the case, provide pinpoint accuracy.

Tambours slide in curved grooves and disappear when opened. Routing matching curved tambour grooves, both S-curved and semi-circular, is no problem with a template (Photo 7).

METHODS OF GUIDING THE ROUTER

The key to making various cuts with a template is to guide the router through the intended path. There are essentially four methods of doing this:

1. Using the guide bearing on the end of a bit;

2. Using a bushing attached to the router's sub-base;

3. Using the sub-base of the router;

4. Using an overarm guide attached to the top of a router table.

THE GUIDE BEARING METHOD

The most convenient method for guiding the router is with the bearing on the end of a bit. Most profile bits have a guide bearing which can be used to shape the edge of a curved surface such as a tabletop. Router bit guide bearings are precisely machined and mounted concentric to the bit's profile. This ensures that the profile's depth remains consistent along the entire edge that's being shaped.

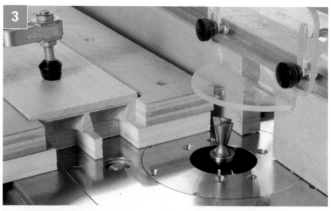

Precision joints can also be made with shop-made templates. I designed this template for routing half-blind dovetails in a drawer front.

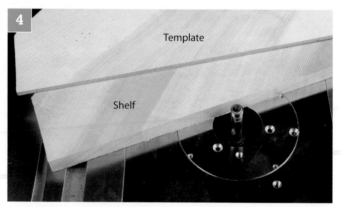

A straight cut that's not parallel to another side is hard to set up on a tablesaw, so it's an ideal candidate for template routing. This is a diamond-shaped shelf for a corner cupboard.

The small diameter of most guide bearings allows the bits to be used to shape tight contours (Photo 8).

Flush-trim bits also use a guide bearing. These bits are ideal for smoothing irregular shapes, such as the sloped edge on the sides of a slant-front desk, as well as smoothing tight bandsawn curves.

Most flush-trim bits have a bearing below the bit, but others have a bearing above the bit, on the shank. These bits are often called "pattern bits" in tool catalogs, and are quite

5

Curved parts, both large and small, can be duplicated by template routing. Here, I'm using a tall flush-trim bit to shape a small serpentine drawer front.

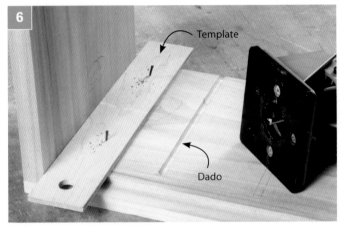

6

Template

Dado

Templates are also useful for routing grooves and dadoes, such as this dado for a partition inside a cabinet. The template precisely locates the dado.

handy when it's more convenient to mount a template on the top of a workpiece, rather than on the bottom.

Some flush-trim bits have two guide bearings, one on the end of the bit and a second bearing on the bit's shank (Photo 9). This design allows you to always cut "downhill" with the grain and avoid tearout. When routing a semicircle, for example, you rout one half of the arc with the template positioned below the workpiece, riding

on the bearing on the bit's shank. To rout the other half, you flip over the workpiece and template, so the template is above the workpiece. Then you readjust the bit's height and ride on the bearing at the end of the bit. This bit is very useful for any S-shaped curve, where the grain of the workpiece is likely to change direction.

Designing a template to use with the guide bearing method is quite simple. Just make the template the exact size and shape as the pattern you wish to duplicate.

THE GUIDE BUSHING METHOD

When cutting on the end of the bit, such as when routing a curved groove, I use a guide bushing. (Guide bushings are also called "template guides" in tool catalogs.) The guide bushing is just a metal ring which fastens to the base of the router (Photo 10). These rings come in a variety of diameters and lengths for use with different diameter bits. When selecting a guide bushing, keep in mind that there must be at least a 1/64" gap between the bit and the bushing, so the bit doesn't cut into the bushing. The inside diameters of many bushings are 1/32" larger than the diameters of commonly used straight bits.

Unfortunately, guide bushings are usually not perfectly concentric to the router collet, because the router's sub-base isn't perfectly centered on the base. This means that the gap between the bit and bushing may be different on one side of the bushing than on another side. The practical result is that the distance between the bit and template may vary, depending on how you orient the router to the template. However, most of the time the

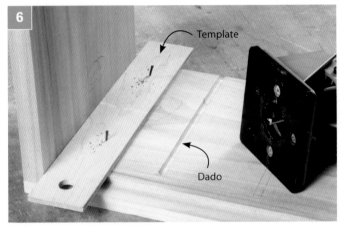

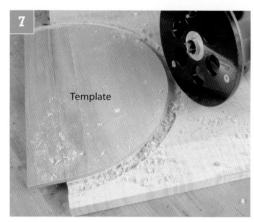

Using a curved template is just about the only way to make a curved groove. This groove will receive a tambour door.

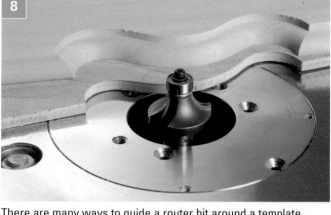

There are many ways to guide a router bit around a template. The simplest method is to use a bit with a guide bearing. Here, the template was fastened to the top of the workpiece.

Some flush-trim bits have two bearings. These bits are ideal for avoiding tearout when routing curves. By flipping the template and workpiece, you can always rout downhill, with the grain.

A bushing mounted in a router's sub-base is also a common method of guiding a bit around a template. This method is well suited for cutting grooves of any width.

slight amount of eccentricity is not an issue. When eccentricity matters, I mark a spot on the base and am careful to always guide the router from that point. This ensures that the distance from the cut to the template remains constant.

When you're designing a template to use with the guide bushing method, first select the bushing and bit and install them in your router. Next, measure the diameter of the bushing and subtract the diameter of the bit (Fig. A). Divide the result in half to give you

the distance between the template and the cutting edge of the bit.

THE SUB-BASE METHOD

Using a router's sub-base to guide a cut is straightforward and convenient, especially when routing certain joints (Photo 11). When using this method, I prefer a square or rectangular sub-base as opposed to a round one. Guiding each cut from the same side of a square sub-base ensures that the spacing is consistent. Some plunge router sub-bases have

A router's sub-base is also a good guide for following a template. Here, I'm routing mortises inside a carcase. Setup is straightforward and convenient.

FIG. A: CALCULATING THE TEMPLATE OFFSET

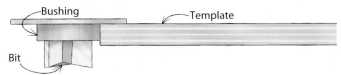

When using a guide bushing, there's always a small gap between the bit and the template. You'll need to know this offset when designing your template. To calculate the offset, measure the diameter of the bit, subtract it from the outside diameter of the guide bushing, and divide the result by two.

one straight side, for example, and I prefer to reference from that side when template routing. I have also made or bought square or rectangular sub-bases for some of my routers to use when accuracy is critical. However, you can also achieve consistent results by guiding off of a round sub-base. Just mark a spot on the sub-base with bright red paint and keep that spot against the template.

When designing a template to use with the sub-base method, you must also factor in an offset, similar to the guide bushing offset

above. Measure the diameter or width of the base, subtract the diameter of the bit, and divide the result in half. This will give you the distance from the template to the cutting edge of the bit.

THE OVERARM GUIDE METHOD

An overarm guide is a shop-built device that mounts on top of a router table (Photo 12). It consists of a long arm whose end is curved to match the smallest radius on the template, a support for the arm, and a bearing securely fastened to the arm. You may purchase the bearing at an auto supply shop or borrow a bearing from a router bit.

This method is similar to using a guide bearing, but unlike a guide bearing, the overarm guide can be positioned eccentric to the bit's profile. This allows for shaping into the interior of the stock where a bearing-guided bit cannot reach. I use this technique when shaping large molding profiles on curved surfaces (see Routing A Gooseneck Molding, page 165). The arm is positioned above the bit and follows the curve of the template. After each cut, the arm is backed away from the bit to increase the depth of subsequent cuts.

Designing a template for use with an overarm guide is usually pretty straight-forward. Make it the same size as the shape you'd like to duplicate, as when using a bearing-guided bit. The offset is created by moving the arm, rather than by adjusting the size of the template.

Template Safety

I teach woodworking to new students each year, and of course I'm particularly concerned that they learn to work safely. We often use templates for routing, and before we get started, I cover these safety guidelines:

1. The template should be large enough to safely distance your hands from the bit.

2. The template should be securely fastened to the workpiece.

3. Screws, nails, and clamps should be positioned out of the bit's path.

4. The template should extend beyond the workpiece, on both ends. This way, the guide bearing or bushing will make contact with the template before the bit comes in contact with the workpiece.

5. Avoid heavy cuts. A light cut is safer and creates a smoother surface.

6. When using a router table, install or make a guard.

7. Never climb cut. (Climb cutting is routing in the same direction that the bit rotates.) Climb cutting can be dangerous because the router bit can grab the workpiece and draw your hands into the bit. Always cut against the rotation of the bit. When routing by hand, the router should be pushed in a counter-clockwise direction for external cuts (see drawing). When the cut is internal, the router should be pushed in a clockwise direction. When the cut is made at a router table, the work should be fed from right to left. An internal cut at the table should be made in a counter-clockwise direction.

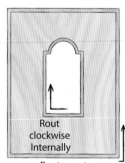

Rout clockwise Internally

Rout counter-clockwise externally

TEMPLATE MATERIAL

One of the most important elements in template routing is the material of the template itself. Although I've used a number of materials through the years, I prefer cabinet-grade plywood, which is solid and stable.

All plywood isn't created equal, though; cabinet-grade plywood is free of voids, which can catch the guide bearing and spoil the cut. Less expensive plywood may have voids, which you won't be able to see until you cut into it. Cabinet-grade plywood is easy to cut and shape, and it is readily available at hardwood lumberyards.

After many uses, the edge of a plywood template can begin to show signs of wear. Before any problems develop, I usually make a new template from the old one with a flush-trim bit.

MAKING THE TEMPLATE

When making a template, I take the time to make it perfect; any irregularity in the template will be duplicated in the workpiece, or dozens of workpieces. On a straight template, I make sure that the edges are truly straight, and the angles are correct. This is not a good time to take anything for granted.

I use a number of methods to draw curves on a template. I may use a compass, a French curve, or draw freehand. Often I draw the shape on the computer with AutoCAD, print the drawing, and glue it to the template with contact cement.

After bandsawing the profile, I carefully smooth the curves with files and sandpaper. This is the fussy part. I carefully inspect the

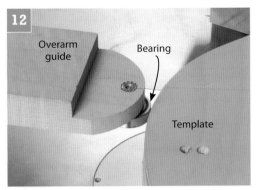

An overarm guide on a router table is a fairly sophisticated device for following a template, but it allows you to use router bits that don't have a bearing, or make cuts where a bearing would get in the way.

template to make sure the curves are fair, checking by eye and by feel. If there's a hump or flat spot, it's back to the file or sanding block.

When making a template, I extend the template ends beyond the length of the workpiece by at least an inch or two (Photo 13). The guide bearing then makes contact with the template before the bit makes contact with the workpiece. This ensures a smooth entry and exit when making the cut.

THE TEMPLATE JIG

I often use a template jig for heavy cuts or for securing small work that would otherwise be unsafe to shape with a router (Photo 14). Template jigs demand a little more work than just making the template. The purpose of the jig is to securely fix the workpiece as it is routed. This requires adding stop blocks on the jig to position the workpiece and to counteract the forces of the spinning bit. I begin by making the template (the jig's base), then glue the stop blocks in position and fasten them with screws.

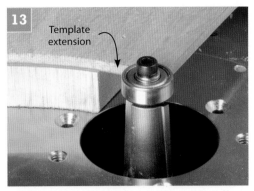

I prefer cabinet-grade plywood for making templates. I design them to extend an inch or so beyond the workpiece, which ensures a smooth entry when starting the cut.

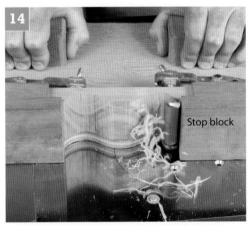

When making a heavy cut or shaping small parts, I build a template jig to securely hold the workpiece. The jig usually has stop blocks to position the workpiece.

SAWING THE WORKPIECE

Once the template or jig is complete, I use it as a pattern for laying out curves on the workpiece. After tracing the template, I use a bandsaw to cut just outside the layout line. I aim for a 1/16" margin. If it's less than 1/16", I run the risk of cutting within the template's outline. A margin greater than 1/16" requires a heavy cut, which can cause tearout or pull the workpiece loose from the template.

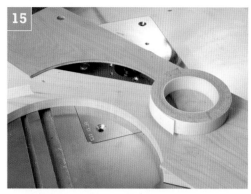

I use brads or screws to attach most templates to a workpiece, but where holes will mar a finished piece, I use woodturner's double-faced tape.

FASTENING A TEMPLATE

I use brads, screws, double-faced woodturner's tape or toggle clamps to fasten the template to the workpiece. The easiest method is just to attach the template with a few brads. This method works well for small work and light cuts; it's fast and the nails grip well. For larger and heavier cuts, I opt for screws.

With either method, it's critical that you position the fasteners out of the path of the bit. Although nails and screws both leave holes in the finished work, that's not necessarily a problem if the holes will be hidden from view.

When holes from a metal fastener will not be acceptable, I use double-faced woodturner's tape (Photo 15). Toggle clamps are ideal for template work, especially when there are a large number of parts to be routed (Photo 16). They open and close quickly and have good holding power. Once your template and stock are prepared, you're ready to make the cut. Remember to adjust the bit's height. If you're using a bearing-guided bit, position the bit so that the bearing makes full contact with the template.

Toggle clamps are ideal for holding a workpiece in a template jig, particularly when you have a lot of duplicate parts to make. Mounting a new part in the jig is quick and easy.

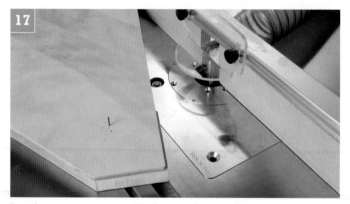

I prefer to use a router table for template routing whenever possible. Even though I'm not using the fence to guide the work, the fence provides dust collection and a guard.

THE ROUTER TABLE IS BEST

Whenever I have a choice between using a hand-held router or a router table, I always opt for the table. This also holds true when template routing. Even though I'm not using the router table's fence to guide the workpiece and limit the cutting depth, the fence provides dust collection and a mounting point for a guard (Photo 17). Using the router table is cleaner and often safer than pushing a router across the work.

Routing a Gooseneck Molding

Making the molding on the top of this clock required an unusual method of template routing: using an overarm guide (see photo below). The overarm guide is attached to the top of a router table, and is really just a long arm with a bearing screwed to its end. The bearing rides against the template, and can follow inside or outside curves and straight sections.

The overarm guide allows you to shape a profile that wouldn't be possible to make with standard bearing-guided bits.

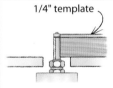

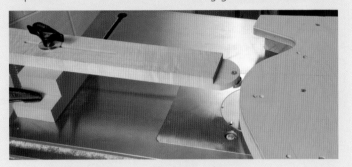

1/4" template — Overarm guide — Bearing

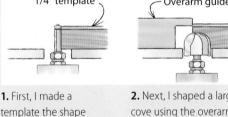
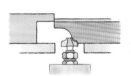
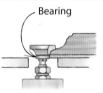

1. First, I made a template the shape of the gooseneck's inside curve. I traced the template onto the workpiece, which at this point is extra-wide, and bandsawed the curve, staying 1/16" away from the line. Next, I fastened the template to the back of the workpiece, installed a flush-trim bit in the router table, and shaped the workpiece to match the template.

2. Next, I shaped a large cove using the overarm guide to bear against the template. This required a number of light cuts, which I accomplished by moving the overarm guide slightly farther back from the cove bit each time. In the final cut, you can see that the center of the bit is offset from the edge of the template. This cut would not have been possible with a bearing-guided bit (unless, of course, it had a custom-made profile).

3. In this step, I cut a small S-shaped curve next to the cove using a standard ogee bit. (I removed the bearing from the bit.) Once more, the overarm guide follows the template. As with the cove bit, this cut would not have been possible with a bearing-guided bit, because the bearing would not have fit within the cove.

4. To complete the profile, I flipped over the workpiece and template, and used a roundover bit. This specialty bit has a bottom bearing which rides directly on the workpiece.

5. I completed the molding by bandsawing the outside curve, then smoothed the curve with an oscillating spindle sander.

by RANDY JOHNSON

Template Routing Tips

CREATE PERFECT PIECES EVERY TIME

I f you want to get the most from your router, you need to master template routing. Once you learn the basics you can spend a lifetime exploring its many possibilities. You'll be able to build more kinds of projects, more accurately, and more easily.

Template routing has two big benefits. The first is repeatability. With template routing you can make one or 100 parts that are exactly alike. Second, template routing simplifies the job of making curved or complex shapes.

A midsize fixed- or plunge-base router is fine for most template routing. We prefer router bits with a 1/2-in. shank for their strength but many 1/4-in. shank bits will do a good job as well.

ART DIRECTION: VERN JOHNSON • PHOTOGRAPHY: RAMON MORENO

BANDSAW GUIDE FOR ROUGH CUTTING

A template-following guide on a bandsaw makes it easy to rough cut workpieces prior to routing. The bandsaw blade sits in a notch about 1/8-in. back from the round end of the guide. The guide follows the edge of the template while the workpiece is cut oversize by 1/8 in., which is just right for most projects. Rough cutting your workpiece removes excess material so your router doesn't have to work as hard. You will also get less chipping and burning.

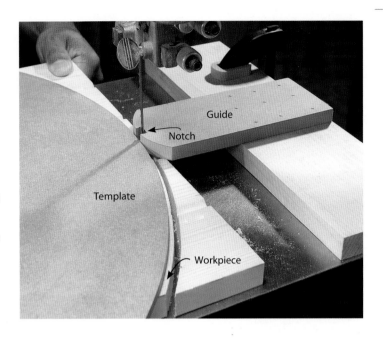

Guide

Notch

Template

Workpiece

Pattern bit

Top bearing

Flush-trim bit

Bottom bearing

Straight bit

Guide bushing

USE THE RIGHT BIT

There are three basic template router bits: a pattern bit with a top bearing, a flush-trim bit with a bottom bearing and a straight bit combined with a guide bushing which fits in a router's baseplate. When possible, use the largest diameter bit that your router, template or wallet can handle, because large diameter bits are less likely to burn, chip, or chatter.

The diameter of the bearing on the pattern bit and flush-trim bit equal the cutting diameter of the bit. This simplifies template design because the template is made the same size as the finished workpiece.

Using a guide bushing for template routing requires the template to be bigger or smaller than the final shape of the workpiece, depending on whether you rout on the inside or the outside of the template. Sizing the template can be a pain, but a guide bushing allows you to use any shape bit that will fit through the hole.

SPAN THE AREA

A wide auxiliary baseplate is the best way to span open template spaces. It can be made of plastic or wood and should be long enough to prevent the router from falling into the template opening. Double-faced carpet tape works well for attaching the auxiliary baseplate to the router's main baseplate.

Auxiliary baseplate

CLAMP IT DOWN

Toggle clamps are hard to beat for their ease of use. They hold the work securely and make it easy to change parts. They are available in various sizes but the 6-1/2-in.-long style shown is a good size for most router jigs.

TOOLS FOR TEMPLATE SHAPING

The two most useful tools for shaping and smoothing router templates are a disc sander for outside curves and an oscillating spindle sander for inside curves. A drum sander on a drill press and a belt sander also work well.

Carpet
tape

PEEL-AND-STICK TEMPLATE

Carpet tape is a quick way to attach a
template when you are only making one or
two parts. Make sure your parts are dust-free
so the tape sticks tight. Once the template is
in place, give it a few raps with a mallet. This
will also help the tape take hold. When you're
done routing, use a putty knife to pry the
pieces apart. Carpet tape sometimes leaves a
residue, but it's easily cleaned off with mineral
spirits. Also, carpet tape comes in different
styles. The indoor/outdoor fiberglass type
works the best, and is available at
home centers.

SECURE IT WITH SCREWS

Screws are a very secure way to attach a template. They do
leave holes but that's not a problem if one side of the workpiece
won't be seen, as in the case of this chair seat.

USE A STARTING PIN FOR SAFE STARTS

Use a starting pin with templates that require routing all the way around. This reduces the chance of kickback and gives you something to bear against, much like a fence does for straight cuts.

To use the starting pin, push your rough-cut workpiece against the pin and then slowly rotate the workpiece into the router bit until it starts cutting. When the bearing of the bit completely contacts the template, you can swing away from the starting pin. Rout around the workpiece in a counterclockwise direction. Keep a good grip on your workpiece while routing. Don't let go of the workpiece while it's in contact with the router bit or your project may turn into a high-speed flying object!

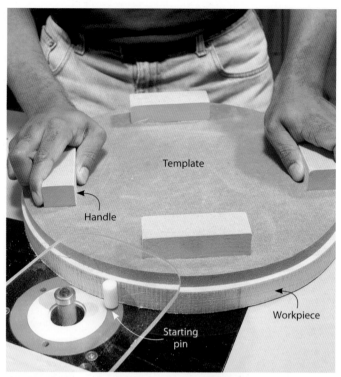

Template

Handle

Workpiece

Starting pin

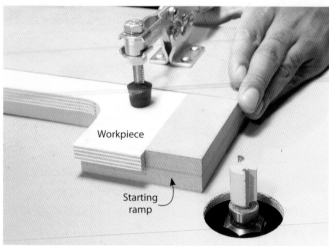

Workpiece

Starting ramp

RAMP-UP FOR EASIER STARTS

A starting ramp provides a safe place for the router bit to contact the template before it starts cutting. A ramp eliminates the need for a starting pin, so build a ramp into your jigs whenever possible. An exit ramp on the other side of the template provides the same advantage at the end of the cut.

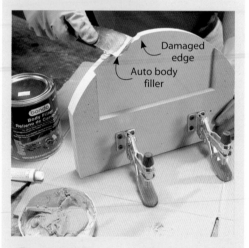

Damaged edge

Auto body filler

Oops!

Here's an easy fix if you accidentally put a gouge in your template with the router bit. Use auto body filler to repair the damage. Apply excess filler to the damaged area and after it's hardened, rasp and sand it to final shape.

Pattern bit

Flush trim bit

SHAPE THICK PARTS IN TWO STEPS

1. Use a top-bearing pattern bit and template-rout the bottom half of the thick part.

2. Use a bottom-bearing flush-trim bit to rout the top half of the thick part. The bearing rides on the surface created in Step 1. The thick part is removed from the template jig and clamped to the table for this step.

DOUBLE-DUTY TEMPLATE

A two-sided template is a great way to rout multiple parts that need to be shaped on two sides. The trick to building the jig is to make one side (A) 1/8-in. wider than the other side (B). That way side A has room for the rough-cut inner edge of the workpiece. Side B is made to final width.

Before using the template, bandsaw the workpieces oversize by about 1/8 in. on each side. Then clamp one workpiece in side A and make the first pass. Next move that part to side B and rout the second side.

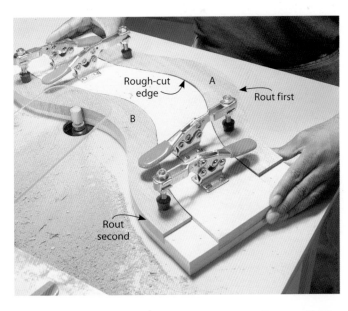

Rough-cut edge

A

Rout first

B

Rout second

Joining Wood with the Router

Examine a well-built piece of furniture and you'll find well-made joints. Traditionally cut with hand tools, most joints can also be cut with a router. Plus, the router is capable of making additional joints that only a router can make. To achieve precise joinery, you must learn how to accurately set up your router, bits, jigs, and router table.

The following chapter includes many setup tips and tricks that will help you quickly master the craft of router joinery. One router joint is the cope and stick, which is used to make frame and panel doors. It requires two complementary bit setups; learning a few of the techniques in this chapter will help you get the perfect fit you need. The sliding tapered dovetail joint is a useful joint that few woodworkers know how to make. When made correctly it becomes a strong durable joint that also displays the skills of the builder. The sliding dovetail is commonly used for jointing case parts such as shelves and sides. Consider it for your next furniture project. If your next project contains drawers, look in this chapter for five different ways to join drawer parts—from a basic lap joint to a locking miter joint—plus many tips on how to get precise results quickly.

« Simple jigs like this one will allow you to make precise cuts every time.

by TIM JOHNSON

3 Router Jigs

MAKE YOUR ROUTER A WORKSHOP WORKHORSE

If you only use your router to rout decorative edges, you're missing the boat. Your router can be the most versatile tool in your shop. The secret to unlocking your router's potential is to use it with specialized jigs. A dovetail jig is a perfect example: With this jig, your router can do the same job as an expensive dovetailing machine.

Fortunately, you can make many useful router jigs in your shop without spending an arm and a leg. I'll show you three simple jigs that will expand your woodworking capabilities by leaps and bounds: one for dadoing, one for mortising and one for making shelf pin holes. Although these jigs have been around since the dawn of routers, they're indispensable additions to any woodworking shop.

DADOES

MORTISES

SHELF HOLES

Bearing

A pattern bit is a flush-trim bit with the bearing mounted on the shaft.

ADJUSTABLE DADOING JIG

This jig (Fig. A) takes the guesswork out of routing dadoes, because setting the exact width is virtually foolproof. Being able to tailor the dadoes' width to precisely match the thickness of shelves is a real blessing when you're building cabinets with hardwood plywood, which is always undersize in thickness.

This jig accommodates wood up to 24 in. wide. Its double T-square design guarantees dadoes that are square to the edges on both left and right cabinet sides. Positioning the jig couldn't be easier—just line up the fixed fence with the top of each dado. This jig must be used with a pattern bit (see photo, left). This combination is perfect for use with nominal 3/4-in.-thick plywood. It allows routing dadoes from 5/8 to 1-1/8 in. wide and up to 1/2 in. deep.

MAKE THE JIG

1. Glue and screw the fixed fence (A) to the rails (B). Make sure the joints are perfectly square.

2. Rout the slots in the adjustable fence (C) on a router table, using the router table's fence and a 5/16-in. straight bit.

3. Use the adjustable fence's slots to locate the rails' carriage bolt holes. Lay the fence on the jig, snug against the fixed fence and flush with the rails. Using a pencil, transfer the slot locations to the rails.

4. Drill and counterbore the holes.

5. Install the carriage bolts.

Cutting List

Part	Name	Qty.	Dimensions
A	Fixed fence	1	3/4" x 5" x 29-7/8" *
B	Rail	2	11/16" x 2-1/2" x 18"
C	Adjustable fence	1	3/4" x 6" x 29-7/8" *

*Length allows cutting both fences from one 60-in. length of Baltic birch plywood

FIG. A: ADJUSTABLE DADOING JIG

Rout perfectly sized dadoes every time!

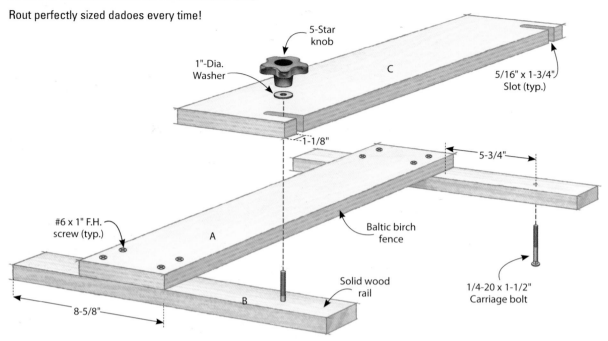

5-Star knob

1"-Dia. Washer

C

5/16" x 1-3/4" Slot (typ.)

1-1/8"

5-3/4"

#6 x 1" F.H. screw (typ.)

A

Baltic birch fence

Solid wood rail

B

8-5/8"

1/4-20 x 1-1/2" Carriage bolt

USE THE JIG

Position the fixed fence on a line indicating the top of each dado. Always orient the jig with the fixed fence at the top of the workpiece. Make sure the jig's rail is firmly seated against the edge. Then clamp both pieces to your bench.

Both rails are square to the fixed fence, so it doesn't matter which rail registers the jig. Out of habit, though, I always register the jig against the front edge of the workpiece.

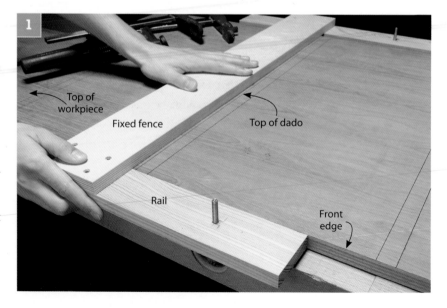

Top of workpiece

Fixed fence

Top of dado

Rail

Front edge

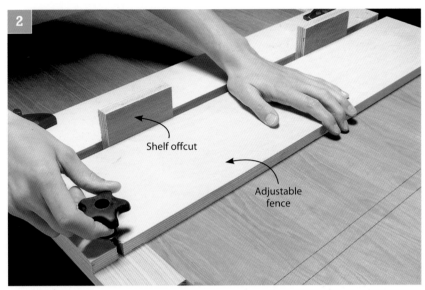

Set the adjustable fence using offcuts from your shelves as spacers. This method guarantees that the dadoes will be exactly the right width.

Rout the dado in two passes. During the cut, the pattern bit's shaft-mounted bearing rides against the jig's fences, so the dado it cuts is exactly the same width as the opening. Bear against the fixed fence during one pass and against the adjustable fence during the other.

An up-cut spiral bit routs a better mortise than a regular straight bit can. It cuts like a drill bit, lifting chips up and out as it spins, instead of jamming them inside the hole. Chatter-free operation and smooth-walled mortises are the result.

Chips

Rotation

VERSATILE MORTISING JIG

If you have a plunge router with an edge guide, you can machine professional-quality mortises without buying an expensive benchtop mortiser. All you need is a plunge-routing bit (see photo, above, right) and this jig (Fig. B).

This jig accepts workpieces of any length. They can be positioned against one end of the jig or extend beyond both ends. Although it accepts stock up to 3 in. wide and 4-1/2 in. thick, this jig is invaluable for routing mortises in narrow pieces, such as door stiles or delicate legs, on which a large, top-heavy plunge router would be tough to balance. By fully supporting the router's base, this jig makes mortising a breeze.

MAKE THE JIG

1. Glue two oversize blanks together. From the glued-up blank, cut the bottom piece (A) to final size.

2. Glue on the sides (B), making sure they're square to the bottom and level at the top.

3. Fasten the clamp rail (C).

4. Drill 1/4-in. holes and install the hanger bolts. Spin a nut all the way onto the bolt. Then use a wrench to thread the bolt into the hole. A doweling jig makes it easy to accurately drill the holes.

5. Make the end stop (D). To make the adjustable stop (E), drill start holes at the ends. Then rout the slots in several passes, using a 5/16-in. straight bit, your router table and a fence. Raise the bit in 1/4-in. increments.

6. Cut stop blocks (F) as necessary for each routing job.

FIG. B: MORTISING JIG

Plunge-rout mortises with ease!

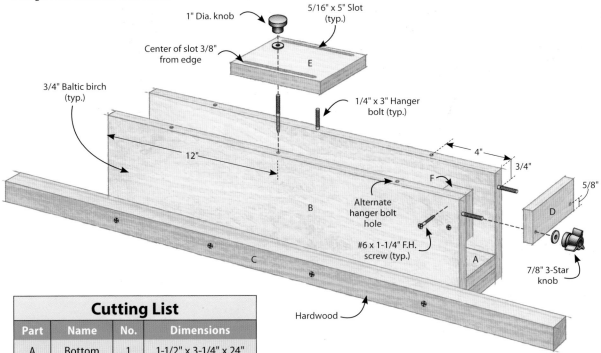

1" Dia. knob

5/16" x 5" Slot (typ.)

Center of slot 3/8" from edge

3/4" Baltic birch (typ.)

E

1/4" x 3" Hanger bolt (typ.)

12"

4"

3/4"

F

B

5/8"

D

Alternate hanger bolt hole

#6 x 1-1/4" F.H. screw (typ.)

A

7/8" 3-Star knob

C

Hardwood

Cutting List

Part	Name	No.	Dimensions
A	Bottom	1	1-1/2" x 3-1/4" x 24"
B	Side	2	3/4" x 6" x 24"
C	Clamp rail	1	1" x 1-1/2" x 30"
D	End stop	1	3/4" x 1-3/4" x 4-3/4" *
E	Adjustable stop	1	3/4" x 4-3/4" * x 6"
F	Stop block	1	3/4" x 1-1/2" x 2-1/2"

* Cut to fit actual jig: plywood thickness is nominal.

USE THE JIG

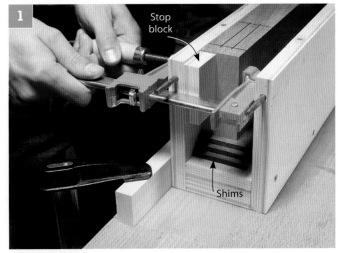

1

Stop block

Shims

Clamp the workpiece in position. First, use shims to raise it flush with or slightly below the top of the rails. Install a stop block when you rout multiple pieces with mortises near the ends, such as this table leg. The width of the stop block determines the location of the top of the mortise. To accommodate wide stock, cut notches for the clamp heads in the back of the jig.

Center the bit on the layout lines by adjusting the router's edge guide. With the router unplugged, use the plunge mechanism to lock the bit in position just above the workpiece's surface. Before you adjust the edge guide, orient the bit's cutting flutes to span the mortise.

Edge guide

Install stop blocks. For the table leg shown here, the end stop determines the top of the mortise and the adjustable stop determines the bottom.

To rout mortises in the middle of a long workpiece, such as a bedpost, remove both stops. Install a second adjustable stop and relocate the first, using the alternate hanger-bolt holes (Fig. B). Center the mortise between the stops when you clamp the workpiece in the jig. If you only have a couple mortises to rout, don't bother with the stops. Just rout to the layout lines.

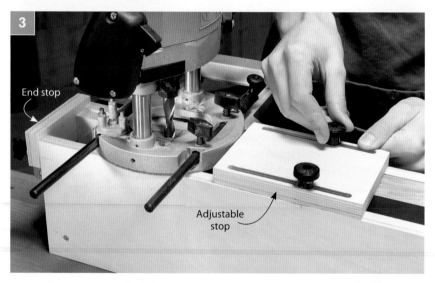

End stop

Adjustable stop

Plunge-rout the mortise in several shallow passes. After routing, square the mortises with a chisel if your tenons are square-shouldered.

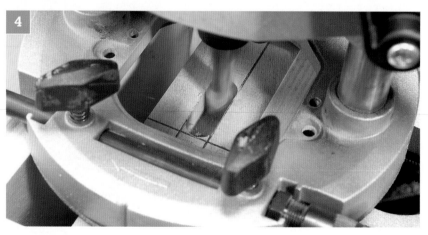

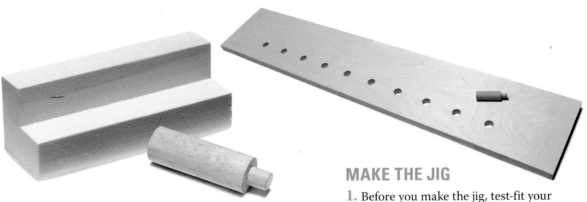

MAKE THE JIG

1. Before you make the jig, test-fit your template in a hole drilled with your Forstner bit. The guide should fit snugly without binding.

2. Lay out the holes.

3. Drill the holes on your drill press, using a fence and a 1/2-in. Forstner bit. Before you drill, set the depth stop so only the center point of the bit goes all the way through the jig.

4. Flip the jig over to finish drilling the holes. This two-step drilling method ensures clean holes on both faces of the jig.

5. Make the alignment pin:

■ Joint one side of a 2x4 and clamp it to your drill press, jointed side down.

■ Using a Forstner bit, drill a 1/2-in. hole all the way through the 2x4.

■ Seat a 1-3/8-in. length of 1/2-in. dowel in the hole so it sits below the 2x4's surface.

■ Without starting the drill press, lower the bit to mark the dowel's center, using the walls of the 1/2-in. hole to guide the bit.

■ Install a 1/4-in. bit and drill a 1/2-in.-deep hole in the dowel, using the center mark you've just made to guide the bit.

■ Glue a 1/4-in. dowel in the centered hole. Then trim it to final length.

SUPER-SIMPLE SHELF-HOLE JIG

Forget about tedious drill press setups or using pegboard as a not-so-accurate template: This jig (Fig. C, page 182) eliminates the onerous task of drilling adjustable shelf holes. And because you plunge-rout the holes, you won't have any of the unsightly tear-out that drill bits frequently cause.

To use the jig, you need a plunge router equipped with a 1/4-in. bit and a template guide (see photo, above). Your router's plunge mechanism must slide smoothly; side-to-side play will result in oversize holes. Operate at a slow (9,000-to 12,000- rpm) speed and use a steady plunge rate.

It's easy to modify this jig. For example, the holes can be spaced differently from the edges or clustered in groups. You may need a shorter version to fit inside a cabinet.

Chips

Rotation

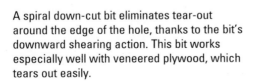

A spiral down-cut bit eliminates tear-out around the edge of the hole, thanks to the bit's downward shearing action. This bit works especially well with veneered plywood, which tears out easily.

FIG. C: SHELF-HOLE JIG

Rout perfect holes for adjustable shelves!

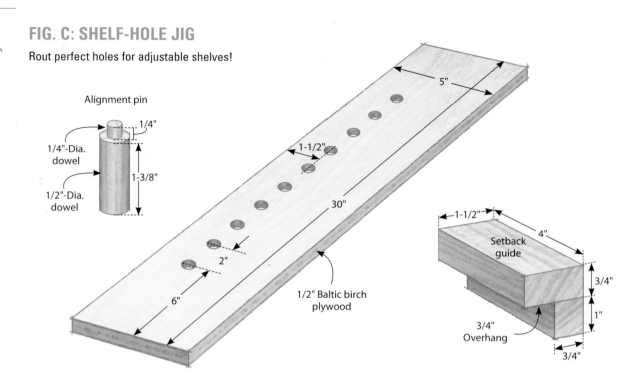

Alignment pin

1/4"

1/4"-Dia. dowel

1/2"-Dia. dowel

1-3/8"

5"

1-1/2"

30"

2"

6"

1/2" Baltic birch plywood

1-1/2"

4"

Setback guide

3/4"

1"

3/4" Overhang

3/4"

USE THE JIG

Position the jig flush with the top and the front edge of the cabinet side. Securely clamp the jig and you're good to go. To rout the back row of holes, flip the jig over and align it flush with the top and the back edge. You can also use this jig inside a completed cabinet. Just register it against the cabinet's top or bottom. If you need to allow room for an inset door or Euro-style hinges, use a pair of setback guides (Fig. C) to move the holes farther back from the front edge.

TOP

Flush

The template guide precisely fits each hole, locking the router in position, so every hole you rout is perfectly located. The guide's collar must extend less than 1/2 in. so it doesn't protrude beyond the 1/2-in.-thick jig. The guide must exactly fit the holes in the jig, but the size of its outside diameter isn't critical. To use a 1/2-in. template guide like the one shown here, drill 1/2-in.-dia. holes; to use a 5/8-in. guide, drill 5/8-in.-dia. holes.

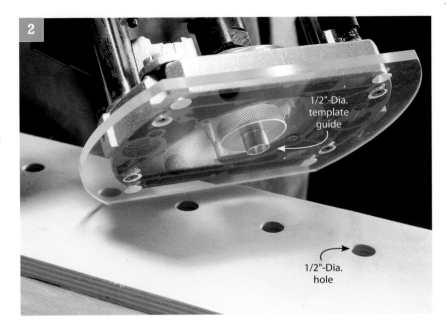

1/2"-Dia. template guide

1/2"-Dia. hole

The alignment pin makes it easy to reposition the jig on long cabinet sides. Installing the pin aligns the jig's top hole with the last hole you've routed. With the pin installed, clamp the jig flush with the front edge and you're ready to rout additional holes.

TOP

Alignment pin

by TIM JOHNSON

Stile & Rail Joinery on Your Router Table

MAKE PERFECT-FITTING FRAMES FOR DOORS AND CABINETS

One of the best buys you can make for your table-mounted router is a set of stile and rail cutters. These cutters allow you to join frame pieces together at right angles by making a decorative version of the tongue and groove joint. It's sometimes called a "cope and stick" joint because the rail is coped to fit around the profile that's "stuck" onto the stile. When assembled, two stiles and two rails form a frame with a groove around its inside edge, perfect for holding a panel.

Stile and rail cutters come in a variety of profiles (Fig. A) and are great for making kitchen cabinet doors and other frame and panel structures. Most manufacturers offer them either as dedicated two-bit sets or as a single "reversible" bit. With the two-bit set you get one bit to make a "profile" cut on long grain (the stile cutter) and another to make a matching "coped" cut on the end-grain (the rail cutter).

With the single, reversible-bit sets you get removable parts that can be configured to make both cuts.

Dedicated sets are best in production shops, but reversible sets are a good choice for anyone working with a budget because they're cheaper to buy and still offer great performance. Using the reversible set is a piece of cake (Photos 1–6), as long as you remember to make the cope cuts face-side up and profile cuts face-side down. Making the changeover from profile to cope cutting (or back) takes only a few minutes. You'll be impressed with the quality of the fit and the speed with which you can make a quantity of doors or frames.

ART DIRECTION: PATRICK HELF AND JOEL SPIES • PHOTOGRAPHY: MIKE HABERMANN AND BILL ZUEHLKE

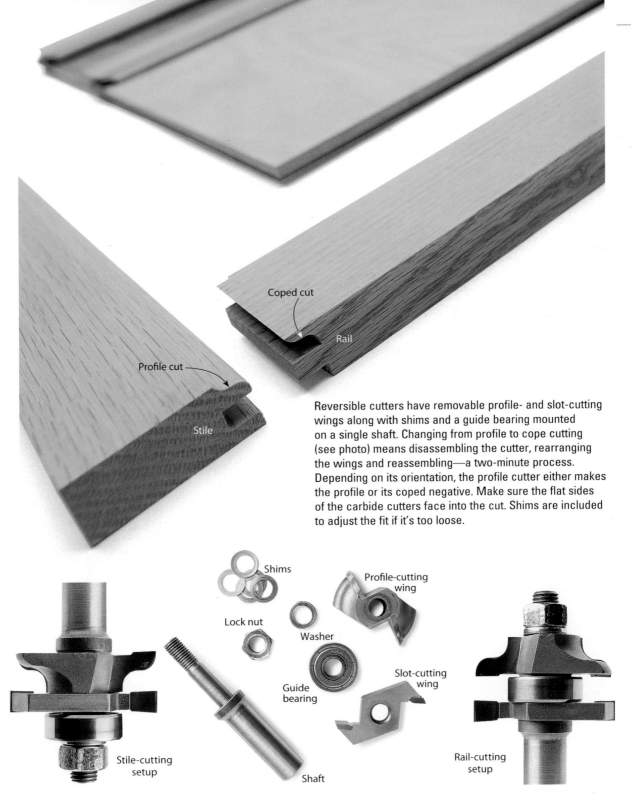

Coped cut

Rail

Profile cut

Stile

Reversible cutters have removable profile- and slot-cutting wings along with shims and a guide bearing mounted on a single shaft. Changing from profile to cope cutting (see photo) means disassembling the cutter, rearranging the wings and reassembling—a two-minute process. Depending on its orientation, the profile cutter either makes the profile or its coped negative. Make sure the flat sides of the carbide cutters face into the cut. Shims are included to adjust the fit if it's too loose.

Shims

Profile-cutting wing

Lock nut

Washer

Guide bearing

Slot-cutting wing

Stile-cutting setup

Shaft

Rail-cutting setup

PHASE 1: MAKE COPED END-GRAIN CUTS

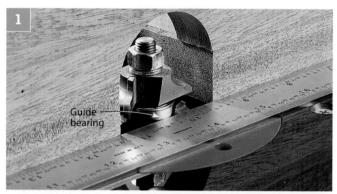

Set the fence flush with the bearing on the rail cutter, using a straightedge to assure a smooth pass.

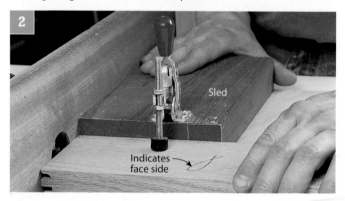

Make test end-grain cuts. You'll need a sled to hold the rail safely and ensure a square cut. Simply glue a block of wood with one squarely cut end onto a larger piece of 1/4-in. plywood, aligned on one edge. Then attach a toggle clamp. Clamp the rails in the sled face-side up for all end-grain cuts.

Set the height of the cutter by making cuts so the rabbet on the bottom of the rail is at least 3/16-in. deep. Otherwise the corresponding bottom shoulder on the stile will be too thin and may break. Once you've got the height set, use the sled and make all of the coped end-grain cuts in the rails.

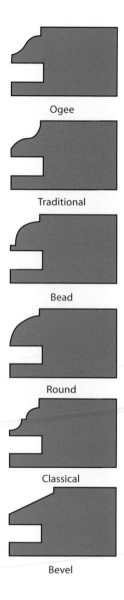

Ogee

Traditional

Bead

Round

Classical

Bevel

FIG. A

Stile and rail cutters come in a variety of decorative profiles.

PHASE 2: CUT PROFILES ON LONG GRAIN

4

Disassemble the cutter to rearrange the pieces for making profile cuts. Leave it mounted in the router when loosening the locking nut—it's a handy way to hold onto the shaft. After rearranging, don't over-tighten the nut or you'll damage the shims.

5

Slot-cutting wing

Tongue

Set the height of the stile cutter by aligning its slot-cutting wing with the tongue on one of the rails. These cuts don't require a sled. Use scrap stock to make a test cut, check its fit with the rails and make adjustments, if necessary.

6

Edge reference mark

Face-side down

Make profile cuts on the stiles and inside edges of the rails with the stile cutter. (Yes, use the stile cutter for this profile cut on the rails!) Orient the pieces face-side down and mark the edge to be routed. Use push blocks to hold the stile against the fence and the table when you guide it past the bit.

by BILL HYLTON

Loose-Tenon Joinery

ROUT 4 VARIATIONS OF THESE SUPER-STRONG JOINTS WITH A VERSATILE SHOP MADE JIG

I've used a number of different methods to create mortise and tenon joints, but I keep coming back to loose tenons, because they're easy, strong, and versatile. Instead of cutting a tenon on one part and a mortise in the other, I rout identical mortises in both parts, and connect them with a fitted strip of wood—a loose tenon.

The only tools you need to start making loose tenon joints are a plunge router equipped with an edge guide, straight bits designed for plunge cutting, and a mortising block—a shopmade jig I've designed that you can make in a day.

You can use off-the-shelf bits and just about any plunge router, but a precision edge guide is a must.

THE MORTISING BLOCK

This jig holds the workpiece, supports the router and controls its movement (Fig. A). The jig consists of the mortising block itself, a top extension, an L-bracket, and a clamp board for bench mounting.

The face of the block has dadoes and mounting-bolt holes for the two work holders—horizontal for edge mortising and vertical for end mortising. The router sits on top of the block (Photo).

Adapt your router to the jig by installing a fence on the edge guide that fits the slot formed by the jig's L-bracket. This keeps the bit aligned as the router slides back and forth. To move the bit laterally, you simply adjust the edge guide.

HOW THE JIG WORKS

- The jig's registration line locates the workpiece.
- The jig's L-bracket tracks the router and keeps the mortise aligned with the edges of the workpiece.
- The mortise's width is determined by the bit's diameter. To create mortises wider than the bit, you reposition the fence and make a second pass.
- The mortise's depth is controlled by the router's plunge mechanism.
- The mortise's length is governed by the jig's adjustable stop blocks.

FIG. A: LOOSE-TENON MORTISING JIG

This jig allows routing both edge and end mortises from a single setup. All you have to do is switch work holders.

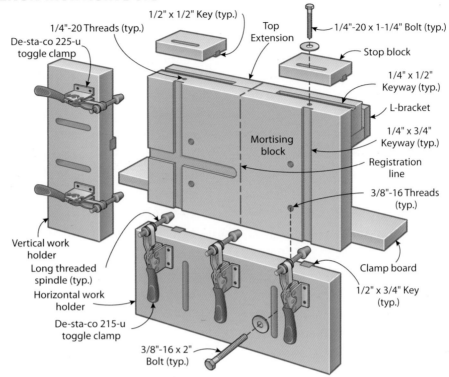

1/4"-20 Threads (typ.)
1/2" x 1/2" Key (typ.)
De-sta-co 225-u toggle clamp
Top Extension
1/4"-20 x 1-1/4" Bolt (typ.)
Stop block
1/4" x 1/2" Keyway (typ.)
L-bracket
1/4" x 3/4" Keyway (typ.)
Mortising block
Registration line
3/8"-16 Threads (typ.)
Vertical work holder
Long threaded spindle (typ.)
Horizontal work holder
De-sta-co 215-u toggle clamp
Clamp board
1/2" x 3/4" Key (typ.)
3/8"-16 x 2" Bolt (typ.)

■ The mortise's lateral (side-to-side) positioning is controlled by the router's edge guide.

BUILD THE JIG

1. Mill stock for the main parts and cut the pieces to final dimensions (Fig. B, page 195). The mortise block's body and the horizontal work holder must be exactly the same length, because you reference from the ends to rout vertical keyways in both pieces.

2. Rout the 1/4" deep vertical keyways in the mortising block and the horizontal work holder.

3. Rout single 1/4" deep horizontal keyways in the mortising block and the vertical work holder. The block's keyhole is stopped.

4. Rout mounting-bolt slots in each work holder, using a plunge router and an edge guide.

5. Plane 1/2" thick stock to fit the work holder keyways. Cut pieces to length to create the keys. Attach them.

6. Clamp the horizontal work holder to the mortising block. Tap a 1/2" brad point drill at both ends of each slot to transfer its location to the block. Remove the work holder and scribe a pair of vertical lines on the block through the four points you marked. Clamp on the vertical work holder, mark the slots, and scribe a pair of horizontal lines.

7. Drill holes for the work holder mounting bolts at the four points where the horizontal and vertical lines intersect.

To secure the 3/8" bolts, I cut threads in the wood itself. To do this, drill the four holes with a 5/16" bit and use a 3/8"-16 tpi tap to cut the threads. No cutting fluid is needed; just turn the tap into the hole, then back it out.

8. Glue and clamp the top extension to the mortising block. Clean off any dried glue after removing the clamps. Then joint the assembly so its top surface is square.

9. Attach a 3/8" thick wood fence to your router's edge guide. Then size the L-bracket parts to create a groove that will house the fence. The fit should be snug, so the fence slides without any wobble. Glue the L-bracket parts together and install them.

10. Make both stop blocks from one long piece of 5/8" by 2-3/4" stock. Rout the 1/4" deep keyway and two mounting bolt slots. Cut the stops to final length. Make keys and attach them.

11. Rout matching keyways in the top of the mortising block.

12. Set the stops in place on the block and mark locations for mounting bolt holes. Drill and tap the holes for 1/4"-20 tpi bolts.

13. Install toggle clamps on the work holders. I used stronger 500-lb. rated clamps on the vertical work holder and installed longer threaded spindles on all the clamps. Be sure to locate the clamps so they don't interfere with the router.

14. Draw a registration line centered on the face and top of the mortising block.

15. Glue on the clamp board.

CREATE THE BASIC LOOSE-TENON JOINT

1. Lay out an edge mortise (Photo 1). It doesn't have to be elaborate, just lines marking the mortise ends and centerline. Only one line is absolutely essential: a centerline across the mortise. This mark aligns with the jig's registration line.

2. Position a test piece on the jig, using the horizontal work holder (Photo 2).

3. Adjust the work holder so the edge of the workpiece is flush with the jig's top. Line up the workpiece centerline with the block's registration line (Photo 3). Adjust the toggle clamps to hold the work securely.

4. Install a bit designed for mortising in the router. Up-spiral bits are popular for making these plunge cuts, but they're not essential.

5. Install the router on the jig and test-slide the edge guide's wood fence in the L-bracket groove. Apply wax, if necessary.

6. Bottom the bit onto the workpiece. Then move the router to center the bit on the mortise centerline (Photo 4).

7. Lock down the edge guide and set the plunge depth.

8. Install the stop blocks to establish the length of the mortise (Photo 5).

9. Rout the mortise (Photo 6). As long as the faces of the workpieces are oriented the same way on the jig, all the edge mortises routed will be the same, regardless of where they fall on the workpiece. Just scribe a centerline across each mortise and align it with the registration line on the block (Photo 7).

10. The only change you have to make to rout the matching end mortises is to switch work holders (Photos 8 and 9).

THE BASIC LOOSE-TENON JOINT

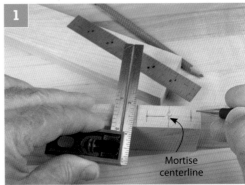

1 Lay out one edge mortise on a test piece to set up the router and jig. The mortise centerline is used for positioning the workpiece on the mortising block—it's the only layout mark required for every mortise.

Mortise centerline

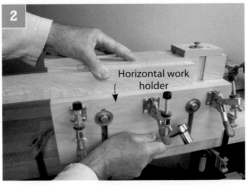

2 Set up the jig to rout the edge mortises. Install the horizontal work holder and position the test workpiece so its edge is flush with the top of the jig. Then tighten the bolts.

Horizontal work holder

3 Align the mortise centerline with the jig's registration line. Then lock the test piece in position.

Registration line

Flush

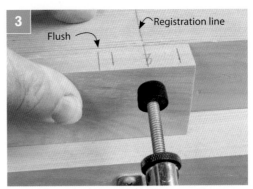

4 Install the router and adjust the edge guide to center the bit on the workpiece. Then adjust the router's plunge-depth stop to the desired mortise depth.

5 Install the stop blocks. Move the router to one end of the mortise and align the bit's edge with the layout mark. Slide the stop against the router and tighten the bolt. Set the second stop the same way.

Rout the mortise with a series of shallow cuts. Plunge the bit about 1/8" and feed quickly to the far stop. Retract the bit, return to the starting position and go again.

Mark your stocks' outside faces and always orient the same face against the mortising block when you rout. Once all the edge mortises are routed, switch to the vertical work holder to rout the end mortises.

To mount the vertical holder, clamp a workpiece with its mortise centerline aligned with the jig's registration line. Slide the holder against the workpiece and tighten the bolts.

Install the router and rout the end mortise. The length, width, depth and placement of the mortise don't change when you switch work holders.

Size a loose tenon blank. Plane a length of stock to fit the mortises. It should slip in without wiggling or binding. Rip the blank to width, slightly less than the mortises' length.

Round the tenon blank's edges to match the mortises. Then cut individual loose tenons from the blank.

REINFORCE A COPE AND STICK JOINT

This variation requires offsetting the rail mortises, so they don't interfere with the panel groove. Start by laying out the offset mortise on a pre-routed rail. Then use this rail to position the vertical work holder.

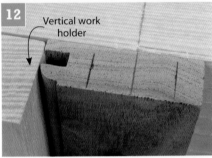

Vertical work holder

Rout the mortises before you rout the cope and stick profiles. Both ends of the rail must be routed with the same face against the block, so the inital set-up shown in Photo 12 positions the mortise in only one end.

To position the mortise in the other end of the rail, install a shim equal to the panel groove's depth between the work stop and the rail.

11. Mill loose tenon stock to complete the joint (Photos 10 and 11).

REINFORCE A COPE AND STICK JOINT

Routed cope and stick joints look great, but their stub tenon construction may not be suitable for large cabinet doors. Adding loose tenons strengthens these joints.

Rout the mortises before you rout the cope and stick profiles, so you don't have to work around stub tenons on the ends of the rails. (The mortises won't interfere when you rout the profiles.) Center the mortises across the thickness of the workpiece. The mortises probably won't align with the stub tenons produced by the cope cuts, but that doesn't matter, because everything will be hidden in the assembled joint.

Start with the end mortises. Offset them away from the rails' inner edges, so the panel groove won't cut into the mortises (Photos 12, 13 and 14). Use the rails' offset end mortises to locate the stiles' edge mortises.

Be aware of the rails' offset mortises when you rout the profile and panel grooves—it's easy to rout the wrong edge.

TWIN MORTISE JOINTS

In post-and-rail constructions made using thick stock, you can make stronger joints by doubling the loose tenons. The rail mortises of these corner joints can all be the same depth, but the inside mortises on the posts will intersect, so they must be shorter, and their tenons must be mitered. The outside post mortises won't intersect, so they can be the same depth as the rail mortises.

TWIN MORTISE JOINTS

Rout twin mortises in two steps. Lay out and rout the first mortises in both the edges and ends. Reposition the bit for the second mortises and go again. Always orient the same face against the fence.

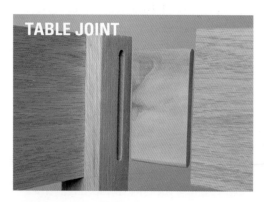

TABLE JOINT

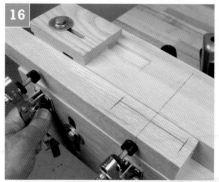

With table joints, the aprons are usually inset from the legs. Mortise the legs first. Clamp the leg with its outside faces against the mortising block and the work holder. Position the bit, set the stops and rout the mortise.

Flip and rotate the leg to rout the second mortise. It doesn't matter that the leg now extends in the opposite direction, because the mortises are centered on the jig's registration line.

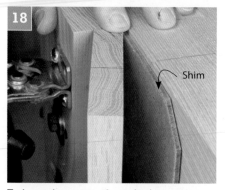

Shim

To inset the aprons from the legs, you offset their mortises by the amount of the inset. Attaching a shim of the desired thickness to the jig automatically offsets the mortise correctly.

FIG. B: DIMENSIONS

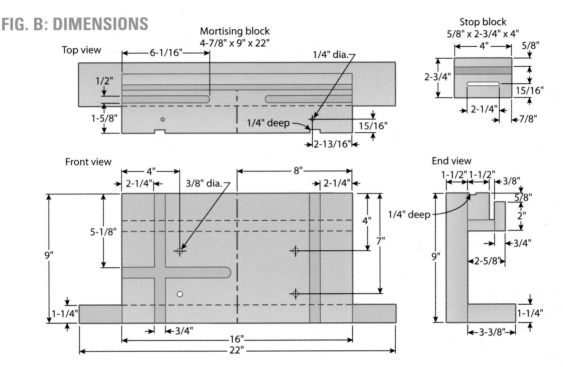

Top view

Mortising block
4-7/8" x 9" x 22"

6-1/16"

1/4" dia.

1/2"

1-5/8"

1/4" deep

15/16"

2-13/16"

Stop block
5/8" x 2-3/4" x 4"

4"

5/8"

2-3/4"

15/16"

2-1/4"

7/8"

Front view

4"

2-1/4"

3/8" dia.

8"

2-1/4"

4"

5-1/8"

7"

9"

1-1/4"

3/4"

16"

22"

End view

1-1/2" 1-1/2"

3/8"

5/8"

1/4" deep

2"

3/4"

9"

2-5/8"

1-1/4"

3-3/8"

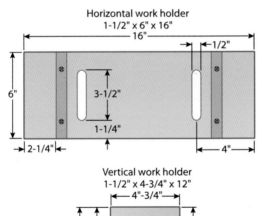

Horizontal work holder
1-1/2" x 6" x 16"

16"

1/2"

6"

3-1/2"

1-1/4"

2-1/4"

4"

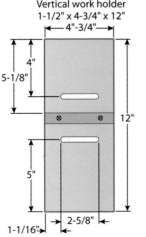

Vertical work holder
1-1/2" x 4-3/4" x 12"

4"-3/4"

4"

5-1/8"

12"

5"

1-1/16"

2-5/8"

Orient the workpieces with their outside faces against the mortising block. Set up and rout all the outside mortises. You'll have to change work holders when you switch from routing edge to end mortises. Reposition the bit and rout all the inside mortises (Photo 15). Reduce the final plunge depth when you rout these mortises in the posts.

LOOSE TENON TABLE JOINT

In this construction, the apron usually is inset from the leg faces. My approach is to set up for the mortises in the legs (Photos 16 and 17). To rout the aprons, I use double-faced tape to install a shim equal in thickness to the inset between the apron and the block (Photo 18). Be sure to install the aprons outside-face in before routing their mortises.

by TOM CASPAR

Router Table Box Joints

THE PERFECT FIT COMES EASILY WITH A SIMPLE SHOP-MADE JIG

Box joints are a cinch to make on a router table. All you need are a sharp bit and a basic plywood jig.

The biggest problem in making box joints has always been getting a precise fit, because the line between success and failure is only a few thousandths of an inch thick. Fortunately, the solution simply requires that your jig be easy to adjust, not difficult to make. I've added a micro-adjust system to my jig that is incredibly precise but takes only a minute to put together.

This jig is specifically designed for a jewelry box project. It's dedicated to only one size of router bit. You can certainly use it for other projects, but there are some limitations. To make wider or narrower box joints, you must build another jig. For box joints wider than 1/2 in., you're better off using a tablesaw and a different kind of jig. If your project requires box joints that are more than 5 in. wide, widen the jig accordingly.

Setting up this jig does require some test cuts. Plan ahead by milling some extra parts from the same wood or wood

FIRST, MAKE THE JIG

1

Jig base

Rout a groove down the length of a piece of plywood to begin making the jig's base (Fig. A). Make the base the same length as your router table.

Use the same size bit that you'll use for the box joints. Here, it's 3/8 in. A spiral bit makes the cleanest joints, but a straight bit works fine.

of equal hardness. In addition, make all the pieces extra wide by 1/4 in. or so. It's much better to rip your pieces to final width after all the box joints are cut. Then the last finger or notch will be exactly the same size as all the others.

FIG. A: BASE

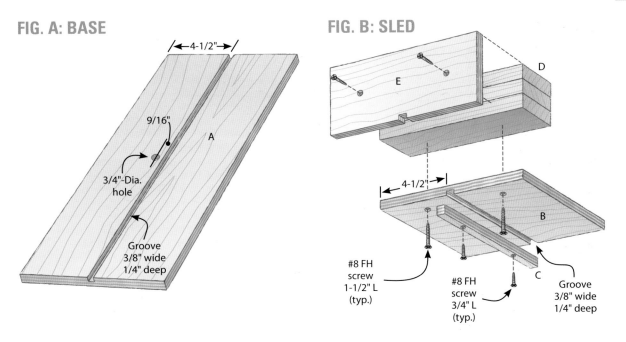

4-1/2"

9/16"

A

3/4"-Dia. hole

Groove
3/8" wide
1/4" deep

FIG. B: SLED

D

E

4-1/2"

B

#8 FH
screw
1-1/2" L
(typ.)

#8 FH
screw
3/4" L
(typ.)

C

Groove
3/8" wide
1/4" deep

Cutting List			
Part	Name	Material	Dimensions
A	Base	1/2" Baltic birch plywood	1/2" x 9-3/8" x length of router table
B	Sled	1/2" Baltic birch plywood	1/2" x 9-3/8" x 9-3/8"
C	Runner	1/2" Baltic birch plywood	3/8" x 1/2" x 10-3/8"
D	Backer	Glued-up 3/4" hardwood	2-1/4" x 3" x 9-3/8"
E	Face	1/2" Baltic birch plywood	1/2" x 2-3/4" x 9"

2

Runner

Fasten a runner to the jig's sled section (Fig. B). The runner's fit in the base is crucial, so begin slightly oversize. Rip the runner on the tablesaw so it barely slides in the base's groove. Then sand one edge with a block until it slides smoothly.

NOW, SET UP A TRIAL CUT

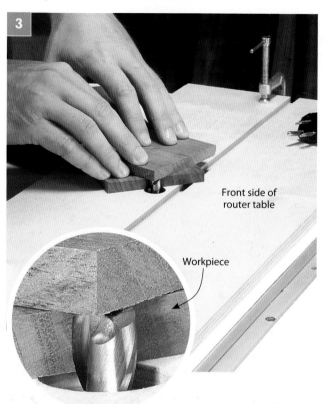

3

Front side of
router table

Workpiece

4

3/8" Router bit

3/8"
Drill bit

Clamp both ends of the base to the router table so the bit is approximately centered in the hole. The base's groove goes in front of the router bit as you face the router table. Raise the bit so it's exactly as high as your workpiece is thick (see inset).

Caution! Unplug your router for all adjustments on this jig.

Position the base so the runner is exactly 3/8 in. away from the bit. Use a drill bit as a measuring device. To adjust the base, withdraw the drill bit, loosen one of the clamps and gently tap the base's edge with a hammer. Recheck the spacing with the drill bit and tighten both clamps.

MAKE YOUR TRIAL CUTS

5

Rout the first notch in test piece A. Mark one edge as the bottom. Butt the workpiece up to the runner, and slide the sled back and forth 1/2 in. or so to cut the notch all the way through. Press down on the sled so it doesn't tip forward.

Caution! Make sure the clamp won't hit the router bit.

6

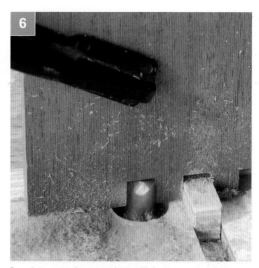

Continue routing notches all the way across test piece A. Lift the workpiece and place each notch onto the runner as you go. This automatically produces a series of fingers that are the same size as the notches.

Caution! Turn off the router between cuts when you are moving the clamp.

7

Rout the first notch in test piece B. This time, one side of the notch lines up with B's bottom edge. To set this up, turn piece A around and clamp it to the sled. Its bottom finger gives you a perfect 3/8-in. spacing. When you're done with the first cut, set aside test piece A.

8

Butt the end notch against the runner and rout again. Continue cutting notches across test piece B, just as you did on piece A.

FINE-TUNE THE SETUP

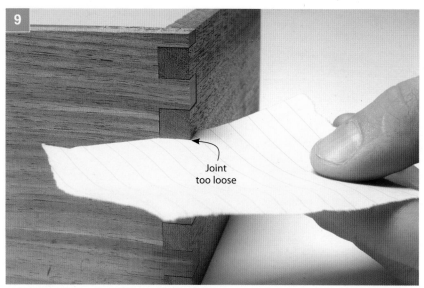

9

Joint
too loose

Assemble the two test pieces. Ideally, they should slide together without any effort. To make gluing easier, the ends of the fingers should be even with or slightly below the surface of the mating piece. Chances are you'll be close on both counts but will still have to tweak the setup. These joints are too loose by a paper's thickness.

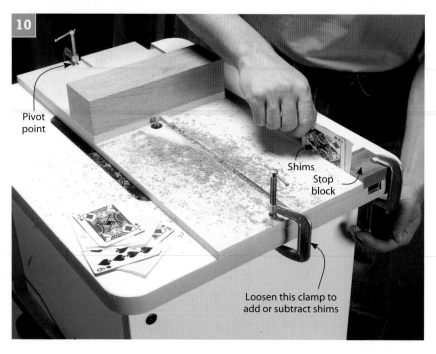

10

Pivot
point

Shims

Stop
block

Loosen this clamp to
add or subtract shims

Add a micro-adjust block to fine-tune the joint's fit. It's simply a stop block, one playing-card shim and one paper shim clamped next to the jig's base (Fig. C). To tighten your box joints, loosen the clamp to the left of the stop block and remove either shim. Then, pivot the base to the right and reclamp it tightly against the block. This slightly increases the distance between the router bit and the sled's runner and widens each finger. To make the joints looser, add another shim.

Fasten a new face to the jig once you've made a pair of test pieces that fit just right. This zero-clearance face prevents your pieces from splintering out. (Half the pieces you rout will have their good sides facing in.) Mark the bottom edge of all your pieces and always begin routing from there.

FIG. C: HOW THE MICRO-ADJUST WORKS

This simple micro-adjust system works by adding and removing thin paper shims. It's extremely sensitive, because the shim is twice as far away from the jig's pivot point as it is from the router bit. Adding or subtracting a shim changes the width of a box-joint finger by exactly half of the shim's thickness.

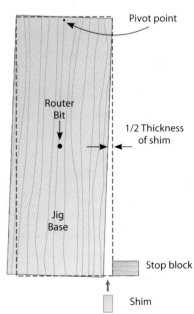

by GEORGE VONDRISKA *and* JIM RODGERS

Lock Miters

THIS SIMPLE SET-UP PROCESS GUARANTEES A PERFECT FIT

Lock miters are strong, attractive joints that make assembly easy. So why the heck don't we use lock miters more? I think it's because they can be a pain to set up. Well, no more excuses. Here's a clever technique. Give it a try and you may become a lock miter enthusiast.

WHAT'S A LOCK MITER?

A lock miter router bit cuts a 45-degree miter with a tongue and groove. When correctly cut, the parts go together at a perfect 90-degree angle and the interlocking tongues and grooves make for lots of mechanical strength and glue surface area. Lock miters are also great at keeping parts aligned during assembly. Use this joint on drawers, boxes or even hollow columns like newel posts. You can cut a lock miter on end grain, as shown in our photos, or on the long grain. Almost anyplace you'd use a miter, you can successfully use a lock miter.

A lock miter router bit.

TOOLING UP

Lock miter bits come in a range of sizes. The size you use depends on the thicknesses of your wood. Even the smallest lock miter bit makes a substantial cut, so I prefer bits with a 1/2-in. shank. They're more stable and result in smoother cuts. Expect to pay $50 to $100 for a bit, depending on the size.

Note: The maximum size lock miter bit you can run in a 1-1/2-hp router is the 2-in. diameter. Larger bits must be run in a 2-hp or higher machine.

It is essential that you run these massive cutters at the right speed—about 10,000 rpm. Your router must have variable speeds so you can slow down for these big cutters.

THE PERFECT SET-UP

Follow the sequence shown in Photos 1 through 7 to produce perfect lock miters on your router table. Remember to have on hand the material required for your project plus six test pieces. It's critical that the test pieces be the same thickness as the project pieces because the bit setup is specific to the thickness of your material. As you get more familiar with the setup procedure you'll need fewer test pieces.

FIRST, CENTER THE BIT ON THE MATERIAL

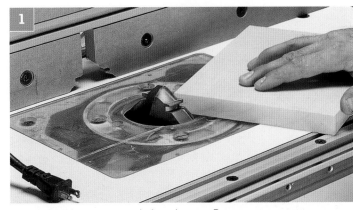

Center the bit on your workpiece by eye. Be sure your router is unplugged.

Adjust the router table fence by eye to its approximate position. Three points must be aligned. The top of the workpiece, the face of the fence and the 45-degree angle of the cutter (Fig. B). This is just a preliminary set up. You'll perfect the fence position later.

Test the height of the router bit by cutting two test pieces. Hold each piece flat on the router table.

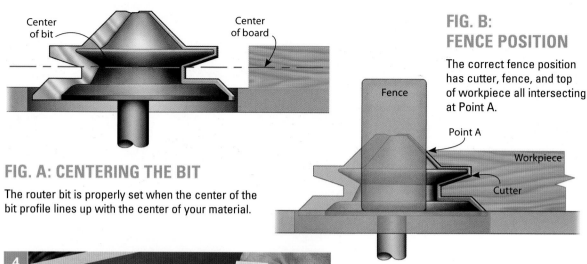

Center of bit

Center of board

FIG. A: CENTERING THE BIT

The router bit is properly set when the center of the bit profile lines up with the center of your material.

FIG. B: FENCE POSITION

The correct fence position has cutter, fence, and top of workpiece all intersecting at Point A.

Fence

Point A

Workpiece

Cutter

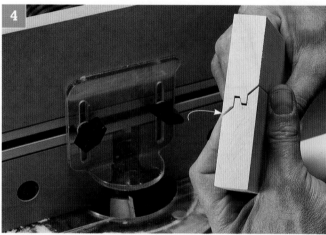

Assemble the test pieces. When the cutter is perfectly centered, the faces of the two pieces will be aligned. Adjust the bit as needed. You must have the bit centered on the material before you start working on the fence position.

5 NOW, SET THE FENCE POSITION

Examine the test cuts to determine if the fence is correctly positioned. If the cut looks like A, the cut is too shallow and the fence must be moved back. If the cut looks like B, the cut is too deep and the fence must be moved forward. Adjust the fence until the cut looks like C; producing a perfect knife edge on the cut.

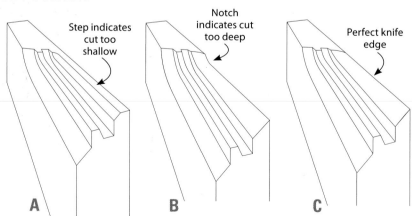

Step indicates cut too shallow

Notch indicates cut too deep

Perfect knife edge

A

B

C

FINALLY, CUT YOUR PARTS.

Machine your parts. One part is held flat on the table. The mating part is held vertically against the fence.

Assemble the pieces. Your careful machining will result in perfect-fitting corners.

Lock Miter Tips

IF YOU FOLLOW THE STEPS YOU'LL BE ABLE TO CUT PERFECT LOCK MITERS.
HERE ARE SOME TIPS TO MAKE IT EVEN EASIER:

Use wide pieces. Your project parts must be cut to the right length before cutting the lock miters, but they can be any width. Leave them 1 in. too wide, and cut them to final width after you've done the routing. They'll be easier to handle, and the "blowout" you get on the back of the cut will be cut off when you machine to final width. If your project calls for narrow pieces, 2 in. to 3 in. wide, machine pieces 6 in. to 7 in. wide and rip them to the size you need.

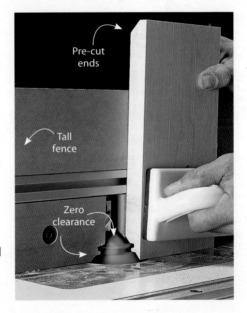

Pre-cut ends

Tall fence

Zero clearance

Use a tall fence. Holding a piece vertically against the fence is a lot easier if the fence is high. Use one that's about 7-in. tall.

Use a "zero clearance" fence. Having the opening surrounding the bit as small as possible helps prevent your workpiece from slipping into the opening.

Precut your parts. A 2- or 3-hp router will hog all the material off in one pass, but it's going to be a lot easier to machine the lock miter if you precut your parts on the tablesaw with a 45-degree bevel. Trim off only about 3/8 in. on 3/4-in. stock.

Use push blocks. Neoprene-padded push blocks will make cutting lock miters easier and safer.

Make a permanent set up piece. When you have all the set-up done, machine a piece and keep it for your next project. If you want to set up the whole operation for the same thickness of material again, use the set up piece to set the thickness of your work, the height of the bit and to position the fence. You'll still need to do some test cuts and some final tweaking, but you'll be darn close.

by RANDY JOHNSON

Lock Rabbet Drawer Joinery

Use a drawer lock router bit on drawer sides from 1/2- to 1-in. thick.

HERE'S A ROUTER-MADE DRAWER JOINT THAT'S QUICK, SIMPLE AND SELF-ALIGNING

For fast, easy, accurate joinery in everything from kitchen-cabinet drawers to jewelry boxes, the lock rabbet is the way to go. Lock rabbets are self-aligning and sufficiently strong for light- and medium-duty drawers.

As with most woodworking techniques, there is more than one way to make a lock rabbet. We experimented with several methods using the tablesaw and router table and settled on this as our favorite. It uses a router bit called a drawer lock bit. And for the wood, we chose 1/2-in. Baltic birch plywood. Its multiple layers and lack of internal voids make it strong and stable.

ROUTER BIT SETUP

Setting up the drawer lock bit is not difficult. Start by aligning this bit with the fence, as shown in Photo 1. Next, adjust the height of the bit to approximately 3/8 in. (Photo 2). Run a couple of test boards (Photo 3) and check the fit (Photo 4). The first test boards you make are unlikely to give you a perfect fit, so adjust the bit's height until the fit is just right.

ART DIRECTION: PATRICK HUNTER • PHOTOGRAPHY: STAFF

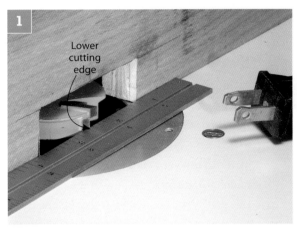

Adjust the router fence until the lower cutting edge just touches the straightedge, which is tight against the fence.

Caution! Be sure your machine is unplugged during this adjustment.

Adjust the height of the router bit to approximately 3/8 in. above the table. This is not the final setting, but a starting point.

Caution! Be sure your machine is unplugged during this adjustment.

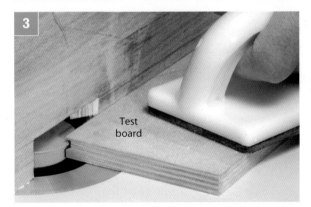

Test the setup by routing a couple of scrap boards.

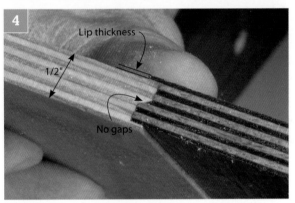

Check the fit. The test joints should fit together easily, but without any gaps. Remember: Lower to loosen and heighten to tighten. Lip thickness will be between 1/16 in. and 1/8 in. when using 1/2-in. material.

MAKING THE DRAWER SIDES

To determine the length of your drawer sides, subtract two times the thickness of the lip on your test board (Photo 4) from your final drawer box length. For example, if you're making a 12-in.-long drawer box and the lip on the test board is 1/16 in., the material for the drawer sides should be 11-7/8-in. long. Here's the math:

1/16" x 2 = 1/8"

12" - 1/8" = 11-7/8"

Prepare your plywood by cutting it into panels that equal the length you calculated with the formula and are two to three drawer-sides wide (Photo 9). Add 1 in. to the width to allow for saw kerfs and edge waste. The edge waste will accommodate the chip-out that usually occurs when the router bit exits the cut. To rout the joint for drawer sides, hold the panel vertically against the fence (Photo 6).

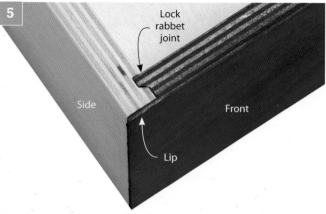

Make both cuts for a lock rabbet joint with one router bit. To clarify the process, we've colored the sides yellow and the front and back blue.

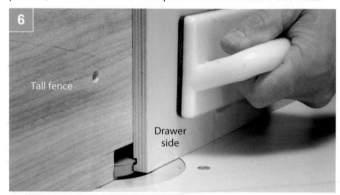

Rout the panels for the drawer sides. Keep even pressure on the panel so it stays against the fence and in constant contact with the table. Use a tall fence for good support.

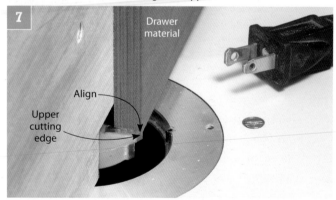

Reset the fence for fronts and backs using a scrap piece of drawer-box material. Move the fence back so the upper cutting edge aligns with the outer edge of the material.

Caution! Be sure your machine is unplugged during this adjustment.

MAKING THE DRAWER BOX FRONTS AND BACKS

Reset your router-table fence before you rout the fronts and backs. Set a scrap piece of your drawer-box material on top of the bit and move the fence back until the cutting depth matches the thickness of the material (Photo 7). Run a test cut with a scrap of drawer-box material and check the fit with the drawer side panels you cut earlier. It should look like the joint in Photo 5. If the lip doesn't flush up with the side panel, readjust the router-table fence and run another test cut until the lip is flush with the side.

The drawer fronts and backs should be as long as the final width of the drawer box because they span the full width (Photo 5). These front and back panels are routed flat on the table (Photo 8).

FINAL SIZING

Now you can saw the drawer parts to final width (Photo 9). Then, saw or rout a 3/16-in.-deep dado in the parts for the drawer bottoms. Make the drawer bottoms out of 1/4-in. plywood and test fit all the parts by assembling a drawer without glue.

ASSEMBLING THE DRAWER BOXES

On small drawers, masking tape works fine as a clamping tool (Photo 10). For larger drawers or thicker material, a few small brads or metal clamps work well. Apply glue to the joints and the dado for the bottom. By gluing the plywood bottom in place, the drawer ends up considerably stronger.

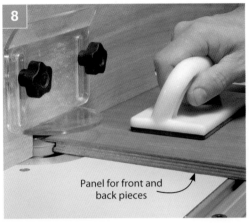

Rout the front and back panels. Hold the panel firmly against the table to prevent it from lifting, or you'll spoil the joint.

Panel for front and back pieces

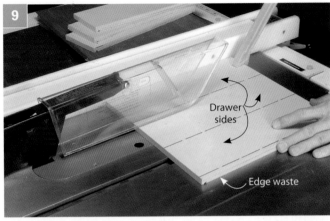

Rip the drawer parts to final width and then saw or rout the dado for the drawer bottoms.

Drawer sides

Edge waste

What about solid or thick wood?

A drawer lock router bit works equally well in solid wood. However, it's not safe to rout anything narrower than 6-in. wide with this technique. For narrower parts, start with a wider board and rip the parts to final width like we did with the plywood.

The bit we used is good for material from 1/2- to 1-in. thick. With thicker material, the settings for the router bit and fence are determined just as they were for our 1/2-in. Baltic birch. You'll notice that if you use thicker material, the lip will also be thicker.

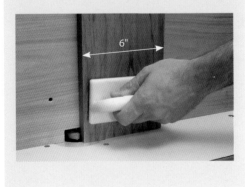

6"

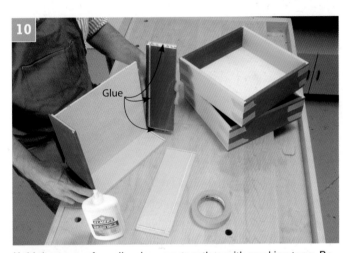

Glue

Hold the parts of smaller drawers together with masking tape. Be sure the boxes are square before setting them aside to dry.

Oops!

We fed this side panel too fast and got lots of chipping. By slowing down the feed rate we were able to keep this from happening. A zero-clearance fence will work wonders, too.

Chip out

by JEFF CORNS

Fast-and-Easy Drawer Boxes

A UNIQUE ROUTER TABLE, WITH TWO MACHINES, DOES THE TRICK

Making drawers can chew up a lot of time—unless you've got an efficient system. I've worked in several cabinetmaking shops where drawers are made fast. I've adopted their methods for my home shop, where I often make cabinets that require lots of drawers. But even if you don't need to work fast, this system works quite well.

As drawers go, this design is pretty simple. It's a classic four-piece drawer box, made from 1/2" Baltic birch. It's intended for utilitarian furniture, not showpieces. The box is dadoed, glued, and nailed together: joinery that's strong enough for a drawer that runs on slides. After the box is built, it receives an applied front, which is usually hardwood or edge-banded plywood.

Let's begin with a drawer-making station I built that saves a lot of set-up time (Photo 1).

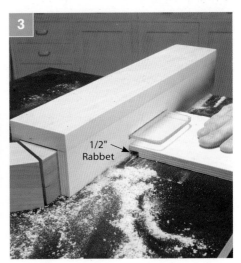

I built a dedicated router table for quickly making lots of drawers. It has two routers: the left machine has a 1/4" straight bit, and the right machine has a 1/2" straight bit. Both bits stick up 1/4".

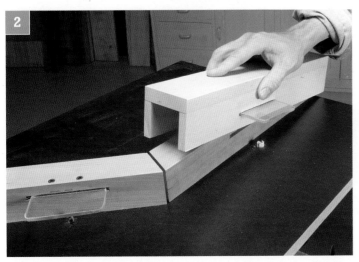

To begin making a drawer, put a box on the right-hand fence. The box has 1/2" thick sides, and the bit is located 1/2" from the fence, so the front side of the box is even with the bit.

Rout rabbets across one end of both drawer sides. The rabbets will receive the drawer front. After routing, remove the box and set it aside.

Rout dados across the opposite ends of the drawer sides. The dados will receive the drawer back.

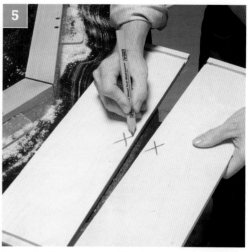

Place the two drawer sides together and mark the sides that will be grooved to receive the drawer bottom.

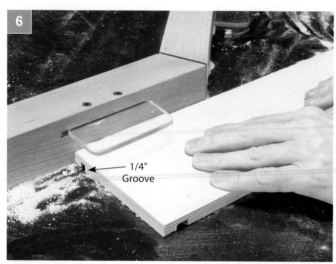

Rout grooves along the inside faces of both drawer sides using the second router in the table. This bit is positioned 3/8" away from the fence.

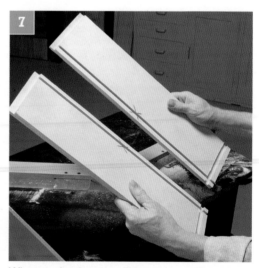

When you're done, you'll have a matched pair of drawer sides. That's it for routing; now move on to calculating the length of the front and back pieces.

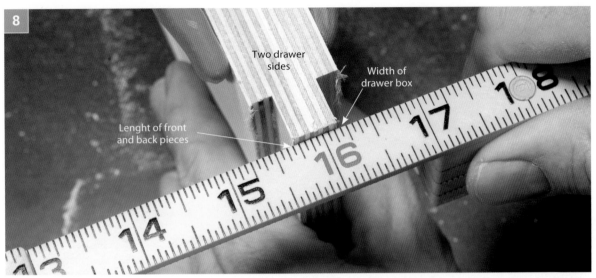

8

Two drawer sides

Width of drawer box

Lenght of front and back pieces

Hold the two drawer sides back-to-back. Place a ruler across the two rabbets to directly calculate the front and back pieces' length. For example, the ruler reads 16-3/16" at right, the size of the finished drawer; at left, the ruler reads 15-11/16", the length to cut the front and back pieces. Rip the fronts the same width as the sides; rip the back piece 5/8" narrower than the sides.

9

Temporarily assemble the drawer. Make the bottom from 1/4" plywood. Rip it 1/32" narrower than the length of the front and back pieces. Crosscut it 1" extra-long. Slide in the bottom and mark its length to be flush with the back.

10

Using a different router table, round over the top edges of the drawer parts using a 1/4" roundover bit. Flip each piece over and rout both sides.

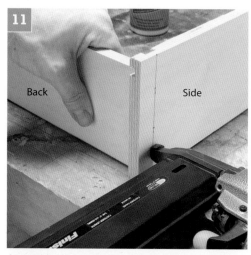

Assemble the drawer using glue and 1" long 18-gauge brads. Place the drawer parts upside down, to align their top edges. Start with the back corners.

Glue and nail the front. Then slide the bottom in almost all of the way, and turn the drawer over.

Run a bead of glue across the end of the drawer bottom, then push the bottom into the front groove. Turn the drawer over.

To make sure the drawer is square, nest it inside two strips screwed to a large piece of plywood. Fasten the bottom using 1/4" crown staples, 3/4" long.

Add glue blocks around the bottom. They're 3/8" square and 2" long. Just rub them in place; they don't need to be nailed. These blocks hold the drawer square and keep the bottom from rattling if it fits loose in the grooves.

15

Add slides and mount the drawer in the cabinet. Attach the solid-wood front piece with double-faced tape, then open the drawer and fasten the front with screws from the inside.

by TIM JOHNSON

Tapered Sliding Dovetails

CREATE PERFECTLY-FITTING JOINTS THAT DON'T NEED TO BE CLAMPED

How would you like to assemble a rock-solid cabinet without using clamps or fasteners? That's the promise offered by tapered sliding dovetail joints. The joint consists of a tapered socket cut into the face of one piece and a tapered dovetail cut on the end of the other. The pieces simply slide together (photos at right). Like dado joints with attitude, tapered sliding dovetails lock mechanically to form rigid 90-degree joints.

Before reliable glues or economical fasteners were available, cabinetmakers relied on these sturdy joints to connect cabinet components. The tapered parts must fit precisely to create a wobble-free joint, so cutting these joints by hand is a real woodworking tour de force.

Fortunately, a dovetail bit, a router table and a simple shop-made jig make tapered sliding dovetails much easier to master. You use the jig (Fig. A) to make the sockets and the router table to make the dovetails. Shims make it easy to create the tapers.

In a tapered sliding dovetail joint, the dovetail and socket both gradually taper from back to front. The parts fit loosely at first, because the dovetail's narrow front end enters at the socket's wide back.

Dovetail

Socket

As the dovetail slides forward in the socket, the fit gradually tightens. The result is a snug clamp-free joint.

TAPER DIMENSIONS

The dovetails and sockets increase in width at the rate of 1/16-in. every 12 inches. (Both sides of each dovetail and socket are tapered, so each side increases by 1/32-in.) Shims milled to 1/32-in.-thickness create perfect tapers on the 12-in.-wide workpieces shown here. To maintain the taper angle on assemblies wider or narrower than 12-in., simply adjust the shims' thickness.

MAKE THE JIG AND ROUT THE SOCKETS

Use a sled to make the jig's tapered guide boards (Photo 1). The sled and both guide board blanks must be squarely cut. Mark the taper's 12-in. run on the sled. Position the sled flush against a block and a stop. Tape a shim on the block, above the mark you've just made on the sled. The shim's 1/32-in. thickness constitutes the taper's rise. Butt the guide board blank against the stop and the shim and nail it to the sled. Mark the tapered edge and the direction of its slope. Then cut the taper (Photo 2).

FIG. A: ROUTING JIG

This jig consists of two parallel rails and two guide boards. The inside edge of each guide board tapers outward at the rate of 1/32-in. per 12-in. length. On a 12-in.-wide board, this jig creates a socket that increases in width by 1/16-in. overall.

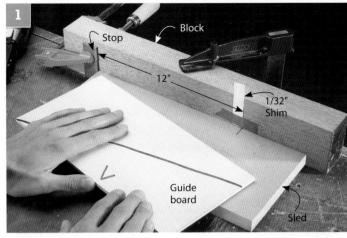

Stop • Block • 12" • 1/32" Shim • Guide board • Sled

Fasten the jig's guide boards to a sled for tapering, using a block, a stop and a shim for positioning. Butt the sled to the stop and the block. Then tape on the shim. It's thickness and location determine the taper's slope. Butt the guide board to the stop and the shim. Then nail it to the sled.

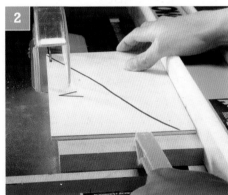

Taper the skewed edge of each guide board. Holding the sled against the rip fence skews the guide board's back end toward the blade. The taper is very slight, so indicate the tapered edge and the taper's direction.

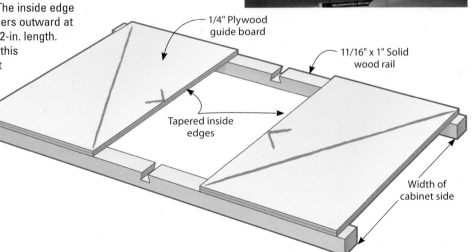

1/4" Plywood guide board • 11/16" x 1" Solid wood rail • Tapered inside edges • Width of cabinet side

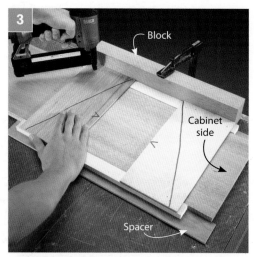

Assemble the jig around the cabinet side. Butt everything against a block to guarantee the jig goes together squarely and the guide board tapers run true. Spacers elevate the rails for fastening the guide boards.

Rout the tapered sockets by bearing against each guide board. Orient the jig's front with the cabinet side's front, so the sockets grow wider from front to back.

To create the tapered dovetails, attach shims at the back edge of each shelf. These shims must be the same thickness as the shim used to skew the guide boards.

Assemble the jig (Photo 3). It should fit snugly over the cabinet sides. Make sure the tapered guide boards angle outward from front to back. The distance between the guide boards at the front of the jig determines the narrow width of the dovetail socket. For example, to make a 5/8-in.-wide socket using a 1/2-in. dovetail bit, the distance between the faces would measure the diameter of your router's base plus 1/8-in. This socket would swell to 11/16-in. at the back of a 12-in.-wide workpiece. Tapered sockets (and dovetails) of this width are perfect for the 3/4-in.-thick stock shown here.

Rout the sockets (Photo 4). The sockets' depth can vary. In 3/4-in.-thick stock, 5/16-in.-deep sockets are ideal.

ROUT THE DOVETAILS AND FIT THE JOINTS

Install the dovetail bit in your router table. Then attach shims to an extra long shelf (Photo 5). Use the shelf's extra length for test cuts while you adjust the bit's height and the joint's fit. The shims hold the back end of the shelf 1/32-in. away from the fence when you rout (Photo 6).

Test the dovetail's fit in a socket. If the dovetail is too wide, the joint won't go

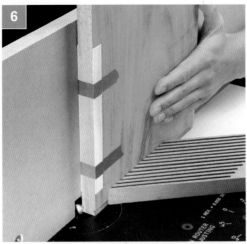

Use a tall fence to rout the tapered dovetails. The dovetails gradually decrease in width from back to front, because the shims hold the back end of the shelf away from the fence.

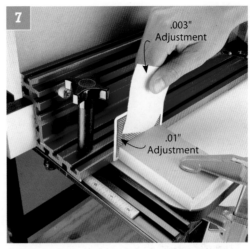

.003"
Adjustment

.01"
Adjustment

A stop and paper shims installed behind the fence allow micro-adjusting the fence to dial in the perfect fit.

The shelf fits perfectly when it can be pushed to within 1-inch of the end by hand. Tap it home with a mallet.

Gluing tapered dovetails is easy. The glue doesn't get forced out because the joints stay loose until the last inch. Once you tap them home, they're rock-solid.

together. If it's too slender, the shelf will slide past the cabinet side's front. I won't lie. These joints are finicky. To dial in a perfect fit, you'll have to be able to make paper-thin adjustments. So when you get close, outfit your router table with a simple micro-adjust system that's up to the challenge (Photos 7 and 8).

Sliding dovetail joints don't have to be glued: They're the predecessors of knock-down hardware. But gluing makes them stronger for the long haul. Apply glue to the beveled sides of the sockets. Slide in the dovetails and tap them home (Photo 9). Give your clamps a rest.

by LUKE HARTLE

More Tapered Sliding Dovetails

TWO JIGS MAKE A COMPLICATED JOINT EVER SO EASY

The tapered sliding dovetail joint is one of the hallmarks of fine craftsmanship. But making it has made many craftsmen pull out their hair! I've made it simple, using a jig with a micro-adjust feature for dialing in a perfect fit.

This exceptionally strong joint was traditionally used to bind solid shelves and dividers to the sides of a carcase. A standard sliding dovetail must overcome a lot of friction to go home, but a tapered sliding dovetail is a cinch to assemble. The jigs I built are sized to fit a bookcase, but it's easy to tailor them to another project.

To reduce setup time, I used two routers to make the joint, but that's not absolutely necessary. You'll need a 1/2-in. top-bearing dovetail bit, a 1/2-in. top-bearing flush-trim bit, a 3/8-in. straight bit, and a 5/8-in.-dia. template guide.

BUILD THE TAIL JIG

1. Make a taper template for routing the tails. First, draw a rectangle (shown in red in Photo 1) the same size as the end of the board that receives the tail. Next,

draw two lines (shown in black) inside the rectangle indicating the amount the dovetail will taper (Fig. A). Each side of this taper has a 1/8-in. rise over the joint's 11-in. length, or run. A 1/8-in. rise works equally well if the joint is a few inches shorter or longer. Rough-cut the template 1/16 in. outside the black lines with your bandsaw.

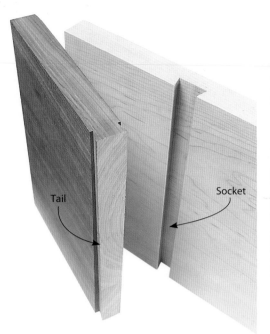

Tail

Socket

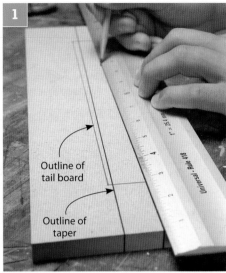

Outline of
tail board

Outline of
taper

Draw an end view of the tail's taper. Rough cut this piece just outside the black lines, to make a taper template.

A sliding dovetail joint has two mating parts: a tail and a socket. It's much easier to assemble when both parts are tapered. As the tail slides into the socket, the joint gradually locks into place until it's rock solid.

2. Cut to the black lines on the router table (Photo 2), using a top-bearing straight bit. Fasten the template to the guide board with screws so the template doesn't flex.

3. Screw the template to a test board (Photo 3). Align the red lines with the board's edges. Position the template so it's exactly centered from side to side, clamp it in place, and drive in the screws.

4. Assemble the rest of the jig on the test board so it fits tightly (Photo 4). Clamp the braces (C) in place first; then add the ends (B, Fig. B).

5. Add two outriggers (D, Photo 5). Stand the jig on a flat surface to ensure these boards are level with the template.

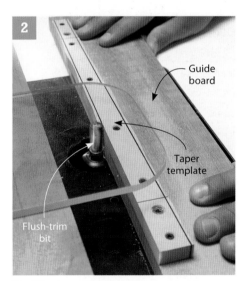

Guide
board

Taper
template

Flush-trim
bit

Rout the taper template using a board as a guide. This guarantees the template will have absolutely straight edges.

6. Rout a test dovetail with a bearing-guided router bit (Photo 6). Lower the bit so it cuts 1/2 in. into the test piece. Unscrew the template and remove the jig.

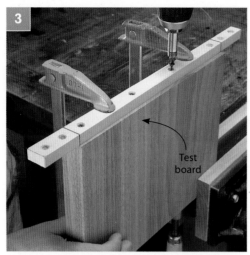

Fasten the taper template to the end of a short test board.

Build a jig for routing the tails. Assemble it on the test board, with the taper template, to fit tightly.

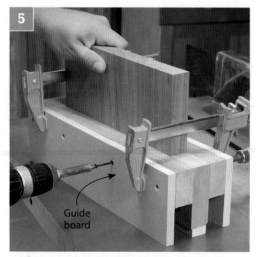

Add two outrigger guide boards to the jig. These pieces will help you balance a router on the taper template.

Rout the dovetail. Follow the taper template with a dovetail bit that has a bearing above the cutter (see inset).

BUILD THE SOCKET JIG

7. Build this jig around a second test board (Photo 7). To position the fixed guide board, use the same 1/8-in. taper you used to make the tail jig. Draw an alignment mark (shown in red) on the guide board perpendicular to the test board's edge. Lay the fixed guide board exactly on the line at one end and offset it by 1/8 in. at the other end. Fasten the guide board to the braces (G). The spacer enables this jig to fit the 12-in. top of the bookcase project.

8. Add the adjustable guide board (Photo 8). Butt it tight to the taper template and a spacer. The spacer makes up for the difference in diameter between the bearing

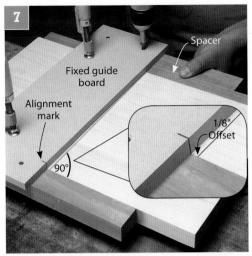

Build the socket jig. Offset a fixed guide board by 1/8 in., the same amount as each side of the template is tapered (see inset).

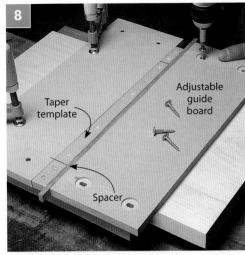

Add a second, adjustable guide board. Use the taper template and a spacer to position this board. Align the red marks.

Rout a test socket. Remove most of the waste with a straight bit (see inset), using a second router with a template guide.

Finish the socket with the bearing-guided dovetail bit.

and the dovetail cutter 1/2 in. up from the bottom (the depth of the tail and socket). Align the template's red line with the alignment mark on the fixed guide board.

9. Rout a test socket (Photo 9). Remove most of the waste with a second router so you don't have to alter the dovetail bit's depth

setting or prematurely dull this special bit. Use a 5/8-in.-dia. template guide and 3/8-in. straight bit. File the template guide to 7/16 in. long, so it's shorter than the thickness of the template material. Make the cut 7/16 in. deep, which is 1/16 in. shy of the socket's final depth.

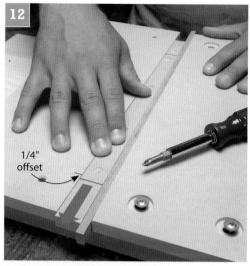

Assemble the joint. It will be very loose until you get near the end, because both parts are tapered. You may have to adjust the width of the socket to make it flush and tight with the tail.

Adjust the socket's width by altering the gap in the jig. Slide the taper template 1/4 in. in or out to micro-adjust the gap's width. Rout a new socket and try the joint again.

10. Rout the socket with the bearing-guided dovetail bit (Photo 10). The socket will be 1/2-in. deep—exactly the same depth as the tail. Remove the jig from the test piece.

TEST THE FIT

11. Test the joint's fit (Photo 11). If the tail won't go home or slides too far, adjust the socket jig (Photo 12). Using the red lines as a reference, shift the template 1/4 in. and rout another test socket. Slide the template in for a looser joint and out for a tighter joint. You may have to cut a couple of test sockets to get the right fit, but once you do, replace the template in the tail jig and you're all set to cut the real tails and sockets (Photo 13).

A perfect fit should only require a few light taps to assemble. The joint should be tight when its two parts are flush.

Cutting List

Part	Name	Qty.	Materials	Dimensions
Tail jig				
A	Template	1	MDF	1/2" x 7/8" x 15"*
B	End	2	Hardwood	1-1/8" x 2" x 3-1/2"
C	Brace	2	Hardwood	1-1/8" x 2" x 15"
D	Outrigger	2	MDF	1/2" x 4" x 15"
Socket jig				
E	Fixed side	1	MDF	1/2" x 5-1/2" x 16"
F	Adjustable side	1	MDF	1/2" x 5-1/2" x 16"
G	Brace	2	Hardwood	1-1/8" x 1-1/2" x 12"
H	Spacer 1	1	Hardwood	1/2" x 7/32" x 17"
J	Spacer 2	1	Hardwood	1" x 1-1/4" x 16"

* Pieces taper 1/4" total over 11" length, 1/8" on each side

FIG. A: TAPER TEMPLATE

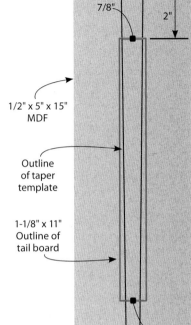

7/8"

2"

1/2" x 5" x 15" MDF

Outline of taper template

1-1/8" x 11" Outline of tail board

5/8"

FIG. B: TAIL JIG

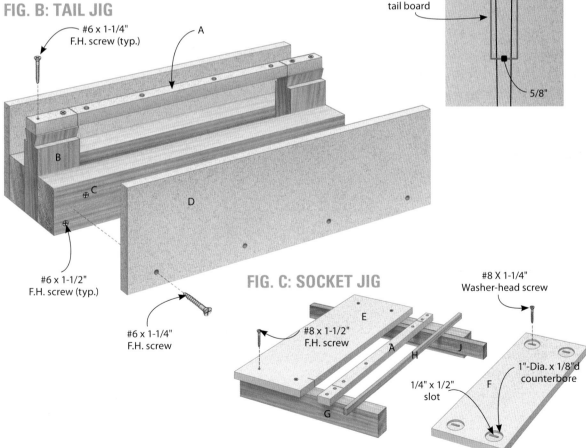

#6 x 1-1/4" F.H. screw (typ.)

A

B

C

D

#6 x 1-1/2" F.H. screw (typ.)

#6 x 1-1/4" F.H. screw

FIG. C: SOCKET JIG

#8 x 1-1/2" F.H. screw

E

A

H

J

G

#8 X 1-1/4" Washer-head screw

1/4" x 1/2" slot

1"-Dia. x 1/8"d counterbore

F

by TOM CASPAR

Sliding Dovetail Drawers

QUICKLY BUILD A STACK OF STRONG DRAWERS USING YOUR ROUTER TABLE

Without question, dovetails are the strongest way to hold a drawer together. Sliding dovetails are often used in production shops, because they're fast to make and easy to assemble. These shops use special equipment, but here's a dovetailing technique that requires only a router table and two ordinary bits.

TOOLS YOU'LL NEED

Accurate dovetailing requires flat, straight stock. You may be able to buy planed wood that's flat and straight already, but often it's cupped or bowed. To be sure your wood is flat, we recommend preparing your own stock with a jointer and planer.

You'll need a router table to make this joint. Our technique is easier to master if your router table has a miter gauge slot, but it isn't required. You'll need two router bits: a 1/2-in.-dia. 14-degree dovetail bit, such as the type used with a half-blind dovetail jig, and a 1/4-in. straight bit. Both bits will perform better if they have 1/2-in. shanks.

Why Use Sliding Dovetails?

■ Fast. The router cuts take no time at all. The joint doesn't require any sanding after you assemble the drawer.

■ Invisible. For a sleek contemporary look, the joint is completely hidden when the drawer is open.

■ Versatile. This joint works with many types of drawers: inset or overlay, with or without slides.

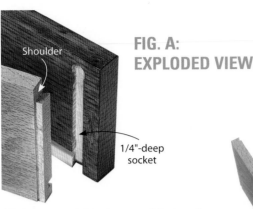

**FIG. A:
EXPLODED VIEW**

Shoulder

1/4"-deep
socket

1/4" x 1/4"
Groove for
bottom

3/8" Space

Groove

All the parts of this drawer slide together.
The front slips down the sides from above.
This makes an invisible joint, because the
dovetailed socket stops short of the top.
The back slides down between the two
sides. The bottom slides in under the back.

MILL THE PARTS

1. Joint and plane lumber for the front,
back and sides (Fig. A, above). The front
can be any thickness over 1/2 in. In this
example, it's 3/4 in. thick. Plane the sides
to 1/2 in. thick. Make some extra sides for
testing the joint's fit.

2. Cut the front to width and length. Cut
the sides the same width as the front. Trim
the sides to length, allowing an extra 1/4
in. for the front dovetails. Leave the back
and plywood bottom oversize for now.

SET UP THE ROUTER TABLE

3. Install a dovetail bit in your router
table. Raise it 1/4 in. above the table's
top. This height determines the depth
of the sockets. It's arbitrary, but routing
a deeper socket can cause a bit to
vibrate excessively.

4. Position the fence 1/2 in. or so away
from the bit. This distance determines the
setback of the drawer sides, so the precise
amount depends on the type of drawer
you're making. If you use 1/2-in.-thick
slides and want a standard 1/16-in. gap on
either side of the drawer front, make the
setback 7/16 in. Use a combination square
to adjust the fence so it's parallel to the
router table's miter gauge slot.

5. Clamp a stop block to the fence (Photo
1). Position the block so your drawer front
fits exactly between the bit and the block.
Without using math or a ruler, this setup
guarantees that the sockets in a drawer
front of any size will be exactly the right
length, stopping 1/4 in. from the top of
the drawer.

CUT THE SOCKETS

6. Rout sockets on the right side of the drawer front (Photo 2). It's easy to get disoriented here, so mark your fronts well. In this step, the socket will be on your right as you face the drawer. When you lower the board onto the bit, you'll make a 1/2-in.-dia. hole. Don't worry; it will be covered by the 1/2-in.-thick drawer side.

7. Move the stop block and rout the drawer front's left side (Photo 3).

8. Without moving the fence or bit, rout sockets in the back of the drawer sides (Photo 4).

ROUT THE DOVETAILS

9. Fasten a tall shop-made fence to the router-table fence (Photo 5). Cut a small notch in the fence to house the bit (Fig. B). Add two 1/4-in.-thick ledges below the tall fence. The ledges narrow the throat opening around the bit, so the workpiece can't tip. Behind the fence, insert four paper shims on each side. You'll be able to micro-adjust the thickness of the dovetails by adding or removing these shims. Hold the workpiece tight to the fence with a featherboard. Push the lower end of the workpiece with a thin stick so it won't tip forward.

10. Raise the dovetail bit until it's slightly less than 1/4 in. above the ledge. This will create a small but important gap between the dovetail and socket, which is 1/4 in. deep. This gap should be 1/32 in. or less and will make assembly easier.

11. Position the fence so the bit makes a shallow cut. Make a trial cut on both sides of a spare drawer side. It's best to make the

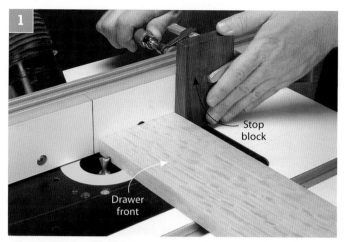

All the joints for this drawer are cut on the router table. Begin by installing a 1/2-in. dovetail bit to make sockets in the drawer front. Clamp a stop block one drawer-front width from the bit.

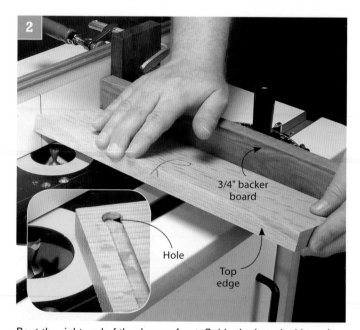

Rout the right end of the drawer front. Guide the board with a miter gauge to keep the board square and tight to the fence. Lower the board onto the bit to make a hole; then continue the cut on through (see inset photo). A 3/4-in.-thick backer board on the miter gauge automatically positions the hole 1/4 in. down from the top.

Rout the left end of the drawer front. Again, position the stop block one drawer-front width away from the dovetail bit. Turn the miter gauge around, push until the backer board hits the stop block and then tilt the drawer front. The result is an identical stopped socket with a hole.

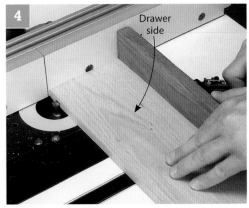

Cut the same socket in the tail ends of the drawer sides. Unlike the sockets in the drawer front, these go all the way across. You won't need a stop block.

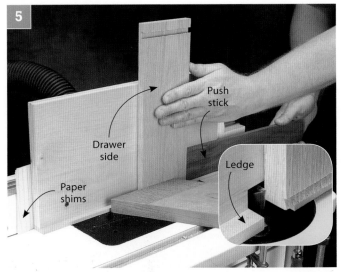

Rout long dovetails on the front end of the drawer sides. These dovetails will slide into the sockets, but it's a fussy fit. Add or remove paper shims behind this micro-adjustable tall fence to fine-tune the depth of cut. The fence's ledge prevents the workpiece from hanging up on the bit's opening or the insert's edge (see inset photo).

dovetail too fat to begin with and then slim it down using the same test piece.

12. Test-fit the drawer side. If it slides all the way down with only a light tap or two, congratulations! If it's too tight, loosen the tall fence and remove one piece of paper from each side of the fence. If it's too loose, reposition the fence or add more shims. As you get closer to the right fit, add or remove shims on one side of the fence only. This effectively changes the depth of cut by one-half the thickness of the shim, less than .002 in.

13. Slide both drawer sides into the front (Photo 6). Cut a spacer board that fits tightly between the sides, and measure the distance between the bottoms of the dovetail sockets. Cut the drawer back to this length. (To be super-precise, subtract twice the gap, about 1/16 in., between the socket and dovetail you made in Step 12 from this length.) Rout dovetails on both ends of the drawer back.

ROUT SHOULDERS

14. Rout a shoulder on the end of each drawer front (Photo 7). If your drawer sides are the same height as the front, move the tall support 1/2 in. back from the bit. Fasten another ledge piece to the bottom of a backer board. Then attach both the ledge and backer board to the miter gauge. Make this cut in multiple passes.

15. Test-fit the drawer side. The shoulder should be deep enough to allow the top of the drawer side to align with the top of the drawer front. It's OK to slightly overcut the shoulder's width. When you assemble the drawer, it's not necessary to push the sides' dovetails all the way to the end of the sockets.

ROUT DRAWER-BOTTOM GROOVES

16. Set up the router table with a 1/4-in. straight bit. Raise the bit 1/4 in. above the table's top. Space the fence 3/8 in. away from the bit.

17. Clamp two stops to the fence and cut a drawer-bottom groove in the drawer front (Photo 8). You don't have to drop the board on the bit. To begin the cut, slide the first socket over the bit, hold the front against the fence and push forward.

18. Remove the stops and cut grooves the full length of the drawer sides. Be careful about orienting the boards, because now you'll be creating left and right sides. The bottom edge of the drawer side faces the fence; the inside face goes down.

Spacer

Assemble the sides and front to calculate the exact length of the drawer's back. Insert a spacer to hold the sides square and measure from the bottom of each socket. Crosscut the back piece and rout its dovetails with the same setup you used for the sides.

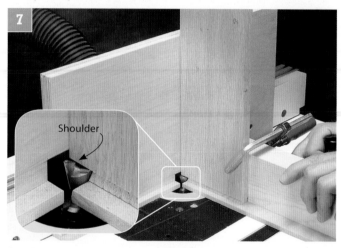

Shoulder

Cut shoulders on the drawer side's dovetails. The shoulder covers the uncut section above the socket. From the last operation, the bit is set at exactly the right height to cut a flush shoulder.

ASSEMBLE THE DRAWER

19. With the grooves cut, you can rip the drawer back to final width. Measure the distance between the top of the groove and the top of the drawer side. Cut the back to this width and assemble the drawer without glue.

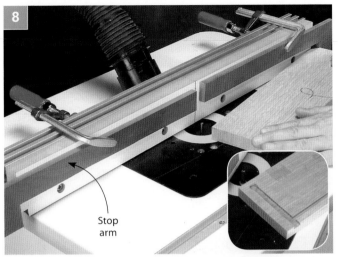

8

Stop arm

Cut a groove in the drawer front for the drawer bottom. Use a 1/4-in. straight bit. This groove starts and stops at the dovetail sockets. To avoid overcutting, which could ruin your day, set up two stops.

9

Glue block

Screw

Add glue blocks around the drawer's perimeter after the drawer is glued and finished. These blocks stiffen the drawer box and keep the bottom from rattling in the grooves. Apply a thin layer of glue to each block and rub it back and forth until it sticks.

FIG. B: TALL FENCE

This fence steadies the workpiece, but it also allows you to fine-tune the sliding dovetail's width. Insert or remove paper shims behind the fence to micro-adjust the router bit's depth of cut.

20. Cut a 1/4-in.-thick plywood bottom to fit the drawer box. The bottom should be 1/32 in. narrower than the distance between the grooves. If it's too tight, you'll have a hard time sliding it in during glue-up.

21. Glue the drawer box. Apply a thin layer of glue to the dovetails and the sockets in the front, sides and back. When the pieces are assembled, slide in the bottom—but don't glue it. The bottom will help make the box square. After the glue is dry, remove the bottom and apply finish to the drawer.

22. Replace the drawer bottom. Rub glue blocks around the perimeter of the drawer to bond the plywood to the box. The blocks prevent the drawer from racking corner to corner, so there's less strain on the front dovetail joints. Finally, screw the bottom to the drawer back.

by ED KRAUSE

Tips for
Router Joinery

NINE SIMPLE WAYS TO MAKE BETTER JOINTS

EDITOR: TOM CASPAR • ART DIRECTION: BARBARA PEDERSON • PHOTOGRAPHY: MIKE HABERMANN

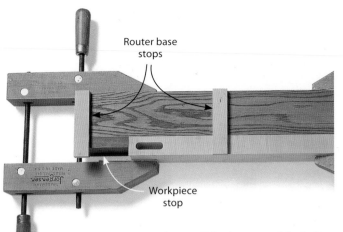

Router base stops

Workpiece stop

1 NO-FUSS MORTISING JIG

Want a dirt simple mortising jig? You know, the kind that can be knocked together in a few minutes, not the fussy kind that takes a whole weekend to make. If you've got a fence for your plunge router, give this no-fuss jig a try.

First, clamp an accurately milled 3- to 4-in. square block to your bench. Then screw on about a 5-in.-long stop block. Butt your workpiece up to it and clamp the workpiece to the large block. (An old-fashioned handscrew-style clamp is ideal for this job because it has a deep reach.) Lay out your mortise on the workpiece and set the router fence so the bit cuts within the layout marks. Finally, add two stop blocks to the top of the big block to limit the back-and-forth movement of your router. These stop blocks define the length of the mortise.

If your mortises are centered, go ahead and cut all of them. If they're offset, simply change the fence setting between cutting right and left legs.

2 UP-CUT SPIRAL BITS FOR MORTISING

A standard straight bit is OK for cutting deep mortises, but the real champ for this work is an up-cut spiral bit. It acts like a twist bit in a drill, throwing chips up and out of the hole. You can plunge straight down to the bottom of a mortise with a spiral bit without burning or sliding sideways.

Solid-carbide up-cut spiral bits can be more than twice as expensive as standard straight bits. However, if you're doing a lot of mortising, I think the extra bucks are worth it. High-speed steel (HSS) up-cut spiral bits are less expensive, but they won't last as long.

Loose 3/4" dado

Tight 23/32" dado

3 PLYWOOD BITS FOR TIGHT JOINTS

Man, was I miffed when I first found out that 3/4-in. plywood doesn't fit in a
3/4-in. dado! It's way too loose to make a good joint. Heck, that 3/4-in. plywood
is a full 1/32-in. undersized. One-half-inch and 1/4-in. plywood is generally
1/64-in. undersized. Now I avoid sloppy joints by using special undersized
router bits. Occasionally I have to lightly sand the end of the plywood to make
it fit, but I'll take a tight joint over a loose one any day.

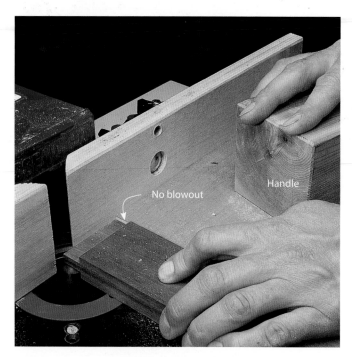

No blowout

Handle

4 RIGHT-ANGLE PUSH BLOCK

How do you hang on to a narrow rail while
cutting a tenon on your router table if you
don't have a miter gauge? You build this push
block, that's how! Make it about 9-in. wide
and be sure to cut it exactly square. Then
attach any kind of handle (a simple block
with a rounded end will do), angling it so the
handle is aimed toward the router bit.

This push block also prevents blowout by
backing up the workpiece. When the block
gets chewed up, simply rip a little off and
you'll have a new solid edge.

5 ONE BASE PLATE, FOUR SIZES OF DADOES

If you're in a pickle and want to rout a 11/16-in.-wide dado but only have a 1/2-in. bit, make a new, graduated baseplate for your router. Each side is progressively 1/16-in. farther away from the bit, so you can easily make four sizes of dadoes using a single bit and one fence setting. Make one cut at the "0" setting to start the groove, then rotate the router to enlarge the groove. The increments can be less or more than 1/16-in., for jobs such as tailoring a groove to fit plywood.

Making the baseplate requires accurate layout. Make it slightly oversized and nibble away at the edges on the tablesaw until the dimensions are perfect.

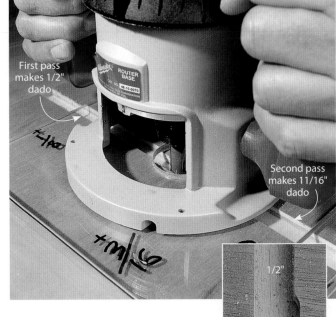

First pass makes 1/2" dado

Second pass makes 11/16" dado

1/2"

9/16"

5/8"

11/16"

6 SET-UP GAUGES SAVE TIME

Setting the bit on a router table by trial and error requires a lot of time-consuming futzing around. Simplify your life by making gauges for the setups you use most often. Go ahead and mill one more piece to save as a gauge every time you make door joints or moldings. Then label it and hang it on a nail nearby. Next time you need the same setup, all you have to do is grab the gauge, adjust the fence and raise the bit height to fit the gauge. A test cut is still a good idea, but you should be darn close.

7 YOUR ROUTER IS ALSO A BISCUIT JOINER

I love the convenience of using biscuits to align boards for a glue-up. However, I never got around to buying a biscuit joiner because I've been using my router to cut biscuit slots.

Standard slot cutters don't work because biscuit slots must be a hair thinner. For less than $45 I bought a special slot cutter and three interchangeable bearings (one for each size of biscuit).

Sliding the bit along the edge of the board about 1 in. makes a perfect biscuit slot. For layout I use a small stick that's 1 in. longer than my router base. I simply line up its center mark with the center mark of the biscuit slot and draw "start" and "stop" marks at either end.

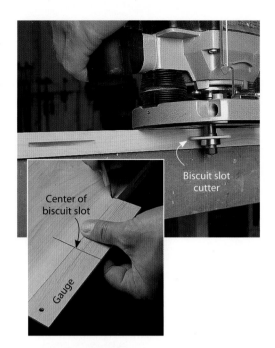

Biscuit slot cutter

Center of biscuit slot

Gauge

Oops!

I was cutting a sliding dovetail when my concentration wandered for a split second, and wouldn't you know it, I turned it into a wandering dovetail!

Using the flat edge of the router seemed foolproof, but I realized that a little twitch can create a huge error.

Now I always use the round edge of the router base as a guide instead. But I found out that my plunge router's collet isn't exactly in the middle of the base. Slightly turning the base for comfort as I routed also made a wandering groove, so I've marked one single spot on the base and keep that spot tight against the fence.

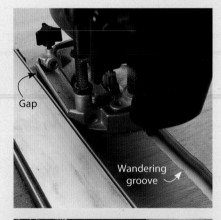

Gap

Wandering groove

1¾ HP

Guide mark

Straight groove

8 EASY LAYOUT FENCE

It's a hassle to set up a single board fence for making dadoes. You have to measure its distance from the dado and square it up at the same time. Eliminate all that bother with a fence shaped like a T-square. Start by cutting two grooves into the crosspiece. Then positioning the fence is as simple as lining up the grooves with layout lines on the workpiece. One clamp holds the fence square.

Make a new fence for each size bit. You'll always be ready to dive right into cutting accurate dadoes or sliding dovetails.

Groove for alignment

Crosspiece

9 PICTURE FRAME MINI-BISCUITS

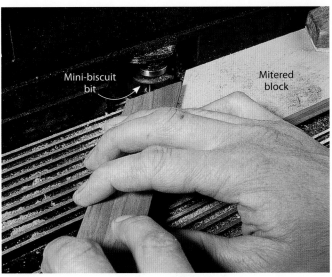

Mini-biscuit bit

Mitered block

All it takes to break the glue joint on a picture frame miter is one careless bump. Reinforce these weak joints with mini-biscuits. Special router bits to make these tiny slots come in three sizes. A bearing limits the depth-of-cut. Install the bit in your router table and clamp a mitered block to the table to guide the cut. These biscuits work well for narrow face frames, too.

Discover these other great books from American Woodworker and Fox Chapel Publishing

Great Book of Woodworking Projects
50 Projects for Indoor Improvements and Outdoor Living from the experts at American Woodworker
Edited by Randy Johnson
An ideal resource for woodworkers looking for a new project or wanting to spruce up their home, this book has plans for 50 projects that can take a few hours, or up to a weekend to complete.
ISBN: 978-1-56523-504-5
$24.95 • 256 Pages

How To Make Kitchen Cabinets
Build, Upgrade, and Install Your Own with the Experts at American Woodworker Magazine
Edited by Randy Johnson
Learn how to build your own kitchen cabinets, and make and install kitchen upgrades with shop-test expert advice from American Woodworker.
ISBN: 978-1-56523-506-9
$24.95 • 256 Pages

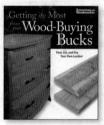

How To Make Bookshelves & Bookcases
19 Outstanding Storage Projects from the Experts at American Woodworker
Edited by Randy Johnson
Build functional yet stylish pieces from a simple wall shelf to a grand bookcase. The experts at American Woodworker give step-by-step instructions using various types of wood.
ISBN: 978-1-56523-458-1
$19.95 • 184 Pages

How To Make Picture Frames
12 Simple to Stylish Projects from the Experts at American Woodworker
Edited by Randy Johnson
Add a special touch to cherished photos or artwork with hand-made picture frames. The experts at American Woodworker give step-by-step instructions using a variety of woods and styles.
ISBN: 978-1-56523-459-8
$19.95 • 120 Pages

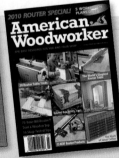

Getting the Most from your Wood-Buying Bucks
Find, Cut, and Dry Your Own Lumber
Edited by Tom Caspar
An essential guide for every woodworker on how to purchase wood wisely for a home workshop. This skill-expanding, money-saving book includes expert advice, detailed drawings, and step-by-step photographs.
ISBN: 978-1-56523-460-4
$19.95 • 208 Pages

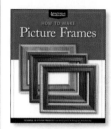

Tool Smarts: Workshop Dust Control
Install a Safe, Clean System for your Home Woodshop
Edited by Randy Johnson
Get wood dust under control with tips for finding the right shop vacuum, dust collector, and air scrubber. Includes practical solutions for making tools work cleaner.
ISBN: 978-1-56523-461-1
$19.95 • 136 Pages

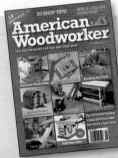

American Woodworker

With American Woodworker, you'll know what the experts know. No other woodworking magazine gives you so many exciting projects, expert tips and techniques, shop-tested tool reviews, and smart ways to improve your workshop and make your shop time more satisfying.

Subscribe Today! Call 1-800-666-3111 or visit *Americanwoodworker.com*

Look For These Books at Your Local Bookstore or Woodworking Retailer
To order direct, call **800-457-9112** or visit *www.FoxChapelPublishing.com*

By mail, please send check or money order + $4.00 per book for S&H to:
Fox Chapel Publishing, 1970 Broad Street, East Petersburg, PA 17520